Introduction to intraNetWare™

NOVELL'S

Introduction to intraNetWare™

KELLEY J. P. LINDBERG

Novell Press, San Jose

Novell's Introduction to intraNetWare™
Published by
Novell Press
2180 Fortune Drive
San Jose, CA 95131

Library of Congress Catalog Card No.: 98-070256
ISBN: 0-7645-4530-2
Printed in the United States of America
10 9 8 7 6 5 4 3 2 1
1P/SX/QU/ZY/FC
Distributed in the United States by IDG Books Worldwide, Inc.
Distributed by Macmillan Canada for Canada; by Transworld Publishers Limited in the United Kingdom; by IDG Norge Books for Norway; by IDG Sweden Books for Sweden; by Woodslane Pty. Ltd. for Australia; by Woodslane New Zealand Ltd. for New Zealand; by Longman Singapore Ltd. for Singapore, Malaysia, Thailand, and Indonesia; by distribuidora Norma S.A-Colombia for Colombia; by Addision Wesley/Intersoft for South Africa; by International Thomson Publishing for Germany, Austria, and Switzerland; by Toppan Company Ltd. for Japan; by Distribuidora Cuspide for Argentina; by Livraria Cultura for Brazil; by Ediciencia S.A. for Ecuador; by Addison-Wesley Publishing Company for Korea; by Ediciones ZETA S.C.R. Ltda. for Peru; by WS Computer Publishing Corporation, Inc., for the Philippines; by Unalis Corporation for Taiwan; by Contemporanea de Ediciones for Venezuela; by Computer Book & Magazine Store for Puerto Rico; by Express Computer Distributors for the Caribbean and West Indies. Authorized Sales Agent: Anthony Rudkin Associates for the Middle East and North Africa.
For general information on IDG Books Worldwide's books in the U.S., please call our Consumer Customer Service department at 800-762-2974. For reseller information, including discounts and premium sales, please call our Reseller Customer Service department at 800-434-3422. For information on where to purchase IDG Books Worldwide's books outside the U.S., please contact our International Sales department at 650-655-3200 or fax 650-655-3297. For information on foreign language translations, please contact our Foreign & Subsidiary Rights department at 650-655-3021 or fax 650-655-3281. For sales inquiries and special prices for bulk quantities, please contact our Sales department at 650-655-3200 or write to the address above. For information on using IDG Books Worldwide's books in the classroom or for ordering examination copies, please contact our Educational Sales department at 800-434-2086 or fax 817-421-5012. For press review copies, author interviews, or other publicity information, please contact our Public Relations department at 650-655-3000 or fax 650-655-3299. For authorization to photocopy items for corporate, personal, or educational use, please contact Copyright Clearance Center, 222 Rosewood Drive, Danvers, MA 01923, or fax 978-750-4470. For general information on Novell Press books in the U.S., including information on discounts and premiums, contact IDG Books at 800-434-3422 or 650-655-3200. For information on where to purchase Novell Press books outside the U.S., contact IDG Books International at 650-655-3021 or fax 650-655-3295.

John Kilcullen, CEO, IDG Books Worldwide, Inc.
Steven Berkowitz, President, IDG Books Worldwide, Inc.
Brenda McLaughlin, Senior Vice President & Group Publisher, IDG Books Worldwide, Inc.
The IDG Books Worldwide logo is a trademark under exclusive license to IDG Books Worldwide, Inc., from International Data Group, Inc.

KC Sue, *Publisher, Novell Press, Novell, Inc.*
Novell Press and the Novell Press logo are trademarks of Novell, Inc.

Welcome to Novell Press

Novell Press, the world's leading provider of networking books, is the premier source for the most timely and useful information in the networking industry. Novell Press books cover fundamental networking issues as they emerge — from today's Novell and third-party products to the concepts and strategies that will guide the industry's future. The result is a broad spectrum of titles for the benefit of those involved in networking at any level: end user, department administrator, developer, systems manager, or network architect.

Novell Press books are written by experts with the full participation of Novell's technical, managerial, and marketing staff. The books are exhaustively reviewed by Novell's own technicians and are published only on the basis of final released software, never on prereleased versions.

Novell Press at IDG Books Worldwide is an exciting partnership between two companies at the forefront of the knowledge and communications revolution. The Press is implementing an ambitious publishing program to develop new networking titles centered on the current version of intraNetWare, GroupWise, BorderManager, ManageWise, and networking integration products.

Novell Press books are translated into 14 languages and are available at bookstores around the world.

KC Sue, Publisher, Novell Press, Novell, Inc.

Novell

Publisher
KC Sue

Marketing Manager
Marcy Shanti

IDG Books Worldwide

Acquisitions Editor
Jim Sumser

Development Editors
Stefan Grünwedel
Kevin Shafer

Copy Editor
Nicole Fountain

Technical Editor
Rowdy Van Cleave

Production Coordinator
Tom Debolski

Graphics and Production Specialists
Mario Amador
Stephanie Hollier
Jude Levinson
Dina Quan

Quality Control Specialists
Mick Arellano
Mark Schumann

Graphics Technicians
Hector Mendoza
Linda Marousek

Illustrator
Jesse Coleman

Proofreader
Nancy Reinhardt

Indexer
Lynnzee Elze Spence

Cover Photograph
tsm/Douglas Whyte, April 1998

About the Author

Kelley J. P. Lindberg, a CNE and award-winning author, worked for Novell for nearly 12 years before becoming a full-time writer. At Novell, she was the project manager for intraNetWare, as well as several previous versions of NetWare. She has written many other books about Novell products, most of them available from Novell Press. She currently lives in Utah.

For my nieces, Lauren and Makenna — dream big, and dream often.

Preface

Networking has become a ubiquitous way of life in today's business world. Few businesses, large or small, are able to work without a net (so to speak). People everywhere need to communicate and collaborate with coworkers, colleagues, clients, suppliers, acquaintances, consultants, experts, and customers — and they need to do it faster and faster every week. Networks are simply the infrastructure that lets that communication and collaboration happen.

Ray Noorda, former CEO of Novell, was fond of saying, "NetWare and intraNetWare should be like underwear. The only time you should really notice it is when it's missing." While this quote had many interpretations (some of which got pretty funny late at night in the engineering labs at Novell), the primary meaning was that a network should just *work*. Once it's up and running, a network should be a silent partner in communication. Users shouldn't need to worry about the network; instead, they should be able to focus completely on their work at hand.

Like any good performer, your networking system should make everything look easy. However, if you're a performer (or a network administrator, for that matter), you know that the key to looking graceful is careful preparation ahead of time.

This book will help you prepare, providing you with a solid foundation in the basics of installing and managing an intraNetWare network.

Why Start with the Basics?

IntraNetWare is an incredibly powerful, complex network operating system. It is designed to accommodate any size network, from a handful of workstations in a dentist's office, to a global conglomeration of thousands of workstations scattered across hundreds of locations. To provide for such a broad range of networking needs, intraNetWare has been built with a flexible, modular design that allows you to start simply, then add, tweak, or turn on additional capabilities that you need or grow into.

If you're new to intraNetWare, or to networking in general, "starting simply" probably sounds like a good idea. You may be surprised, however, to learn that "starting simply" is also a good idea for even experienced network administrators, because basic, straight-out-of-the-box intraNetWare is preset and optimized for most average networks. In other words, it's designed to run extremely well on most small-to-medium networks, without all of that tweaking.

After the network administrator has learned more about the advanced capabilities of intraNetWare, or when network needs begin to expand or change, it's very easy to add or enhance the network. This can be done by taking advantage of intraNetWare's built-in, advanced features, or by adding additional Novell or third-party products designed to fit smoothly into an intraNetWare network.

You've probably heard about the old 80-20 rule: 80 percent of the people use 20 percent of the features in any high-tech product. Chances are good that you're in the 80 percent when it comes to running an intraNetWare network — and you're in good company. And this book is for you.

Novell's Introduction to intraNetWare introduces you to the fundamental concepts and management procedures you need to install and run your intraNetWare network. In this book, you'll find:

- ▶ Explanations of the basic concepts you need to know about networking, intranets, and the Internet.

- ▶ Step-by-step instructions showing the easiest (and often the most efficient) ways to install servers, workstations, and printers.

- ▶ Clear descriptions of how to get your users working (and how to keep them working) on the network, while making sure they don't compromise your network's security.

- ▶ Troubleshooting hints and suggestions.

- ▶ An "Instant Access" page at the beginning of each chapter that helps you immediately identify the concepts and procedures discussed in the chapter.

- ▶ A "Beyond the Basics" section at the end of each chapter, showing where you can go for more information when you're ready to learn about advanced features of intraNetWare.

What's the Difference Between intraNetWare and NetWare 4.11?

IntraNetWare is the latest product in Novell's long line of networking software. Previous versions of this networking software were called NetWare. In fact, the core network operating system inside intraNetWare is still called NetWare 4.11. Novell changed the product's name to intraNetWare because they added several advanced components (such as the Novell IPX/IP Gateway, the Web server, and the Multiprotocol Router) that allow workstations to easily access intranet and Internet services.

It's actually possible to purchase NetWare 4.11 by itself, without the extra components that make it intraNetWare. However, most people purchase intraNetWare, and few people purchase just NetWare 4.11 (especially because you can get intraNetWare for the same list price as NetWare 4.11).

Because intraNetWare and NetWare 4.11 are essentially the same product, all references to intraNetWare in this book hold true for NetWare 4.11. In fact, you'll probably notice the same thing in the intraNetWare software — some places in utilities or installation programs may refer to intraNetWare, while others may refer to NetWare 4.11. Don't get confused by this; the names can be considered interchangeable.

What You Need to Know

Novell's Introduction to intraNetWare is designed to provide you with the fundamental concepts and procedures you need to understand, install, and manage a basic intraNetWare (or NetWare 4.11) network.

This book assumes that you are familiar with the operating systems that run on the workstations you'll be maintaining, such as DOS, Windows 3.1, and Window 95. Advanced features and concepts of intraNetWare networks are mentioned only briefly, with references to places you can go for more information about them.

TIP

You should have access to the online documentation that came with your intraNetWare operating system, in case you need more detailed instructions or explanations of the advanced concepts and procedures that aren't covered in this book.

Another resource for learning more about intraNetWare's advanced features is the book *Novell's IntranetWare Administrator's Handbook*, from Novell Press. It is a quick-reference handbook, which concisely covers all of the features of intraNetWare, including the advanced features, without delving too deeply into conceptual information.

What This Book Contains

The basic components of intraNetWare are explained in the chapters and appendix of this book.

- ► Chapter 1 describes the components that make up a network—network hardware, network software, network topologies, and network cabling architectures—and the intraNetWare features, such as Novell Directory Services and security features, that make the components work together.

- ► Chapter 2 explains how to install an intraNetWare server, how to upgrade a server from a previous version of intraNetWare, and how to manage the server after it's installed.

- ► Chapter 3 describes how to install network workstations that are running Windows 3.1 and Windows 95.

- ► Chapter 4 provides an overview of Novell Directory Services (NDS) and explains how to plan your NDS tree and the objects in the tree. It also describes how to set up the NetWare Administrator utility on your workstation.

- ► Chapter 5 includes instructions for creating and managing users and groups on the network. It also explains how to set up login scripts to automatically set up your users' access to network directories and applications.

- ► Chapter 6 covers the various security tools provided in intraNetWare, which you can use to make sure your network is as secure as you need it to be.

- ► Chapter 7 discusses file management, including tips on how to plan the directory structure, how to work with files and directories, how to salvage deleted files, and how to back up and restore files.

- ► Chapter 8 explains the Quick Setup method for setting up intra-NetWare print services.

- ► Chapter 9 describes how to set up and use the online documentation that came with your intraNetWare network operating system.

- ▶ Chapter 10 provides tips on how to plan ahead so you can restore your network quickly after a disaster (such as a fire or even a crashed server). It also describes a variety of additional resources you can turn to for more help or information (such as user groups, Novell's Internet site, Novell publications, and so on).

- ▶ The appendix is an alphabetical reference to all of the utilities and NLMs (NetWare Loadable Modules) you can use in intraNetWare.

This book also includes a glossary and, of course, an index to help you get to the information you need quickly.

Acknowledgments

I've always believed that the key to success is to surround yourself with bright, talented people — and then *listen* to them. Fortunately for me (and for you), that's exactly the situation I found myself in while writing this book. Now is my opportunity to thank these terrific people for helping me create this book.

First, I want to thank the Novell Press people at IDG Books Worldwide, Inc. They are some of the nicest, most talented folks I've ever worked with. You know all those stories you hear about the evil publishing empires and the vicious, back-stabbing people who work there? Apparently, everyone at IDG Books missed that day at publisher's school, because they are always wonderful to work with. I especially want to thank Jim Sumser — he's tops on my list. His confidence in me is an anchor; his friendship is a bonus. All writers should be so lucky as to have someone like Jim behind them. (Now that this book is finished, I hope his dreams about intraNetWare no longer keep him awake at night!)

Of course, a writer's best ally is a darn good editor. Thank goodness I had one for this book — Kevin Shafer, top-notch developmental editor and all-around good guy. Working with him was painless, yet very fruitful. That's a combination most writers only dream of.

Rowdy Van Cleave (my technical editor) and Nicole Fountain (my copy editor) are more examples of that valuable IDG talent that contributed to making this book as good as it could possibly be. Many thanks to both of them, and to all the other people working behind the scenes — illustrators, desktop publishers, the production coordinator, indexer, and everyone else who makes a Novell Press book happen.

I want to thank the employees of Novell, Inc., for creating the best networking software in the world. The technology invented inside those buildings has changed the world, and leads the competition by light years. The engineers, writers, testers, project managers, and other miracle workers there are the finest you could ever hope to meet.

I send many, many thanks to my brother-in-law, Bill Lindberg, for spending some of his vacation installing Ethernet cable throughout my new offices so I could set up my network without creating that "clothes-line" look in every room.

As usual, my friends and family were extremely supportive and encouraging, and always ready to preserve my sanity by knowing just when to invite me to lunch. I don't know what I'd do without all of you.

And finally, I want to thank my husband, Andy, for being the brightest, warmest part of my life.

Contents at a Glance

Contents

Chapter 10 Disaster Planning and Troubleshooting   253

Appendix IntraNetWare Utilities and NLMs   265

Starting an intraNetWare Network

Instant Access

Understanding Network Components

▶ A network consists of hardware components (such as computers, cables, network boards, printers, and so on) plus software components (such as the network operating system, drivers, client software, and protocols).

▶ The type of network cabling hardware you use is your network architecture. Common network architectures include Ethernet, Token Ring, AppleTalk, and newer fiber-optic architectures, such as FDDI.

▶ Networks can be laid out in three basic topologies (or sometimes a combination of): bus, star, or ring.

▶ To manage users and resources on the network, intraNetWare uses Novell Directory Services (NDS), which is a database of information about each object on the network.

Controlling Network Security

▶ IntraNetWare's login security controls who may access the network.

▶ IntraNetWare's NDS security controls how users access and work with other objects in the network.

▶ IntraNetWare's file system security controls whether users can access files and directories to delete, change, or create them.

The Internet Versus the Intranet

▶ The Internet is a giant network of computers and networks located all over the world. Anyone can connect to the Internet and use browsers to search for, and read, the data published and made available to the public.

▶ An intranet is a private network that publishes information just like the Internet — browser readable. An intranet is private, however; only authorized users (usually within a company or organization) can access it. Outside, unauthorized Internet users cannot access the information on an intranet.

What Is a Network?

If you do business in today's world, you're probably using a network. There's no escaping the need to be in constant communication with coworkers, clients, and competition — and networks help us stay connected.

All computer networks perform the same basic function — they connect computers, printers, plotters, modems, the Internet, and any other resources we may be using. The difference in networks is how those components are connected, how well they work once connected, and how easy they are to use.

In this chapter, we'll look at the components that make up an intraNetWare network.

Network Building Blocks

Like all networks, an intraNetWare network consists of hardware and software working together. One of the characteristics of Novell networks is that you have a tremendous choice of hardware and software to use.

Early on, Novell established itself as the *freedom of choice* networking company. While most other manufacturers in the fledgling networking industry were making products that connected only one type of computer (such as an all-PC network, or an all-Macintosh network), Novell was connecting everything to everything else. PCs, Macintoshes, minis, and mainframes all became part of the Novell networking universe. The operating system (OS) you use on those computers is also up to you. DOS, Windows and all its flavors (3.1, 95, NT, and so on), UNIX, OS/2, Mac OS — Novell's NetWare and intraNetWare products support them all.

Despite the wide variety of options available to you, it is still easy to talk about the basic building blocks that make up an intraNetWare network.

NETWORK HARDWARE

First, take a look at the types of hardware that typically make up a network, as illustrated in Figure 1.1. A network generally consists of a server, workstations, printers, storage devices, various other peripherals, and lots of cabling.

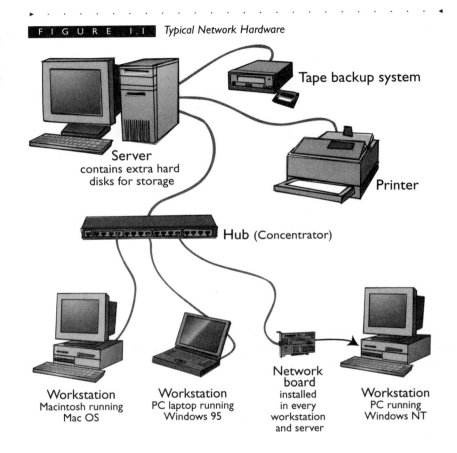

FIGURE 1.1 *Typical Network Hardware*

Tape backup system

Server
contains extra hard
disks for storage

Printer

Hub (Concentrator)

Workstation
Macintosh running
Mac OS

Workstation
PC laptop running
Windows 95

Network
board
installed
in every
workstation
and server

Workstation
PC running
Windows NT

The Server

The "brains" of the intraNetWare network are contained within the server. The server is just a computer with intraNetWare's network operating system running on it.

The computer you use as a server must be a PC (it can't be a Macintosh), but it doesn't have to be a special type of PC. It can be any PC-based computer, so long as it has enough memory and storage space to do the job properly.

Imagine that you have a small network (say, a half-dozen workstations), and you expect your users to store their files and primary applications on their own workstations. You also expect your users to use the server to access the occasional application and the office printer. In this situation, you may not need the top-of-the-line machine. You might get away with a lower-end or older computer, such as a Pentium 166MHz machine with one or two gigabytes of disk space and 32MB of RAM.

If, however, you intend for your users to store all their work files on the server and run all their applications from the server, you will probably discover that a lower-end machine won't be able to keep up with your needs. Instead, you'll want to choose a more powerful machine with lots of expandable storage capacity and RAM.

NOTE

The server on an intraNetWare network is a single-minded machine. It can't be used as a workstation if you're using it as a server (unlike some of the lower-end networking products you might have used before).

In the past, Novell created and marketed versions of NetWare (the precursor to intraNetWare) where the server performed double-duty as both a server and workstation. The demand for this type of product from Novell was low, however. While this feature is adequate for very small networks (five or so workstations), it doesn't expand well to support larger networks. The dedicated server proved more reliable and useful for customers needing larger networks, more power, greater capacity, and more features.

Workstations

Workstations on an intraNetWare network come in all shapes and sizes, including desktops, laptops, and notebook computers (as shown in Figure 1.2). A workstation is nothing more than the computer on which a user does work. You can select a variety of operating systems to run on your workstations. The following types of workstations can be used on an intraNetWare network:

- ▶ DOS and Windows 3.1 workstations
- ▶ Windows 95
- ▶ Windows NT
- ▶ Macintosh
- ▶ OS/2
- ▶ UNIX

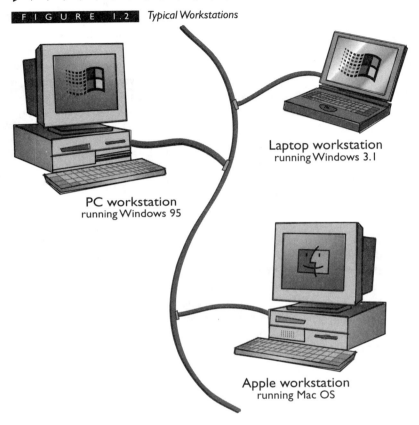

Laptop workstation
running Windows 3.1

PC workstation
running Windows 95

Apple workstation
running Mac OS

You use a network workstation the same way you would use a standalone workstation. You use the same OS you're used to (such as Windows 95), and you work with files in the same manner. For the average network user, a network is just an extension of the workstation — more storage space and printers, faster access time, easier backups (because someone else can do them!), and so on.

Printers, Plotters, and Other Fun Things

Just about every network has at least one printer attached to it; however, many networks don't stop there. You can install a variety of printers, plotters, scanners, modems, and other types of equipment on a network, so long as those machines have suitable drivers that enable them to talk to the network. (Drivers are software programs that let hardware communicate with other parts of a computer or network.) These types of equipment are often referred to as *peripherals*. Figure 1.3 shows some of the typical peripherals on a network.

FIGURE 1.3 *Typical Peripherals*

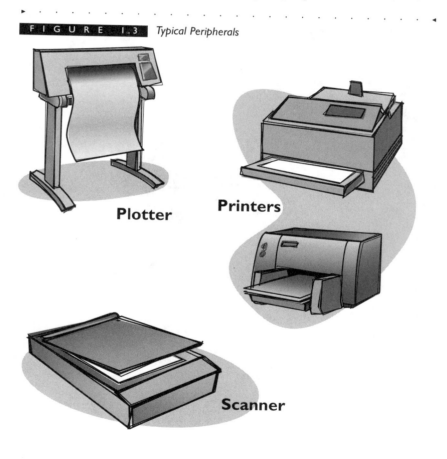

Plotter **Printers**

Scanner

Storage Devices

Just as every house seems to need more closet space, every network seems to need more storage space. Fortunately, manufacturers are happy to oblige.

When your server begins to run short of storage space, there are several types of products you can use to extend your network's capacity. Your solution can be as simple as adding a larger hard disk, multiple disks, a CD-ROM drive, or an optical CD storage system to your server. It can also involve installing tape drives. (Some examples of storage devices are shown in Figure 1.4.)

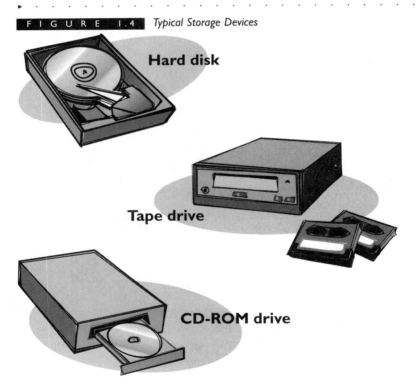

FIGURE 1.4 *Typical Storage Devices*

Hard disk

Tape drive

CD-ROM drive

Each hard disk or other type of storage device installed in your server has its own *controller board*. The controller board is a circuit board on the storage device that plugs into the computer. Through this board, the computer and the disk communicate. Sometimes this board comes preinstalled and you never see it. Other times, you may have to install it yourself.

Many of these products can be used in conjunction with your server and your intraNetWare network. Check with the manufacturers to be sure they'll work for you.

Some type of backup system is an essential element of your network. Whether you use a tape backup system or a system that uses CD-ROMs or other optical media, you can't afford to skimp on this piece of equipment. Backups are essential to make sure you minimize the amount of work you lose if something happens to your original files.

Cabling and Network Boards

When you thought of network hardware, did you think about cabling? Maybe not, this type of hardware is often invisible and forgotten when it works, but a royal pain when it doesn't.

Network cabling is used to connect all of the network's hardware components (such as workstations, servers, and printers) together. It comes in many forms, from coaxial cable (like your TV cable), to twisted pair and shielded twisted pair, to fiber optic cable. Some devices use more exotic forms of connections (such as infrared wireless connections), but currently, most networks still use physical cables. Figure 1.5 shows some typical examples of the different types of cabling used by networks.

FIGURE 1.5 Types of Cables

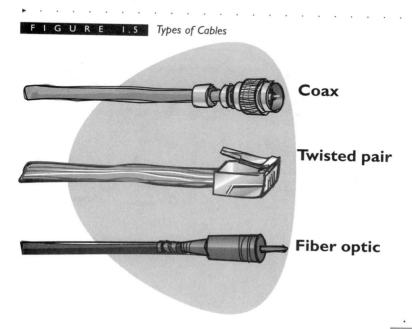

Coax

Twisted pair

Fiber optic

The type of network cabling you choose will also dictate another type of hardware you need—connection hardware (such as connectors, terminators, and hubs). Your connection hardware must match your network cabling. Figure 1.6 shows some examples of the different types of connection hardware.

FIGURE 1.6 *Examples of Connection Hardware Used with Network Cabling*

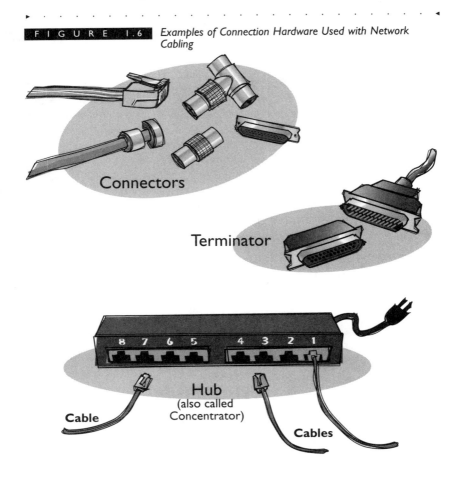

Connectors

Terminator

Hub
(also called
Concentrator)

Cable

Cables

The three types of connection hardware shown in Figure 1.6 are as follows:

▸ Connectors join cables together or connect them to other pieces of hardware. Connectors come in a wide variety of shapes and sizes, depending on the type of cable and equipment with which they're designed to work.

▸ Terminators may be required by your cabling system. Terminators are attached to the open ends of any cables. They keep electrical signals from reflecting back across the network, corrupting information or communications.

▸ Hubs, which are used with some cabling systems, are a piece of equipment into which all workstation cables must feed before being connected to the main network cable. Passive hubs simply gather the signals and relay them. Active hubs (sometimes called concentrators) boost the signals before sending them on their way.

Now that you have cables to connect your computers, you may be wondering where to plug them into the computer. The cables plug into a *port* (connector) on the computer's network interface board.

Each device (computer, printer, and so on) on a network must contain a network interface board (also called *network boards*). A network board is a special type of circuit board that allows the machine to connect to the network. With computers, you often need to purchase these network boards separately. However, some computers and devices, such as printers, may have these boards (or their equivalents) built in during manufacturing.

The type of network board you use depends on your cable type. Figure 1.7 shows a common type of network board. Figure 1.8 shows where the cable connects to the network board when the board is installed in a computer.

NOTE

Network interface boards may also be referred to as network cards, network interface cards (NICs), and network adapters. If they're built into the machine (rather than purchased and installed separately), they may be called built-in adapters.

FIGURE 1.7 *A Typical Network Board*

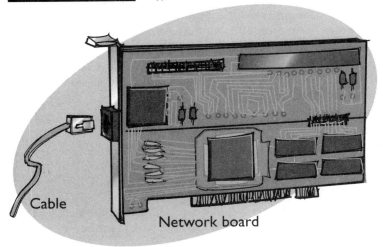

Cable

Network board

FIGURE 1.8 *A Network Board Installed in a Computer*

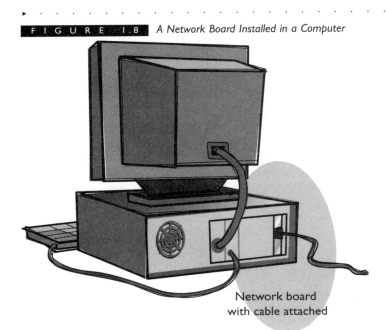

Network board
with cable attached

Network Architectures and Topologies

All of the cabling, connectors, and boards used in a network must work together. The cabling scheme that allows these components to interoperate is called the *network architecture*. The following network architectures are the most common ones used today:

- ▶ Ethernet — This is the most common network architecture. It provides good performance at a reasonable cost, and is relatively easy to install.

- ▶ Token Ring — Token Ring works well in situations that involve heavy data traffic because it is reliable. It is also fairly easy to install, but more expensive than Ethernet networks.

- ▶ AppleTalk networks — AppleTalk is a networking protocol suite built into every Macintosh. It runs on several different network architectures (including LocalTalk, EtherTalk, and TokenTalk), and provides peer-to-peer networking — serverless networking — between all Macintoshes and Apple hardware.

- ▶ High-speed architectures — The newer high-speed architectures, such as Fiber Distributed Data Interface (FDDI) and Fast Ethernet, are becoming more prevalent. They are capable of supporting speeds up to 100Mbps. Most of these architectures use fiber-optic cabling.

Because each of these network architectures handles data in a different way, each requires a unique type of network hardware. Before installing any network hardware, be sure to refer to the hardware manufacturer's documentation. The manufacturer's documentation should indicate specific restrictions or suggestions for their hardware, such as length limits for cables.

Although all devices on a given network must use the same network architecture, you can easily connect two networks that use different architectures. You use a *bridge* to join the two architectures so communication can flow between the two networks. Users don't know they're using two different physical networks. The bridge appears seamless, making the two networks look like one continuous network.

The network architecture determines the type of hardware used in a network. The way the hardware is laid out, however, is called the *network topology*. There are three basic topologies that can be used with most architectures:

- ▶ Bus — In this topology, all of the network components are laid out sequentially along the main network cable (see Figure 1.9).

▸ Star—All of the network components in this topology radiate out from a central location (usually a hub or concentrator), as shown in Figure 1.10.

▸ Ring—In this topology all of the network components form a ring. Any network communication goes one direction around the loop until it finds the desired component. Figure 1.11 shows a ring topology.

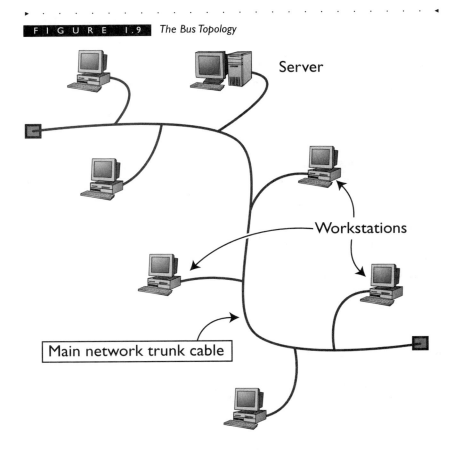

FIGURE 1.9   *The Bus Topology*

Server

Workstations

Main network trunk cable

FIGURE 1.10
The Star Topology

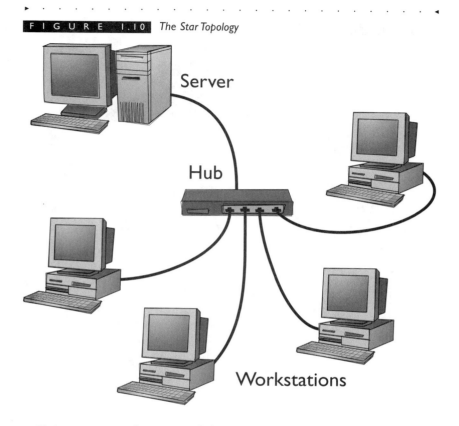

Server

Hub

Workstations

Variations or combinations of these topologies are commonly used. The network architecture mentioned previously can support the following basic topologies:

- ► Ethernet — Ethernet can support either bus or star topologies.

- ► Token Ring — Token Ring is cabled like a star topology, but actually acts like a ring. Data flows from workstation to workstation around the ring until it finds its destination.

- ► AppleTalk — AppleTalk has an Ethernet variation (called EtherTalk) that runs on bus or star topologies. It also has a Token Ring variation (called TokenTalk) that runs on a ring topology.

FIGURE 1.11   *The Ring Topology*

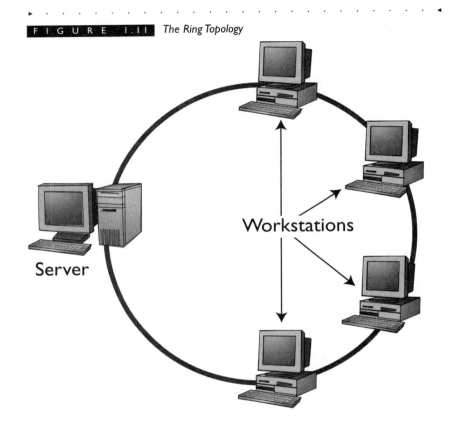

Workstations

Server

NETWORK SOFTWARE

Now, consider the software components that enable all of the network hardware to work. You need the network operating system, client software, print servers (and other types of servers), drivers, protocols, and routers and gateways.

The Network Operating System (the Server)

First, go back to the brains of the network. The intraNetWare server is a computer with the intraNetWare network operating system installed on it. The network operating system (sometimes called the NOS) replaces the computer's regular operating system (such as DOS or Windows 95). The network operating system manages all communication taking place over the network.

On an ordinary computer, the OS (such as Windows 95) controls how data is transferred and how files are stored within the computer. It also dictates how attached pieces of hardware (such as disk drives or printers) communicate with the computer.

When intraNetWare takes over the computer, it does the same tasks but on a larger (network-wide) scale. It controls data transfer over the network, the way users' files are stored on the server, and all communication between the network and attached hardware (such as network printers). In addition, intraNetWare manages network security (providing access to authorized users only), handles communication between multiple networks, and regulates other network activities.

Normally, a computer running an operating system such as Windows will have a single hard disk, and that hard disk will have a single *partition*. A disk partition is just a portion of the hard disk that is formatted in such a way that it can store and handle files. (In most cases, the entire disk belongs to the partition, but it is possible to create more than one partition on a single hard disk.)

You have probably formatted floppy disks before. When you format a floppy disk, you prepare the disk's magnetic surface in a particular structure that will be recognized by the operating system you're using. If you've ever tried to use a Macintosh-formatted floppy disk in a PC, you know that different operating systems expect entirely different disk formats.

Hard disks are formatted for operating systems in the same manner as floppy disks. One difference between hard disks and floppies, however, is that you can divide a hard disk into more than one partition. That way, you can format one partition to meet one operating system's structure, and another partition to meet a second operating system's structure. Few people ever do this on standalone computers because there are few reasons why this is necessary — most people only use a single OS on their standalone computers. For an intraNetWare server, however, this feature is very valuable.

When you install intraNetWare on your server computer, you divide the server's hard disk into two partitions. One partition — a very small one — will be formatted with DOS so that the computer can boot up normally and run any DOS programs that the server needs. The other partition — which is the bulk of the hard disk — will be formatted with the intraNetWare operating system. While this is a different format than DOS, it performs many of the same functions. It enables all network files and directories (or folders) to be created and stored on the server's hard disk, just as they would be stored on a DOS disk. The main difference is simply that intraNetWare requires some specific formatting characteristics to handle all of its security and management features.

NOTE

Disk partitions are not physical sections of the disk — you can't see the partitions by opening up the computer and looking at the hard disk. Partitions are simply portions of the hard disk's storage area that are programmed to handle different operating systems. You create the partitions by using the DOS commands FDISK and FORMAT, as described in Chapter 2.

Client Software (the Workstations)

To allow workstations to communicate with the network, you must install some special intraNetWare software on each one. This workstation software is called *client software*, because it acts like a client, requesting services from the network server.

In simple terms, intraNetWare's client software on the workstation forms a connection with the network. This enables users to log in, transfer data across the network, and find and use network resources (such as printers).

Novell's intraNetWare client software doesn't replace the workstation's regular OS, such as Windows 95. Instead, the client software allows the workstation's own OS to handle normal processing tasks, and then steps in whenever a task requests a network service. When a network request comes along, the client software manages the request and data transfer across the network.

When you install the intraNetWare client software, you also get some additional utilities to help you use the network more efficiently. These utilities are explained in Chapter 5.

The Print Server

The print server is a software program that runs on the intraNetWare server. It manages the method in which print jobs are handled by the network and its printers.

With a print server on the network, users can easily send their print jobs to network printers. Print servers control print traffic, manage the order and priority of print jobs, and verify that users are permitted to use the printers they select.

TIP

Other companies — most notably Microsoft — also produce client software that can be used with networks. If you're using intraNetWare, you should replace Microsoft's client with the intraNetWare client, because the intraNetWare client is optimized to run with intraNetWare.

What Does the Term Client/Server Really Mean?

Think of the server as the software that services clients. When a client (such as a workstation, application, or peripheral) needs to access a network resource or service, the server manages that access.

The term client/server, which has been a common buzzword for several years, is used to describe this relationship. Applications, such as database programs, are client/server applications if the processing is distributed so that some of the work is done by multiple clients, and other parts of the work are done by the main (server) portion of the program.

Novell has moved away from the term client/server, and now uses the term *client/network*. This is because intraNetWare no longer views a single server computer as the center of the network. Instead, intraNetWare weaves multiple servers, and all of the network resources and services, into a seamless web of a network. That way, clients who access network services may access them from any number of servers or locations. Servicing clients then becomes more of a network role than a single server role.

Other Types of Servers (Web, Mail, and Fax)

You may have additional types of servers, such as fax servers or mail servers, installed on your intraNetWare network. These servers are similar to print servers — they are software programs that manage the communication traffic associated with that type of product (for example, faxes or e-mail). A Web server is basically software that is used to post and control information on the World Wide Web (WWW).

Some of these specialty servers may be programs installed and running on the intraNetWare server. Other specialty servers may be running on separate computers connected to the network. For example, if you have a smaller network, you could have a mail server running within your intraNetWare server. On a larger network, you may decide to dedicate a separate machine for the mail server.

NOTE

The term *server* is often used to describe any software program that provides a service to network clients. Technically, the term *server* seldom refers to a physical computer. When users refer to the mail server, they really mean the primary servicing portion of the e-mail software program.

In common usage, however, people often use the word *server* when referring to both the program and the machine it's running on (such as the intraNetWare server). This is especially true when a single computer houses a single server program for the sake of efficiency.

Drivers

Drivers are small software programs associated with a piece of hardware. A driver enables the hardware device to communicate with the computer it's installed in. You are probably familiar with some of the drivers involved with a standalone computer, such as a mouse driver (which controls how your mouse works with your computer) and drivers for devices such as monitors and sound cards.

On a network, you also encounter LAN drivers, which enable a network board to communicate with the computer it's installed in. When you buy a network board, the package usually includes a diskette with the board's associated LAN driver on it. Most network boards require their own matched brand of driver.

Disk drivers are another important type of drivers. They make it possible for the computer to communicate with its hard disk (actually, with the hard disk's controller board). CD-ROM drives and tape drives also have their own corresponding drivers. The term *device drivers* is sometimes used as a generic name for all the hardware-related drivers your computer may require. When you install intraNetWare, the installation program looks at your hardware and attempts to find a matching LAN driver and disk driver. It then attempts to install them automatically from the set of drivers shipped on the intraNetWare CD-ROM. If it can't find a driver it needs, the installation program will ask you to insert a diskette with the necessary driver on it.

TIP

Novell's intraNetWare includes a large selection of the most common types of LAN drivers. However, board manufacturers frequently update their drivers, so if you're installing a network board, check with the manufacturer for an updated driver. (Web sites are a good place to check for updated drivers.)

Protocols

A protocol is a set of defined rules that controls how processes or machines communicate. For example, a protocol regulates how two computers establish a connection so they can communicate, and how they terminate the connection when finished. In addition, protocols control how data is transferred over a network. When data is sent across the network, it (the data) is packaged in small units, called *packets*. Think of these packets like the packages you mail at the post office. Each packet includes a small amount of data, plus addressing information to ensure the data gets to the right destination. The packets may also include information that informs the receiving station of the data's safe arrival, and other helpful tidbits. A protocol dictates exactly how these packets should be formed, so that every device on the network can understand the packets that it receives.

Several different types of protocols have been developed by various organizations to control how information is exchanged across a network. Many of these protocols are supported by intraNetWare. Each protocol forms packets in a unique way.

Discussions about protocols can be very confusing because there are so many different types of protocols, as well as protocols that layer on top of each other. Protocols are associated with several types of characteristics, such as:

- ▸ The network architecture they support
- ▸ The way they transmit data
- ▸ How they determine where data should go
- ▸ The types of communication they're facilitating

By default, intraNetWare supports a protocol developed by Novell, called IPX/SPX. It can also support both the IP protocol (used by the Internet) and the AppleTalk protocol (used by Macintoshes).

For a workstation to communicate on the network, it must use the same protocol that is used on the network. Fortunately, intraNetWare networks can be configured to use different protocols, or even multiple protocols at the same time.

NOTE

Because using multiple protocols is an advanced feature of intraNetWare, this book will assume your network is using the default — and more efficient in many situations — IPX/SPX protocol.

Routers and Gateways

Routers are software programs that enable network communication to travel across mixed networks. Routers take packets of data from one network, and reformat them (if necessary) to conform to the next network's requirements. The routers then send the packets along to their destination.

Many people think of routers as hardware components, too, because the router programs are sometimes housed in their own hardware devices. The actual routing of packets from one network to the other is controlled by the software. The router's hardware forms the necessary physical connection by linking the cabling systems together.

Routing software is built into the server in intraNetWare. The server machine itself forms the physical connection between two networks — for example, the server may have both an Ethernet network board and a Token Ring network board installed in it. The router software then manages the flow of data packets between the two networks via their respective network boards. Figure 1.12 illustrates two networks joined by routing software in a server.

FIGURE 1.12 *A Router Running in a Server*

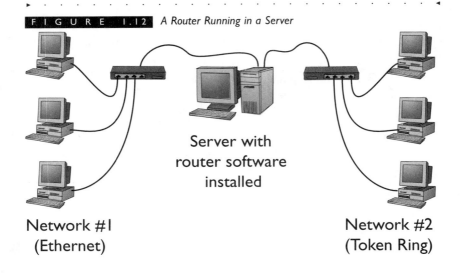

Server with
router software
installed

Network #1
(Ethernet)

Network #2
(Token Ring)

Other companies also create extremely good routers that can work with intraNetWare. These third-party routers are usually contained within their own specialized hardware to make routing work more efficiently with their routing software.

Routers can track routes between servers or networks. They keep track of which servers are up and running, which route between two servers is shortest, and so on. This ensures that network communication isn't interrupted or slowed down unnecessarily.

Routers can also connect two networks that are using different protocols — they take data packets from one protocol and reformat them to work on the next protocol down the line.

Gateways are another product that can translate one protocol's format into another, and back again. The difference between routers and gateways is a little confusing, and with advancements in technology, the line between them is getting somewhat blurred.

One way to look at the difference — though it's not necessarily a precise definition — is that a router links multiple networks so they appear to be one seamless network. If your company has hundreds of servers scattered all over the globe, you're using a large number of routers every time you communicate with someone. The routers work together to scatter information across a spider web of connections to get the data to its destination. A piece of data, traveling across the network, may go through a variety of paths. If one router is down, the data can travel through another router on a different path, but still wind up at the same destination.

A gateway generally connects your network to a completely different type of network or computer system, through a single point. If, for example, you're using a workstation on a network and you want to connect to a mainframe computer, your communications can go through a gateway installed somewhere on the network. The gateway takes your data and transfers it to the mainframe, reversing the process when the mainframe replies to you. If the gateway is down, you won't be able to communicate with the mainframe. There usually isn't another gateway that is set up to automatically retrieve your data and send it on an alternate route to the mainframe.

How intraNetWare Ties the Blocks Together

Now you have a bunch of hardware and a bunch of software all hooked up together. You need a powerful system to connect everything and ensure that the whole network runs smoothly, users can gain access, security is controlled, and nothing falls through the cracks. The tool for this job is intraNetWare.

The first key to managing a complex system is to impose a structure on it that will organize and simplify all of the components. Novell Directory Services (NDS) is intraNetWare's foundation for organizing the network.

First, let's look at the fundamentals of NDS. Next, we'll look at how intraNetWare regulates security. Finally, we'll see how intraNetWare pulls it all together so the network administrator can manage the network.

NOVELL DIRECTORY SERVICES (NDS)

NDS is simply a database that contains information about every object in the network. Using this database, intraNetWare can identify each object and know where it's supposed to be in the network, who's permitted to use it, and to what it's supposed to be connected.

Every physical component on the network, such as a server, printer, or workstation, has its own unique NDS object defined in the NDS database. Software entities, such as print servers, print queues (directories that contain pending print jobs), and volumes, also have their own NDS objects. In fact, all users and organizations (departments, companies, or even project teams if you like) have their own objects defined in the NDS database. If a user, server, or other type of entity doesn't have an NDS object defined for it in the database, that user or device can't access network services.

If your network is small and contains only one server, the NDS database is stored on that server. If you have more than one server on your network, all of them share a single, distributed NDS database. That way, any object defined anywhere in the network will be recognized by all of the servers in that network.

Having a distributed database makes the database itself more flexible and easier for the network administrator to use. For example, instead of being limited to a single server, an administrator can make changes to the database from any number of servers, and all of those servers will receive the same updates.

In addition, a distributed database means that a single server can't make the whole network fail. If one server goes down, the whole database still exists on other servers, so users can still log in, most services will still be available, and so on. In most cases, the only problem a downed server may cause is to prevent a user from accessing files stored on that particular server. If, however, the user stored files on his or her workstation, the user can still print those files on network printers, send e-mail to other users, and the like.

NOTE

One of the beauties of NDS is that all servers on the network share a single NDS database. Before NDS, if you wanted to work on three different servers, you had to get the administrator to define you three different times — once on each server. Now, however, all servers share the same information, so once you're defined, any server on the network will recognize you.

Likewise, you no longer need to know which server contains the service you need, such as a particular printer. Because all servers recognize the printer, you can get straight to the printer without having to locate a specific server first.

The NDS database is structured in a hierarchical format, which means that objects in the database can be at different levels or grouped into subordinate divisions. By using this format, NDS objects can be organized into groups and subgroups, so it's easier to manage all of them. If, for example, you group all your marketing users under a single Organization object, it is easy to change the user accounts of every marketing user simultaneously by just manipulating the Organization object under which they're grouped.

The structure of NDS objects, and the way they are grouped together, is called the Directory tree (or, sometimes, the NDS tree). The discussion throughout this book talks about the Directory tree, and where objects — and you — are located in it.

The Directory tree is called a tree because a diagram of the NDS objects in your network's NDS database will look like an upside-down tree, with a root at the top and branches and subbranches fanning out beneath it, as shown in Figure 1.13.

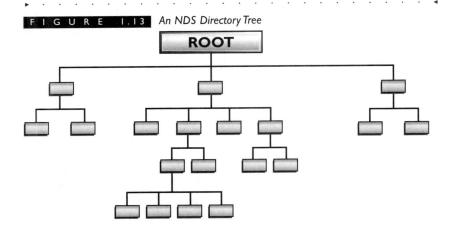

FIGURE 1.13 *An NDS Directory Tree*

NOTE

Most small- or average-sized intraNetWare networks have a single NDS tree (and a single NDS database) that defines the entire network. Larger networks may have multiple trees, though this isn't always necessary. For example, a large company that consists of three different subsidiaries who seldom communicate with each other might have a separate tree for each subsidiary.

NDS makes it easy for network administrators to keep track of their networks and update new information as users or network devices come and go. By defining objects once for an entire network, administrators cut out a lot of the repetitive work they once had to do with earlier versions of NetWare and other network products. Chapter 4 goes into more explanation about NDS objects and trees.

SECURITY

An object defined on the network can be recognized and accessed by any server on the entire network. Some people are concerned the first time they hear this, worrying that it means anyone can have free access to every object on the network. Rest assured, the network doesn't have to be a free-for-all.

By using a distributed, shared database, NDS ensures that an object on the network can be recognized by any other object on the network. However, that doesn't mean that every other object will be *allowed* to access the object. A powerful array of security features is included with intraNetWare. These security features control exactly what an object is allowed to do once it's on the network.

The three primary types of security features contained within intraNetWare are:

- ► Login security — This controls whether or not users can log in to the network. (You can also specify such restrictions as when they can log in and what kind of password they use.)

- ► NDS security — NDS regulates how objects can use other objects. (For example, you can specify whether or not User A can change User B's permissible login times, or whether User C can delete or change a print server.)

- ► File system security — This specifies whether individual users or groups can open, change, delete, or create new files and directories.

These three types of security offer enough flexibility and protection to secure networks from nearly any type of intrusion, or unintended or accidental access. The network administrator controls this security, allowing as much (or as little) access as necessary. The administrator can also share security duties with other users, so different people control access to different parts of the network. Chapter 6 explains intraNetWare security in greater detail.

NETWORK MANAGEMENT

IntraNetWare provides a host of tools that network administrators can use to manage the entire network. Its utilities enable the administrator to create and change NDS objects, modify security features, detect trouble on the network, back-up (archive) and restore files safely, regulate printing, and so on.

Depending on the size and complexity of the network, the amount of time an administrator spends managing it can be minimal or a full-time job. In a simple, small network, the administrator's tasks usually involve setting things up (such as installing a new workstation for an employee), upgrading applications every once in a while, creating a new user object when a new hire arrives, backing up files, and the like.

In a large, complex network for a company that's changing rapidly, the administrator may carry out those same tasks, but at a much faster pace and in greater numbers. In addition, larger networks tend to have more complexity of hardware, protocols, and applications that keep a network administrator hopping to keep up.

Regardless of the size of the network, intraNetWare management tools help the administrator keep the network running smoothly.

Networks, the Internet, and Intranets

Just as the whole world seemed to get the hang of the Internet, a new buzz-word was invented, and the computing industry began another one of its typical feeding frenzies. That new buzzword was *intranet*. Intranets are really just a merging of the Internet idea with the networking idea.

Network is a fairly generic term for linking several computers and related equipment. A network can be small (a few workstations in a dentist's office, for example) or it can be huge (thousands of workstations across a global organization, all linked together). There are no real restrictions on what a network can comprise.

The Internet is a specific, giant network. Originally, it was started as a way to link various research, defense, and education systems together. Since then, it has grown by leaps and bounds as thousands of other networks have connected to it. Universities, corporations, individual users, small businesses, nonprofit organizations, and anyone else wanting to join the party have connected into the Internet, stretching its borders around the globe.

The allure of the Internet is that it expands your network of communication far, far beyond your own organization. Entering the Internet is like entering the largest library in the world. Avenues for information are seemingly endless. You can find the equivalent of "study groups" or round-table discussions on nearly any topic. You can also be as passive or as interactive as you care to be with the information you find.

These aspects of the Internet (libraries of archived information, active discussion groups, and so on) quickly proved useful to the corporations and organizations that accessed them. Before too long, some of those organizations realized that the same type of forum would be extremely useful to disseminate internal information to employees. They wanted to put a Web server on their internal network and make it so no one outside the company could see it. Novell was one of the first companies — if not the first — to call this type of network an intranet.

With an intranet, employees can access the company's Web server, and the information on it, through the same browsers they use to surf the Internet. The only difference between an intranet and the Internet is that the intranet can only be accessed by people on the company's own network — outsiders can't access it.

On an intranet (more specifically, on the company's private Web site), employees can post information that internal employees may need, without posting it to the entire world on the Internet. For example, a company's internal Web site might include forums for:

▶ Project information (such as schedules, status reports, and product specs)

▶ Information about employee benefits (such as online employee handbooks, holiday schedules, and phone numbers for health plan doctors)

▶ Databases of technical information for use by customer service employees

▶ Product descriptions

▶ Even fun and after-hours topics, such as employee "for sale" bulletin boards, the cafeteria lunch menu, employee newsletters, or information about upcoming company parties

NOTE Novell changed the name of its flagship product from NetWare to intraNetWare when they added a Web server and browser. These components enable companies to turn their networks into intranets for their employees. With intraNetWare's security features, a company can go beyond restricting the outside world from its intranet; it also lets the organization restrict how (and which) internal employees can access the information.

At that time, Novell also added features that enable companies to connect their intranet to the Internet, without compromising security. That way, employees can surf out, without intruders surfing in.

Beyond the Basics

This chapter introduced you to the fundamental basics of an intraNetWare network. Later chapters in this book will go into detail on some of these features. You'll find the following topics addressed later in this book:

▶ For more on NDS objects and Directory trees, see Chapter 4.

▶ For more on intraNetWare security, see Chapter 6.

▶ The intraNetWare management tools you're most likely to need are discussed throughout this book, for example:

　▶ To manage users, see Chapter 5.

- ▶ To manage security, see Chapter 6.
- ▶ To manage files and applications on the network, see Chapter 7.
- ▶ To manage print services, see Chapter 8.

Some features or aspects of an intraNetWare network that were touched on in this chapter are more advanced than the scope of this book — specifically, network architectures and protocols. You can find more detailed information about those features in Novell's online documentation (which came with your intraNetWare package) and in *Novell's IntranetWare™ Administrator's Handbook* (from Novell Press), which can be used as an advanced companion to this book. For more information about connecting to the Internet, you may also want to see *Novell's Guide to Internet Access Solutions* from Novell Press.

CHAPTER 2

Installing and Managing intraNetWare Servers

Instant Access

Preparing to Install or Upgrade a Server

- Prepare the computer that will become the server by installing appropriate RAM, network boards, and hard disks, and by creating a DOS partition on the first hard disk.

- Ensure that the server is protected by placing it in a secure room, bracing it against earthquakes, and installing a UPS or surge suppressor.

Installing an intraNetWare Server

- To install the server, use the INSTALL utility and choose the Simple Installation.

- To upgrade a server, use the INSTALL utility and choose Upgrade.

- During the installation or upgrade, you will specify the server's information (such as its name and hardware) and set up the NDS tree (or place the server into an existing tree).

Managing the Server

- You can use two types of utilities to manage the server: console utilities and NLMs (NetWare Loadable Modules).

- You can use Remote Console to control the server from a workstation. Your workstation's monitor and keyboard become the monitor and keyboard for the server, from which you can execute server commands.

- STARTUP.NCF and AUTOEXEC.NCF are the two primary startup files for the server. You can edit them by loading EDIT.NLM.

- You can use MONITOR.NLM to monitor the server's activities and performance.

- You can monitor the server's error log files to see if any errors have occurred on the server while it was running.

The First Step — Installing the Server

The first step in getting an intraNetWare network up and running is to install the server. After the server is installed, you can use the server to manage network activity.

In a nutshell, when you install the server, you:

► Set up the network's data storage on the server's hard disk.

► Create the NDS Directory tree structure, if this is the first server in the network, or add the server into an existing tree if one already exists.

► Create the first user in the network (user ADMIN, who has complete security access to the network after installation).

► Specify the type of network architecture the network will be using (such as Ethernet).

► Install all of the intraNetWare utilities that both the network administrator and the users need when working on the network.

Because this book discusses the basics of intraNetWare, we'll look at the easiest way to install a new intraNetWare server in this chapter: the Simple Installation.

NOTE

The Custom Installation is another option for installing a new intraNetWare server. The Custom Installation assumes that you are familiar with all of the advanced features of intraNetWare, such as time synchronization and protocols, and that you want to make specific changes to the default setup. The Custom Installation is not explained in this book. Many network administrators, especially for smaller networks, find that the Simple Installation is entirely adequate for their needs.

For more information about the Custom Installation, refer to either the Novell online documentation or to Chapter 2 of *Novell's IntranetWare Administrator's Handbook.*

In many cases, you may be upgrading an existing NetWare 3 or NetWare 4 server to intraNetWare. Therefore, this chapter will also look at the easiest way to upgrade an existing server (which, coincidentally, uses the same utility as a brand new installation).

Finally, the chapter will end with a look at some of the basic management activities you can do with the server after it is set up.

NOTE

In some cases, you may have a network that is running a previous version of NetWare. However, instead of upgrading the existing server, you decide you want to replace the old server with a completely new machine. In this case, you won't use the regular upgrade procedure described in this chapter.

Instead, you will use a procedure called *migrating* to transfer the network data off of the old server machine, across the network, onto the new machine. Once the new machine is functioning as a server, you can take down the old machine and get rid of it (or turn it into a workstation). To *migrate* a server this way, use the DS Migrate utility and the File Migration utility. These advanced utilities aren't explained in this book.

For more information about the migration procedure, refer to the Novell online documentation.

Preparing to Install or Upgrade a Server

Before you install or upgrade your server, you need to make sure you're prepared. There are three steps to preparing for the installation:

▶ Make sure the server itself is ready, with the necessary amount of memory installed, a smaller DOS partition created, network boards installed, and so on.

▶ Ensure the server is going to be protected.

▶ Arm yourself with all of the necessary information you'll need to answer questions during the installation procedure.

GETTING THE SERVER READY

Before running the installation program, you need to make sure the server hardware is ready. As mentioned in Chapter 1, a server can be any PC-based computer (at least a 486 processor or higher is recommended). The server should have enough processor speed, memory, and hard disk space to suit your needs. The larger your network, the more powerful your server will need to be. The server also needs a CD-ROM drive to run the installation program, and a network board (such as an Ethernet or Token Ring board) to connect to the rest of the network.

IntraNetWare requires a minimum of 105MB of hard disk space (15MB on the DOS partition and 90MB for the NetWare partition). However, this doesn't allow for any additional files (such as applications, work files, and so on) to be stored on the server, and allows no room for growth. You will probably want to have much more disk space available. In fact, you may decide you want to have multiple hard disks installed in the server.

Planning the Server Memory

One of the most important characteristics of your server — more important in many cases than processor speed — is memory. You need to make sure that your server has enough memory to keep things humming along smoothly.

Officially, an intraNetWare server should have a minimum of 20MB of RAM. Depending on the size of the network (the number of servers, number of users on the server, total disk space on the server, and so on), you will probably want more memory than that.

Novell recommends that you multiply the amount of your server's disk space by 0.008, and then add that amount to the base 20MB of RAM. For example, assume you have a 2GB disk (approximately 2000MB). Thus, 2,000 times 0.008 equals an additional 16MB of RAM.

Then add another 1 to 4MB for additional cache buffer RAM, to increase performance. The more memory you add here (up to 4MB), the better the performance will be.

Therefore, if you decide to add 4MB of cache buffer RAM to the example 2-gigabyte hard disk, you end up with a minimum of 40MB of RAM:

$$20 + (2000 \times 0.008) + 4 = 40MB$$

RAM is relatively inexpensive for the benefit you receive from it, so don't skimp on it unnecessarily.

Installing the Network Boards

If you install and configure the network board(s) in the server before installation, the installation program will be capable of analyzing the hardware and (in most cases) automatically will load the necessary LAN driver. Refer to the network board manufacturer's documentation for configuration instructions.

If this is not the first server in the network, connect the server to the rest of the network by installing the network board in the server, and connecting a network cable from the network board to a hub or other network connection. By connecting the server's cable to the network before the server is even installed, you allow the installation program to automatically identify the existing Directory tree and other important network information.

Installing Additional Hard Disks

If you need to add extra hard disks to the server—now is the time to do it. Install all hard disks according to the manufacturer's instructions. Then the installation program will automatically recognize the disks and treat them accordingly.

Creating a Small DOS Partition

Before you run the installation program to install a brand new server, you will want to reformat the server's hard disk to create a smaller DOS partition than usual. (Chapter 1 explained why the disk needs to be partitioned.)

NOTE

If you're upgrading an existing server, you don't need to reformat this disk. An existing server will most likely have a DOS partition and a NetWare partition on it already.

Normally, when you purchase a new computer, the hard disk is preformatted to support the workstation's operating system (DOS, Windows 95, or the like).

When you want to turn a computer into a server, you will need to reformat the hard disk so it can contain two separate partitions, each formatted in a different way.

The first disk partition you will create is a DOS partition. The DOS partition is the portion of the hard disk that is reserved for DOS system files and other DOS files that you want to store on the server. The files needed to boot the machine and let it communicate with its fundamental hardware are located in the DOS partition. In addition, some intraNetWare files will exist on the DOS partition. The DOS partition does not need to be as large as the NetWare partition.

The rest of the disk becomes a NetWare partition, which stores the majority of the intraNetWare files and all of the network data. Plan for at least a 20MB DOS partition, but a rule of thumb is to add 1MB to the DOS partition for every MB of server RAM installed. A safe plan is to create a minimum DOS partition of about 60MB, to ensure you have enough room for any files you want to load.

The first hard disk in the server will have a DOS partition and a NetWare partition. If the server contains additional hard disks, each of them can have only one NetWare partition (as shown in Figure 2.1).

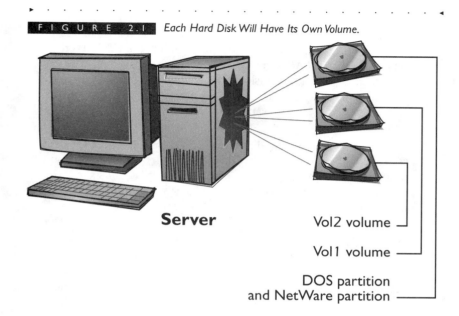

FIGURE 2.1 *Each Hard Disk Will Have Its Own Volume.*

Server

Vol2 volume

Vol1 volume

DOS partition
and NetWare partition

NOTE If the computer you are turning into a server is currently running Windows 95, you'll need to reformat the computer's hard disk to support DOS instead. IntraNetWare doesn't need to have Windows 95 on the hard disk, so there's no need to retain Windows 95 on this machine.

To eliminate Windows 95 and format the DOS partition, boot the computer from the intraNetWare License diskette (put the diskette in drive A and turn on the computer). This diskette contains the DOS utilities called FDISK and FORMAT. By running these utilities, as explained in the following procedure, you'll reformat the disk to support DOS.

You should create the DOS disk partition before running the installation program. (The installation process will create the partition for you if you want, but it's generally easier to do it yourself so you can avoid having to reinstall the CD-ROM drive's drivers and other configuration information after the installation program runs.) Here are the basic steps to format the DOS partition (refer to your computer manufacturer's documentation for more specific instructions):

1. First, save the computer's disk drivers (including the CD-ROM driver), AUTOEXEC.BAT, and CONFIG.SYS onto a diskette so you can copy them back onto the disk after you've reformatted it. You may also have other files that are loaded by the AUTOEXEC.BAT file (or other boot files) that you want to retain. Copy those files to the diskette, too.

2. Use DOS's FDISK command to create a DOS partition of at least 60MB. Use the formula described earlier to determine the size you need. (If the computer you're using doesn't have DOS installed, you can boot from the license diskette that came with intraNetWare. The necessary DOS commands to reformat the server's hard disk are contained on that diskette.) To run FDISK, make sure you're at the DOS prompt, and then type FDISK. Follow the instructions on the screen to delete the current DOS partition and then create a new primary partition.

3. Use DOS's FORMAT command to format the partition. To use this utility, type the following command at the DOS prompt. The "/X" option formats a hard disk, and the "/S" option copies the DOS COMMAND.COM file to the disk.

   FORMAT /X /S

4. Leave the rest of the disk space alone for now — that space will be converted to the NetWare partition during the installation program.

All of the disk space in the NetWare partition will be assigned to one volume. (A volume is the same thing as a root directory — the highest directory or folder in the file system.) This volume, called SYS, is created automatically by the Simple Installation. If the server has more than one hard disk attached, each additional disk will have its own separate NetWare volume, named VOL1, VOL2, and so on.

TIP

You must choose the Custom Installation if you want the option of changing the sizes and names of the volumes before intraNetWare creates them, or if you want to create more volumes than just SYS on the first hard disk. The Custom Installation is not discussed in this book. Refer to the online Novell documentation for more information.

Installing the CD-ROM Drive

If the CD-ROM isn't already installed in the server, install it (as a DOS device) according to the manufacturer's documentation. Most CD-ROM drives have an automatic installation program that you run after you've connected the drive to modify the AUTOEXEC.BAT and CONFIG.SYS files. This way, the CD-ROM's drivers can load and work properly.

Verifying the Date and Time Using the DOS DATE and TIME commands, verifies that the server's time and date are set correctly, and changes them if necessary.

To use the DATE command, go to the DOS prompt and type DATE. The computer will display what it thinks is the current date, and then it will ask you to enter a new date. If the date is wrong, type in the new date in a mm-dd-yy format. If the date is already correct, just press Enter and the date will remain unchanged. The TIME command is used the same way.

PROTECTING THE SERVER

Protecting the server is a very important safeguard that cannot be over-looked. Damage to the server can affect the entire network.

Preventing Physical Damage

If the server is in an exposed public area where anyone can have access to it, accidents may happen. For example, someone might trip over the power cord or turn off the server thinking it was a regular computer that had been left on accidentally. After-hours janitorial people are notorious for unplugging computers to plug in vacuum cleaners.

Of more concern than accidents, however, is the possibility of deliberate tampering. Computer specialists will tell you over and over again that the best security software in the world, such as intraNetWare's, can't protect your server if an unauthorized person can gain physical access to the server. If an intruder can get to your server physically, he or she can remove hard disks, reboot the server, load virus programs from diskette, and so on.

In other words, if you really want to protect your server, and the data on it, lock the server in a secure room, and hide the key. In fact, you may also want to remove its keyboard and monitor, and access it only with the Remote Console feature when necessary. (Remote Console is explained later in this chapter.)

Bracing Against Earthquakes

If you work in an earthquake-prone area, you should also secure the server to a desk or counter. A good-sized shake, such as the one that hit San Francisco a few years ago, can send computers flying across the room. A moderate one can tip over the racks on which the computers are sitting. Don't risk losing your network simply because the server fell off the table.

Minimizing Electricity-Related Problems

The electrical power coming from the power company into your office is not always consistent. Because of this, you need to make sure your server will not be damaged and files won't be corrupted if a brownout, spike, surge, or blackout occurs.

The best protection for your server is to use an *uninterruptible power supply* (UPS). A UPS provides the server with a backup battery that takes over in case of a power outage. This backup battery allows enough time for the UPS to shut down the server cleanly, leaving no open files exposed to corruption. A good UPS also protects against spikes, surges, brownouts, and line noise (interference on the wire).

If possible, attach each workstation to a UPS, too. If a UPS isn't feasible, at least use surge suppressors on the workstations and peripherals (such as printers) to prevent electrical surges and spikes from damaging the equipment. Figure 2.2 shows a typical UPS and surge suppressor.

NOTE

UPS's and surge suppressors can be found at many computer equipment stores (and even some of those big warehouse stores that sell computer and office supplies). Depending on your needs, these protection devices can be fairly inexpensive. Before purchasing one, check recent reviews in the trade press for top-ranking products, or at least verify what type of equipment the device is designed to protect.

For example, surge suppressors come in a variety of "strengths" — meaning that some can withstand higher voltage spikes and surges than others. Make sure you get devices that will adequately protect the equipment you have. If you're unsure, don't hesitate to call the manufacturer (or look up their Web site) for recommendations. One of the top UPS and surge suppressor manufacturers, APC (American Power Conversion), has a Web site at www.apcc.com. Their Web site contains useful information about power and APC's products.

When Power Corrupts

A *brownout* (also called a *sag*) occurs when power in the area is diminished, but doesn't go out completely. Generally, lights grow dimmer and appliances run slower, sporadically, or not at all. These can be caused by too many machines trying to start up at the same time or by a single heavy-load machine. Power companies may deliberately cause brownouts when electrical demand exceeds supply (such as on hot summer days when all the air conditioners are running), thereby allowing customers to avoid a total blackout. Brownouts can put undue stress on your computer's components, causing damage.

A *spike*, which is often caused by lightening strikes, occurs when the electrical voltage suddenly and drastically increases, usually doubling (or more) the normal peak voltage. This is the type of power problem than can fry your electrical appliances if they're plugged in, and the reason why experts say you shouldn't talk on the telephone during thunderstorms. Spikes can also occur when power is turned back on after an outage.

A *surge* is a brief increase in power, but not as great an increase as a spike. Surges may occur when a heavy-load machine is turned off and power surges to other devices that were on the same circuit. While a surge may not destroy your computer, it can stress delicate parts and cause premature failure.

A *blackout* is a complete power outage. Obvious problems with this are that you will lose any unsaved data instantly. But this kind of instant outage can also corrupt open files, including files that keep track of where everything is on your hard disk. More damage can be caused by the spike that might occur when the power comes back on.

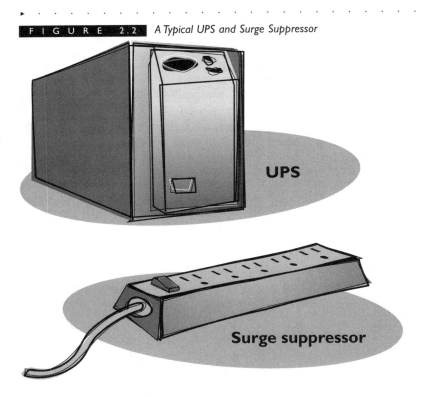

FIGURE 2.2 *A Typical UPS and Surge Suppressor*

UPS

Surge suppressor

INFORMATION YOU'LL NEED
BEFORE INSTALLING THE SERVER

Regardless of whether you are upgrading or installing a new server, there are several decisions you have to make about your server. You'll need to provide the answers to some of these questions during the installation, so make sure you know what you want before you begin.

Novell Directory Services (NDS) objects and Directory trees were introduced in Chapter 1.

TIP

During the Simple Installation, you will create a basic Directory tree. This Directory tree will have only one Organization object, named with the name you enter for your organization. (The tree will have the same name as this Organization object to make it easier to identify.) An Organization object is sometimes referred to as a container object, because it contains other objects.

The server you're installing, its hard disk volumes, and a user named ADMIN will all be created as NDS objects underneath this Organization object.

If you are installing a server into an existing Directory tree, the installation program will ask you to select the existing tree into which you want to install this server. In this case, this server's object (and its volumes) will be created underneath the pre-existing Organization object.

This chapter assumes you are installing a relatively simple network, and that you only require a single Organization object to contain all of your users, servers, printers, and so on.

However, you can specify additional layers of container objects underneath the Organization object, should you so desire. These "subcontainer" objects are called *Organizational Unit objects*. If you think of an Organization object as your company's name, an Organizational Unit object might be equivalent to a department name.

If you want to learn more about NDS objects and trees before you go through the installation program, you can refer to Chapter 4.

Before starting the installation or upgrade, you should have the following information about the server:

▶ *The server's name.* You can choose any name between 2 and 47 characters long, using letters, numbers, hyphens, or underscores.

▶ *The server's time zone.* You'll need to know the acronym for the server's time zone and whether that time zone supports Daylight Saving Time. (This information will probably be filled in automatically during the installation, but you'll want to verify it.)

▶ *The name of your organization* (for instance, your company name). This Organization object name will become the Directory tree's name, as well. (If you're installing a server into a pre-existing tree, you'll need to know the name of the existing tree.)

▶ *The types of network boards you will install in the server.* You'll need to know the type of network board inside the server and the name of its corresponding LAN driver. In many cases, intraNetWare will automatically detect the board and load the correct driver without even asking you. However, if intraNetWare doesn't recognize the necessary LAN driver, you'll need to supply the driver on a separate diskette (usually available from the manufacturer) along with the driver's settings. Check the manufacturer's documentation for information on the correct settings to use. (Settings may include the interrupt that the board uses, the slot it's installed in, or the like.)

▶ *The name of the disk controller board's driver.* You should know the name of the disk driver required by your hard disk. Again, intraNetWare will recognize most common disks and automatically load the correct driver for them, but you'll need to have the driver on hand if the installation program can't recognize it.

▶ *How you plan to install the intraNetWare client software on your work-stations.* Note that the client software included on the CD-ROM is an older version than client software available on Novell's Web site. It's highly recommended that you download the newer client from the Web instead of using the older client on the CD-ROM. Instructions for this are in Chapter 3. However, if you do not have access to the World Wide Web, you can use the client software on the intraNetWare CD-ROM:

  ▶ If you have workstations that have never been connected to a NetWare or intraNetWare network before, you will need to make a set of installation diskettes from the CD-ROM. The server installation program has an option for making these diskettes. You will use the diskettes to install the client software on those computers. (If all the new workstations have CD-ROM drives, you can install clients directly from the intraNetWare CD-ROM, so making diskettes may not be necessary for your situation.)

  ▶ If you plan to upgrade existing workstations that are already running a previous version of NetWare client software, you can choose to copy all of the client installation files from the CD-ROM onto the server instead. This way, you can upgrade the existing workstations directly from the network, eliminating the need for making diskettes. See Chapter 3 for more information about installing workstations.

▶ *Whether you want any volumes to support Mac OS or UNIX files, or whether you want any volumes to support the long file names allowed by OS/2, Windows 95, or Windows NT.* By default, the server supports DOS files, which only use short (11 character) file names. This default setting also supports OS/2, Windows 95, and Windows NT files, but doesn't allow them to have longer file names. This default does not support Mac OS or UNIX files, because those files require completely different file formats.

To support the long file names and the different file formats used by other operating systems, you will have to load a special program, called a name space module, for those files after installation. Then you will assign that name space to the volume where you want to store those files. The steps for this will be explained at the end of the installation procedure.

The following name space modules support the different file formats and file name restrictions, as shown in Table 2.1.

TABLE 2.1 Name Space Modules

NAME SPACE MODULE	FILES SUPPORTED
LONG.NAM	Windows 95, Windows NT, OS/2
MAC.NAM	Mac OS
NFS.NAM	UNIX

Installing a New intraNetWare Server

To perform the Simple Installation of intraNetWare, complete the steps in the following sections.

BEGINNING THE INSTALLATION

To begin the installation, perform the following steps:

I. Set up the server hardware, as described in the previous sections.

    a. Install and configure any new memory, network boards, and hard disks in the server.

    b. Using the DOS FDISK and FORMAT commands, create a DOS disk partition. Leave the rest of the disk space free.

   c. If necessary, install the CD-ROM drive as a DOS device on the
      server, and then reboot the server to make sure the drive is recog-
      nized by the computer and that its settings take effect.

   d. Using the DOS DATE and TIME commands, verify that the
      computer's time and date are set correctly, and change them if
      necessary.

2. Insert the *NetWare 4.11 Operating System* CD-ROM into the computer's
    CD-ROM drive.

3. From the DOS command prompt on the server, change to the CD-
    ROM drive's letter (often D), and enter the following command:

      INSTALL

4. Choose the language you want to use (as shown in Figure 2.3).

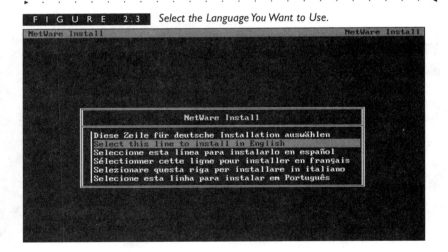

FIGURE   2.3   *Select the Language You Want to Use.*

5. A screen called "Novell Terms and Conditions" will appear. This
    describes the legal terms and conditions you must agree to in order to
    install intraNetWare. Press any key to page through the document.

6. Choose Readme Files if you want to read the information in the
    readme files that was written too late to be printed in the manuals.

7. Choose NetWare Server Installation → NetWare 4.11 → Simple
    Installation of NetWare 4.11 (see Figure 2.4).

FIGURE 2.4 *Select Simple Installation of NetWare 4.11.*

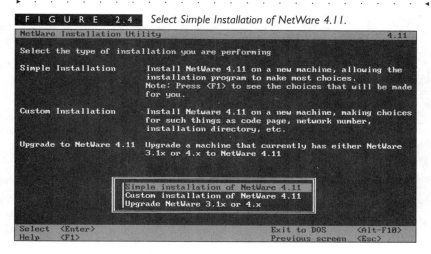

Now the installation program will begin; continue with the instructions in the next section to specify the server's information.

SPECIFYING THE SERVER'S INFORMATION

To specify the server's information, perform the following steps:

1. Enter a name for this server, as shown in Figure 2.5.

2. In some cases, you may be asked to specify the country code, code page, and keyboard mapping for your server. If you're using United States English DOS, you probably won't see this screen, so skip this step. Different countries have slightly different versions of DOS developed to support varying languages, and some countries or languages have their own unique types of keyboards. This screen will only appear if intraNetWare detects that you may be using a different combination of these settings, so that you can specify them. (If this screen appears, press Enter and choose the correct selections from the lists that appear.)

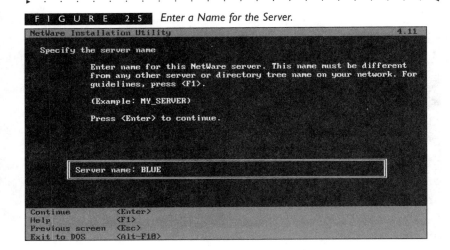

F I G U R E   2.5   *Enter a Name for the Server.*

```
NetWare Installation Utility                                        4.11

  Specify the server name

          Enter name for this NetWare server. This name must be different
          from any other server or directory tree name on your network. For
          guidelines, press <F1>.

          (Example: MY_SERVER)

          Press <Enter> to continue.


      ┌─────────────────────────────────────────────────────────────┐
      │ Server name: BLUE                                             │
      └─────────────────────────────────────────────────────────────┘


  Continue            <Enter>
  Help                <F1>
  Previous screen     <Esc>
  Exit to DOS         <Alt-F10>
```

NOTE

At this point, boot files are copied from the CD to the DOS partition on the server. This will take some time. Then, the server will automatically load a file called SERVER.EXE, which is the operating system, and other necessary programs. When the process is completed, the installation program will begin looking for disk and LAN drivers for your server.

3. The installation program can automatically detect many brands of hard disk controller boards and automatically select and load the necessary disk drivers that support those boards. If the installation detects and loads your disk drivers, skip to Step 4. If the installation doesn't detect your disk drivers, select the disk drivers you need for your server's hard disk controller board and CD-ROM drive controller board (if necessary) from the list that appears, and specify their settings. If a driver you need doesn't appear in the list, press Ins and insert the diskette that contains the driver, then press F3 to specify the correct path to the driver. (Most manufacturers supply you with the necessary disk drivers on a diskette that comes with the hard disk you purchased. Check with the manufacturer if you can't find the necessary driver.)

4. The installation program can automatically detect many network boards and automatically select and load the necessary LAN drivers. If the installation detects your LAN drivers, skip to Step 5. If the installation doesn't detect your LAN drivers, select the LAN drivers for your server's network boards from the list that appears, and specify their settings. If the driver you need doesn't appear in the list, press Ins and insert the diskette that contains the driver, then press F3 to specify the correct path to the driver. (Most manufacturers supply you with the necessary LAN drivers on a diskette that comes with the network board you purchased. Check with the manufacturer if you can't find the necessary LAN driver.)

5. When the program has located all the necessary drivers (or after you've selected them), it will display a screen asking you to verify the drivers it found, as shown in Figure 2.6. If the drivers are correct, select Continue Installation. If you need to change the drivers, choose Select Additional or Modify Selected Disk and LAN drivers.

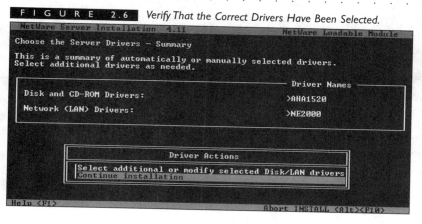

FIGURE 2.6 *Verify That the Correct Drivers Have Been Selected.*

6. In some cases, you may need to select whether to access the CD-ROM as a DOS device or a NetWare volume. If so, tell INSTALL to mount the CD-ROM as a NetWare volume. (This means the CD-ROM will be available to network users just like the volumes on the server's hard disks. However, all you really need to know about this now is that the preferred option is to load it as a NetWare volume.) If the keyboard locks up, repeat the installation and choose Continue Accessing the CD-ROM via DOS option instead. Either method can work; the NetWare volume method is preferred mainly because it could avoid a possible driver conflict.

7. If you are asked whether to delete any existing nonbootable partitions, select Yes. At this point, more files are copied to the server's hard disk. This is called the *Preliminary Copy*, as shown in Figure 2.7, and can take up to 20 minutes.

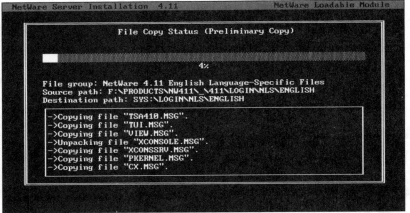

FIGURE 2.7 *The Status Screen, Showing the Progress of the Preliminary Copy*

When the boot files are copied, the Installation program will ask you to set up NDS on this server. Continue with the steps in the following section to set up NDS.

SETTING UP THE DIRECTORY TREE

To set up the Directory tree, complete the following steps:

1. If you are installing this server into an existing Directory tree, select the correct tree into which this server will be installed. (To create a new tree, press Ins.) If this is the first server in the tree, select "Yes, this is the first NetWare 4 server."

2. Select the time zone in which this server will exist.

3. If this is the first server in the Directory tree, enter the name of your organization (such as your company name). Keep the name short. This will become the name of your Directory tree and your only Organization object.

4. Enter a password for the ADMIN user. If this is the first server in the tree, enter any password you want. (You will have to enter it twice to verify the spelling.) If this server is being installed into an existing NDS tree, an ADMIN user already exists, so type in the ADMIN password that has already been assigned.

NOTE

If this is the first server in a tree, NDS will now be installed. After NDS is installed, you'll see a screen that indicates the name you gave your Directory tree (the same name as the organization), the *Directory Context* (or location in the tree) where your server has been installed, and the Administrator user's full name.

When an object is created, it has a name, such as "BlueSky" or "Fred" or "Printer1." It also has a longer name, called a full name (or full distinguished name), that indicates its position in the tree. Basically, an object's full name consists of the object's name, followed by the names of each of the objects above it. Each name is separated by a period. For example, if a user named Fred is located under an Organization object called BlueSky, the user's full name will be Fred.BlueSky.

Sometimes, the type of object is also indicated in a full name. If an object is an Organization, the indicator "O=" will be added to the beginning of that object's name. If the object is an Organizational Unit, "OU=" is used. All other noncontainer objects, such as users, servers, printers, and the like, are designated with "CN=". This abbreviation stands for "Common Name." (These object types are designated by official naming standards set in the industry, and are described more fully in Chapter 4.) Therefore, Fred's full name would be CN=Fred.O=BlueSky.

5. If you are installing this server into an existing tree, you will see a screen showing you the server's context. The *server context* (also called *name context* or *Directory context*) is basically just the server's location in the Directory tree.

By default, the screen will show the name of the Organization at the top of the screen. Also by default, the server context (at the bottom of the screen) will indicate the name of the Organization, showing that the server's NDS object is going to be created immediately underneath the Organization's object.

The three additional levels of Organizational Unit objects are optional. If you want to put the server's object under a subcontainer in your tree (such as in a Marketing Department underneath the Organization), you can fill in a name for the first level, to create that new Organizational Unit object. You can specify up to 3 levels of Organizational Units in this screen, or you can leave the Organizational Unit blanks empty and create the server immediately under the main Organization object.

By entering the name of the organization (such as your company) and the names of descending levels of Organizational Units (such as a division and a department), you actually create the branch of the NDS tree that will contain this server if the branch doesn't already exist.

If Organizational Unit objects already exist in a branch, and you want to put this server under them, press Enter on each field and select the Organizational Unit objects you want. See Chapter 4 for more information about NDS tree structures.

6. When prompted, insert the license diskette. When the server has accepted the license, it will begin the "main file copy," copying the intraNetWare files to the server's SYS volume. This process can take up to half an hour.

When these files have finished copying, the main portion of the installation is complete. Now, you can follow the steps in the next section to select some optional, additional tasks, and to exit the installation program.

FINISHING THE INSTALLATION

To complete the installation, follow these steps:

1. After the remaining files are copied to the server, the Other Installation Options screen appears.

   If you want to make a set of installation diskettes to install client software on your network workstations, choose the Make Diskettes option.

   If you plan to upgrade existing workstations that are already running a previous version of NetWare client software, you can choose the Create Client Installation Directories on Server option. This will place the client installation files into the volume SYS, under the directory (folder) PUBLIC so you can upgrade the existing workstations directly from the network.

   See Chapter 3 for more information about installing workstations.

TIP

Before choosing to make client diskettes or copy client files to the server, note that the client software included on the CD-ROM is an older version than client software available on Novell's Web site. It's highly recommended that you download the newer client from the Web instead of using the older client on the CD-ROM. Instructions for this are in Chapter 3.

2. Choose Continue Installation to finish the server installation.

3. When the final installation message appears on the screen, press Enter to exit the program. You will be returned to the server's console prompt. The server is now functioning.

4. If you want the server to be able to store Mac OS files, UNIX files, or the longer file names that Windows 95, Windows NT, and OS/2 allow, you must load the appropriate name space on the server. Then you must add the name space to one or more volumes.

    a. To allow the server to store non-DOS files or long file names, enter the following command at the server console. Replace *name* with MAC for Mac OS files, NFS for UNIX files, or LONG for Windows 95, Windows NT, or OS/2 files:

    LOAD *name*

    For example, to make the server support Windows 95's long file names, type **LOAD LONG.**

    b. Then specify a particular volume that will store these files by using the ADD NAME SPACE command. Type this command in the following format (replace *name* with MAC, NFS, or LONG, and replace *volumename* with the name of the volume, such as SYS or VOL1):

    ADD NAME SPACE *name* TO VOLUME *volumename*

    For example, to add the LONG name space to volume SYS, type:

    ADD NAME SPACE LONG TO VOLUME SYS

5. Reboot the server to make all the necessary changes take effect. To reboot the server, type **DOWN** and then type **RESTART SERVER.**

You've finished installing your server. IntraNetWare is now running on the computer. To see what you can do with the server now, skip to the section titled "After the Installation — Managing the Server," later in this chapter.

Upgrading from Previous Versions of NetWare

To upgrade an existing NetWare 3.1x, 4.01, 4.02, or 4.1 server to intraNetWare, use INSTALL.NLM and choose the Upgrade NetWare 3.1x or 4.x option. This is the simplest way to upgrade a server.

For NetWare 4.x servers, INSTALL.NLM will copy new intraNetWare files and the new intraNetWare operating system onto the existing server. It will also upgrade Novell Directory Services (NDS).

When upgrading a NetWare 3.11 or 3.12 server, the server's existing network data (stored in a database called a *bindery*) is upgraded into an NDS database. All of the server's bindery objects become NDS objects, and they are all placed in the same location (name context) in the Directory tree as the server.

TIP

In most cases, it's best to upgrade all NetWare 4.0x and 4.1 servers to intraNetWare as soon as possible, to avoid maintaining a network with multiple versions of NDS on it. IntraNetWare fixed several problems with the older versions of NDS, and it is easier to maintain NDS if all servers are operating at the same level.

Because NetWare 3.1x did not use NDS, it is not necessary to upgrade all NetWare 3.1x servers quickly. There is no conflict between NetWare 3.1x servers and the intraNetWare NDS.

NetWare 3.x binderies were a simpler form of network database than the NDS database. Binderies were flat instead of hierarchical, meaning all objects were at the same level, and couldn't be grouped into containers. In addition, binderies were specific to particular servers. This means that if you wanted user John to access three different NetWare 3.1x servers, you had to create John as a separate user on all three servers.

NDS is an great improvement over a bindery because it is much more flexible, letting a network administrator have more control over how the network is organized is managed. With NDS, a single NDS database is common to all servers in the network. Therefore, you only need to create John once, and then just give him trustee rights to files on those three servers.

Keep this in mind if you are upgrading several NetWare 3.1x servers into a NetWare 4.11 Directory tree. If you have three instances of user John on three different NetWare 3.1x servers, and you install all three servers into the same location (underneath the same Organization), the installation program will ask you if you want to delete, rename, or merge the user with the one that already exists. If one of the NetWare 3.1*x* users named John is actually a different person than the other two Johns, you should rename one of them before starting the upgrade to ensure that they don't merge.

TIP

To upgrade a NetWare 4.*x* server to intraNetWare, the NetWare 4.*x* server must be currently running a compatible version of NDS. The main NDS program is called DS.NLM, and this program must be at least version 4.89 or higher. Very few networks still have an older version than 4.89 running on them, so this is seldom a concern. However, it's still a good idea to check it.

To see the DS.NLM version, go to the server's keyboard and type MODULES. This command will display the version of all NLM programs (NetWare Loadable Module programs) currently running on this server. Watch for the version number of DS.NLM.

If the version number is not 4.89 or above, you must update the existing DS.NLM before you can upgrade the server to intraNetWare. Do this by following the instructions in the readme file on the intraNetWare CD-ROM. If you are running NetWare 4.0*x*, see the READUPGD.TXT and DSREPAIR.DOC files in the PRODUCTS\NW402\ENGLISH directory. If you are running NetWare 4.1, see the READUPDS.TXT file in the PRODUCTS\NW410\ENGLISH directory.

Use the instructions in the following sections to upgrade your existing NetWare 3.1*x* or 4.*x* server to intraNetWare.

If you are upgrading from NetWare 3.1*x* and you want to upgrade your printing services from NetWare 3.1*x* to NetWare 4.11, you will also have to use PUPGRADE.NLM. (You do not need to run PUPGRADE if you are upgrading from NetWare 4.*x*.) For information on how to upgrade your NetWare 3.1*x* printing setup, see Chapter 8.

BEGINNING THE UPGRADE

To begin the upgrade, follow these steps:

1. Make two backups of all network files.

2. While the server is still running the older version of NetWare, locate the server's LAN drivers and a file called AUTOEXEC.NCF in the SYS volume. Copy the LAN drivers and AUTOEXEC.NCF file onto a diskette, so you can have backups of these files if necessary.

(AUTOEXEC.NCF is a server configuration file that intraNetWare uses to configure the server every time it boots. This files loads programs the server needs.)

3. Bring down the existing server by typing the following commands at the server's keyboard:

   ```
   DOWN
   ```

   and then

   ```
   EXIT
   ```

   Now the computer is just running DOS. The intraNetWare operating system has been halted.

4. From the server's boot directory, copy the server's boot files (.BAT files, .NAM files, disk drivers, INSTALL.NLM, SERVER.EXE, STARTUP.NCF, VREPAIR.NLM, and V_*namespace*.NLM files) to the same diskette you used in Step 2. (These are files that boot up the server and that allow you to fix problems that may occur. You'll learn more about them in later chapters.)

5. If you are upgrading from NetWare 3.1*x*, locate the SERVER.31*x* directory, and rename it to NWSERVER. (In many versions of DOS, you can use DOS's RENDIR command to change the directory's name, by typing **RENDIR SERVER.31*x* NWSERVER**.)

6. Insert the NetWare 4.11 Operating System CD-ROM into the computer's CD-ROM drive; change to the CD-ROM drive's letter (usually D), and type:

   ```
   INSTALL
   ```

7. Choose the language you want to use.

8. A screen called "Novell Terms and Conditions" will appear. This describes the legal terms and conditions you must agree to in order to install intraNetWare. Press any key to page through the document.

9. Choose Readme Files if you want to read the information that was written too late to be printed in the manuals.

10. Choose NetWare Server Installation → NetWare → 4.11 Upgrade NetWare 3.1*x* or 4.*x* (see Figure 2.8).

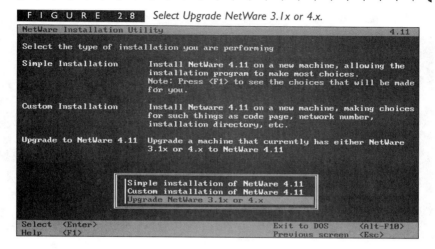

FIGURE 2.8 *Select Upgrade NetWare 3.1x or 4.x.*

Now the upgrade version of the installation program will begin; continue with the instructions in the next section to specify the server's information.

SPECIFYING THE SERVER'S INFORMATION

To specify the server's information, follow these steps:

1. Specify the destination directory, which is the directory that will contain the server boot files (C:\NWSERVER). The new server boot files are now copied to this directory. (This will take several minutes.) Whenever the server boots up, it will look in this directory for its boot files.

2. If necessary, change the country code, code page, and keyboard mapping for your server, as displayed in Figure 2.9. (To select these, press Enter and choose the correct selections from the lists that appear.) In most cases, you won't have to change these settings. These settings specify the country and language that your computer is supposed to use. (Different countries have slightly different versions of DOS developed to support varying languages, and some countries or languages have their own unique types of keyboards.)

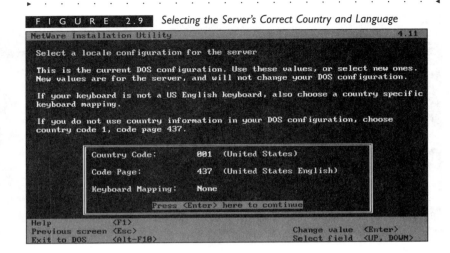

Selecting the Server's Correct Country and Language

NetWare Installation Utility   4.11

Select a locale configuration for the server

This is the current DOS configuration. Use these values, or select new ones.
New values are for the server, and will not change your DOS configuration.

If your keyboard is not a US English keyboard, also choose a country specific
keyboard mapping.

If you do not use country information in your DOS configuration, choose
country code 1, code page 437.

Country Code:	001	(United States)
Code Page:	437	(United States English)
Keyboard Mapping:	None	

Press <Enter> here to continue

Help	<F1>	
Previous screen	<Esc>	Change value <Enter>
Exit to DOS	<Alt-F10>	Select field <UP, DOWN>

NOTE

Now, the upgrade program will execute a file called
SERVER.EXE, which is the server operating system, and other
necessary files. Then it will begin looking for drivers.

3. The installation program will automatically load any disk drivers it
finds listed in the original STARTUP.NCF file of the server you're
upgrading. (STARTUP.NCF is a startup file that was created when the
server was first installed. It contains information that lets the server
boot up, including instructions to load the server's hard disk driver.)

If it cannot find a disk driver listed in that file, the installation program can detect many disk types and automatically select and load
the necessary drivers from the intraNetWare CD-ROM.

The upgrade program will display a screen listing the currently loaded
disk drivers, and it will ask if you want to select additional drivers. If
the list of loaded drivers is correct, select Continue Installation.

If the installation doesn't detect your hard disk driver, choose Select
an Additional Driver and select the disk drivers for your server's hard
disk controller board and CD-ROM drive controller board from the
list that appears, and specify their settings. If the driver you need
doesn't appear in the list, press Ins and insert the diskette that contains the driver. Then press F3 to specify the correct path to the driver.

(The hard disk manufacturer should supply you with a driver for the hard disk and controller board that you purchased.)

4. In some cases, you may need to select whether to access the CD-ROM as a DOS device or a NetWare volume. If so, tell INSTALL to mount the CD-ROM as a NetWare volume. (This means the CD-ROM will be available to network users just like the volumes on the server's hard disks. However, all you really need to know about this now is that the preferred option is to load it as a NetWare volume.) If the keyboard locks up, repeat the installation and choose Continue Accessing the CD-ROM via DOS option instead. Either method can work; the NetWare volume method is preferred mainly because it could avoid a possible driver conflict.

5. After some files (called unicode files) are transferred, a message appears saying that the AUTOEXEC.NCF file will be scanned for any LAN drivers that don't have a frame type specified. A frame type is a particular "flavor" of the Ethernet protocol. IntraNetWare uses a different default frame type (called 802.2) than some previous version of NetWare, so this message is just telling you that it will set the network to use this new frame type unless another one is specifically set. In most cases, you should just press Enter to accept this and continue the installation. After you press Enter, the upgrade program will update driver, utility, and name space files.

6. When prompted, insert the License diskette and press Enter.

7. When the message appears describing a temporary AUTOEXEC.NCF file, you can press F3 to review it to see if you must edit it. In most cases, however, you probably don't need to edit this file (as this is a simple upgrade). Just press Enter to execute the file and continue the installation.

In this temporary file, commands that may cause problems during the upgrade are disabled with a REM command. Edit the file only if there are commands that you know must execute, and then continue with the installation.

8. The installation program can automatically load any LAN drivers (called "network drivers" by the upgrade program) it finds specified in the original AUTOEXEC.NCF file of the server you're upgrading.

If it cannot find a LAN driver listed in that file, the installation program can detect many network boards and automatically select and load the necessary LAN drivers from the CD-ROM.

The upgrade program will display a screen listing the currently loaded LAN drivers, and it will ask if you want to select additional drivers. If the list of loaded drivers is correct, select Continue Installation.

If the installation doesn't detect your LAN drivers, select the LAN drivers for your server's network boards from the list that appears, and specify their settings. If the driver you need doesn't appear in the list, press Ins and insert the diskette that contains the driver. Then press F3 to specify the correct path to the driver. (Most manufacturers will supply a diskette with the required LAN driver for the network board you purchased.)

Now the upgrade program is ready to set up NDS on this server (if you're upgrading a NetWare 3.1x server) or add the server to an existing Directory tree. Continue with the steps in the following section to set up NDS.

PLACING THE SERVER INTO THE DIRECTORY TREE

To place the server into the Directory tree, follow these steps:

1. (NetWare 4.x upgrades only) If you are upgrading a NetWare 4.x server, enter the password for the pre-existing user ADMIN when prompted. A message will appear, telling you that the NDS schema will be updated. (This is okay.) Press Enter to continue, then skip to Step 6.

2. (NetWare 3.1x upgrades only) If you are upgrading this NetWare 3.1x server into an existing NetWare Directory tree, select the correct tree. If this is the first server in the tree, select "Yes, this is the first NetWare 4 server," and then specify a name for the new tree.

3. Select the time zone in which this server will exist, and accept the time synchronization information that appears. (Time synchronization is an advanced feature. The default settings are usually adequate.)

4. Now you will see a screen showing you the server's *context*. The server context (also called *name context* or *Directory context*) is basically just the server's location in the Directory tree.

   By default, the screen will show the name of the Organization at the top of the screen. The server context (shown at the bottom of the screen) will indicate the name of the Organization and any Organizational Units under which this server will be installed.

   The three levels of Organizational Unit objects are optional. If you want to put the server's object under a subcontainer in your tree (such as in a Marketing Department underneath the Organization), you can fill in a name for the first level, to create that new Organizational Unit object. You can specify up to three levels of Organizational Units in this screen, or you can leave the Organizational Unit blanks empty and create the server immediately under the main Organization object.

By entering the name of the organization (such as your company) and the names of descending levels of Organizational Units (such as a division and a department), you actually create the branch of the NDS tree that will contain this server if the branch doesn't already exist.

If Organizational Unit objects already exist in a branch, and you want to put this server under them, press Enter on each field and select the Organizational Unit objects you want. See Chapter 4 for more information about NDS tree structures.

5. Enter a password for the ADMIN user. If this is the first server in the tree, enter any password you want. If this server is being installed into an existing tree, the ADMIN user already exists. Enter the ADMIN password that has already been assigned.

6. You may receive messages telling you about changes the upgrade program has made to your AUTOEXEC.NCF file. Review the new AUTOEXEC.NCF file that appears on the screen. Information you entered during the upgrade process so far is already placed into this file. Press F10 to save the file and continue.

At this point, the main portion of the upgrade is complete. Now, you can follow the steps in the next section to select some optional, additional tasks, and to exit the installation program.

FINISHING THE UPGRADE

To complete the upgrade, follow these steps:

I. After the remaining files are copied to the server, the Other Installation Options screen appears.

From this screen, choose the Make Diskettes option if you want to make a set of installation diskettes to install client software on your network workstations.

If you plan to upgrade existing workstations that are already running a previous version of NetWare client software, you can choose the Create Client Installation Directories on Server option. This will place the installation files into SYS:PUBLIC so you can upgrade the existing workstations directly from the network.

See Chapter 3 for more information about installing workstations.

TIP

Before choosing to make client diskettes or copy client files to the server, note that the client software included on the CD-ROM is an older version than client software available on Novell's Web site. It's highly recommended that you download the newer client from the Web instead of using the older client on the CD-ROM. Instructions for this are in Chapter 3.

2. Choose any other installation options or additional products you want to install, or choose Continue Installation to finish the upgrade.

3. When the final installation message appears on the screen, press Enter to exit the program. You will be returned to the server's console prompt. The server is now functioning.

4. Reboot the server to make all of the necessary changes take effect. To reboot the server, type **DOWN** and then type **RESTART SERVER**.

After the Installation — Managing the Server

The intraNetWare server's primary function is to run the network. There are a variety of utilities on the server to help you see how well it's doing its job. You can also use these utilities to change how the server is working.

The following sections discuss:

▶ The types of utilities that run on the server itself.

▶ How to access and control the server from your workstation.

▶ How to bring down and reboot the server.

▶ The error log files you may want to read periodically.

CONSOLE UTILITIES AND NLMS

There are two primary types of utilities (helpful programs or tools) that run on the intraNetWare server: console utilities and NetWare Loadable Modules.

Console utilities are commands you type at the server's console (keyboard and monitor) to change some aspect of the server or view information about it. These console utilities are built into the operating system, just as internal DOS commands are built in to DOS. To read online help for console utilities, type the following command at the server's keyboard:

HELP

NetWare Loadable Modules (NLMs) are software modules that you load into the server's operating system to add or change functionality. Many NLMs are automatically installed with the intraNetWare operating system. Others are optional; you can load them if your particular situation requires them.

There are four different types of NetWare Loadable Modules that you can use to add different types of functionality to your server:

- ▶ NLMs

- ▶ Name space modules

- ▶ LAN drivers

- ▶ Disk drivers

These NLMs are described in Table 2.2. Many third-party software manufacturers create different types of NLMs to work on intraNetWare.

TABLE 2.2		*Different Types of NLMs*
TYPE OF NLM	**FILENAME EXTENSION**	**DESCRIPTION**
NLM	.NLM	Changes or adds to the server's functionality. Such an NLM might allow you to back up network files, add support for another protocol, or add support for devices such as a CD-ROM drive or a UPS (uninterruptible power supply).
Name space module	.NAM	Allows the operating system to store Macintosh, OS/2, Windows NT, Windows 95, or NFS files, along with their long file names and other characteristics. Name space modules support file naming conventions other than the default DOS file names.
LAN driver	.LAN	Enables the operating system to communicate with a network board installed in the file server.
Disk driver	.DSK	Enables the operating system to communicate with a disk controller board installed in the file server.

You can load and unload NLMs while the server is running.

Many NLMs have their own status screen that displays on the server. Because several NLMs may be running on the server simultaneously, several different screens may be active on the server (similar to having multiple windows open on a Windows workstation). There are two ways to move between active NLM screens on the server's console:

▶ Use Alt-Esc to cycle through the available NLM screens.

▶ Use Ctrl-Esc to bring up a list of available screens, from which you can select one.

To work with NLMs, you can use commands from the server console. These commands are shown in Table 2.3. (The server console may be either the physical console or the Remote Console, as explained in the next section.)

T A B L E 2 . 3 *NLM Commands*	
COMMAND	**DESCRIPTION**
LOAD *nlmname*	Loads the NLM. You do not need to type the NLM's filename extension. In most cases, if an NLM requires that other NLMs also be loaded, it will automatically load them.
UNLOAD *nlmname*	Unloads the NLM.
MODULES	Lists all the currently loaded NLMs.

USING REMOTE CONSOLE TO CONTROL THE SERVER FROM A WORKSTATION

To control the server from a workstation, you can temporarily transform your workstation into a "remote console." With the Remote Console feature running, you can enter console utilities and load NLMs, and the commands you execute will work just as if you were using the server's real keyboard and monitor. Using Remote Console allows you to access the server from any workstation on the network, which gives you greater freedom when administering your network.

You can use Remote Console on a workstation that is directly connected to the network, or on a workstation that connects to the network via a modem. The following sections explain how to run Remote Console both ways.

Running Remote Console over a Direct Connection

To run Remote Console on a workstation that is connected directly to the network, complete the following steps:

1. Load REMOTE.NLM on the server by typing the following command at the server's keyboard:

    LOAD REMOTE

2. When you load REMOTE.NLM, you are asked for a password. Enter any password you choose. (You will have to supply this same password when you use Remote Console from the workstation.)

3. Load RSPX.NLM on your server by typing the following command at the server's keyboard:

    LOAD RSPX

4. From the workstation you want to turn into a Remote Console, map a search drive to SYS:SYSTEM to give the workstation access to the Remote Console files. (See Chapter 5 for more information on how to map search drives.)

5. To execute the Remote Console on the workstation, type the following command at the workstation's DOS prompt:

    RCONSOLE

6. When prompted for a connection type, select SPX, as shown in Figure 2.10.

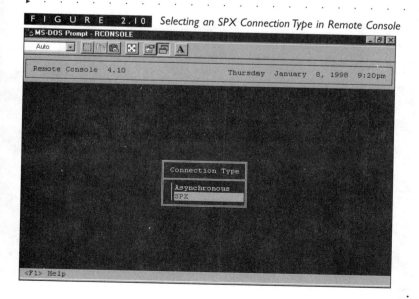

F I G U R E   2.10   *Selecting an SPX Connection Type in Remote Console*

7. Select the server you want to access.

8. Enter the Remote Console password you assigned when you loaded REMOTE.NLM.

Running Remote Console over a Modem

You can run Remote Console on a workstation that connects to the server via a modem (called an *asynchronous* connection). To run Remote Console over a modem, complete the following steps:

1. Load REMOTE.NLM on the server by typing the following command at the server's keyboard:

```
LOAD REMOTE
```

2. When you load REMOTE.NLM, you are asked for a password. Enter any password you choose. (You will have to supply this same password when you use Remote Console from the workstation.)

3. Load RS232.NLM, AIO.NLM, and AIOCOMX.NLM on the server by typing the following three commands at the server's console:

```
LOAD RS232

LOAD AIO

LOAD AIOCOMX
```

4. Copy the following files from the SYS:SYSTEM network directory to a directory on the workstation:

RCONSOLE.EXE

RCONSOLE.HEP

RCONSOLE.MSG

IBM_RUN.OVL

_RUN.OVL

IBM_AIO.OVL

_AIO.OVL

TEXTUTIL.HEP

TEXTUTIL.IDX

TEXTUTIL.MSG

5. To execute the Remote Console on the workstation, type the following command at the workstation's DOS prompt:

```
RCONSOLE
```

6. When prompted for a connection type, select Asynchronous, as shown in Figure 2.11.

7. Select the server you want to access.

8. Enter the Remote Console password you assigned when you loaded REMOTE.NLM.

FIGURE   2.11   Selecting an Asynchronous Connection Type in Remote Console

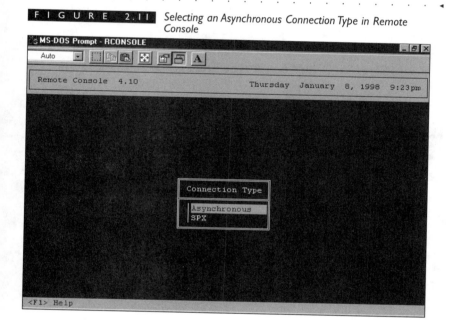

Using Remote Console

When you are running a Remote Console on your workstation, you can use the following keystrokes to navigate through the Remote Console screen:

KEYSTROKE	DESCRIPTION
F1	Displays help
Alt-F1	Displays the Available Options menu
Alt-F2	Quits the Remote Console session
Alt-F3	Moves you forward through the current server screens
Alt-F4	Moves you backward through the current server screens
Alt-F5	Shows this workstation's address

BRINGING DOWN AND REBOOTING THE SERVER

If you need to bring down the server or reboot it, you can use the methods listed in Table 2.4.

TABLE 2.4 *Utilities Used to Bring Down or Reboot the Server*

TASK	HOW TO DO IT
Bring down the server, but leave it connected to the network.	Enter the command DOWN
Bring down the server, and exit to DOS. (This disconnects the server from the network.)	Enter the command DOWN then enter EXIT
Reboot the server.	Enter the command DOWN then enter RESTART SERVER

MODIFYING SERVER STARTUP ACTIVITIES

When you start up or reboot the intraNetWare server, several startup files work in sequence to start and configure the server. These boot files execute in the following order:

1. The DOS system files load, then run AUTOEXEC.BAT. This boot file sets up a basic environment and can be set to execute SERVER.EXE automatically.

2. SERVER.EXE is the actual intraNetWare operating system. When this file executes, the computer is turned into the server.

3. STARTUP.NCF automates the initialization of the intraNetWare operating system. It loads disk drivers, loads name space modules to support different file formats, and executes some additional parameters that modify default initialization values. This file is created during the server installation, and contains commands that reflect the choices you made during the installation.

4. AUTOEXEC.NCF loads the server's LAN drivers, specifies the server name and internal network number, mounts volumes, loads any NLMs you want loaded automatically (such as MONITOR), and executes additional server parameters. This file is also created during the server installation, and contains commands that reflect the choices you made during the installation.

5. Additional .NCF files, if they've been created, can be called from the AUTOEXEC.NCF file or executed from the server's console. These additional files may be created by optional products you install on the server, and they contain configuration information to make the server work better with the product that is installed on it.

You can edit the STARTUP.NCF and AUTOEXEC.NCF files after installation to add new commands or modify existing ones if you'd like. If you install other products on the server, those products' installation programs may edit these files automatically to add necessary commands. You can also edit these files manually, if you need to (however, it is seldom necessary to do this).

To edit either .NCF file, you can use EDIT.NLM, which is a simple text editor that runs on the server. To use EDIT.NLM, type the following command:

```
LOAD EDIT
```

Then specify the file you want to edit. When the file opens, edit it like you would any other text file. Save it when you're finished, and then exit EDIT.

MONITORING THE SERVER'S ACTIVITIES

MONITOR.NLM is a useful management utility for seeing how the server is performing. When you load MONITOR on the server, you can see a tremendous amount of information about the server, its disk information, its processor utilization, its memory utilization, file activity, workstation connections, and the like. Figure 2.12 shows Monitor's main menu.

F I G U R E   2.12 *MONITOR.NLM's Main Menu*

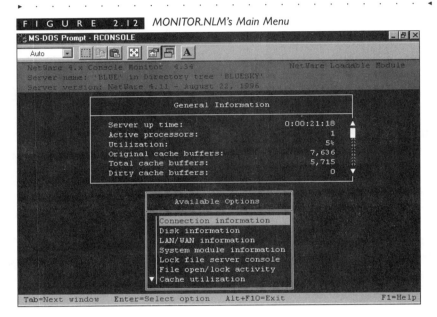

For the most part, the information that MONITOR displays is highly technical and useful primarily to advanced network administrators who know how to interpret the information and "tweak" it to optimize the server's performance. However, some of the more commonly used options offer useful information even to new network administrators:

▶ Select Connection Information to see the users that are currently logged in to the server.

▶ Select System Module Information to see a list of all the software modules running in the server. This includes LAN and disk drivers, as well as NLMs.

▶ Select Lock File Server Console to lock the console. (You will be asked for a password that will later be required to unlock the console.) Locking the console disables the keyboard, so that no one can enter any commands. To unlock the console, enter the password you assigned when you locked the console.

▶ If you leave MONITOR unattended for a few minutes, it will bring up a screen saver (often called "the snake" because it is a simple cursor that snakes around the screen). Many administrators leave MONITOR loaded and running at all times so that the screen saver will be active.

If you'd like to learn more about all the information displayed in MONITOR, see the Novell documentation.

MONITORING THE ERROR LOG FILES

There are three different error log files that you can monitor to see if your network generated any error messages. You should make a practice of reviewing these files on a regular basis to ensure that nothing out of the ordinary is happening to your network.

▶ SYS$LOG.ERR logs error messages for the server. It is stored in the server's SYS:SYSTEM directory. All of the messages or errors that appear on the server's console are stored in this file.

▶ VOL$LOG.ERR logs error messages for a volume. Each volume has its own log file, which is stored at the root of the volume. Any errors or messages that pertain to the volume are stored in this file.

▶ ABEND.LOG tracks any *abends* that may have happened on the server. (An abend, short for "abnormal end," is a serious error that stops the server from operating.) IntraNetWare has a new feature that allows the server to shut itself down and restart automatically after most abends, so you may not be aware that the server has abended unless you view this file. This file is created on the server's boot partition but gets copied to SYS:SYSTEM when the server restarts.

To view any of these error log files, you can either use a text editor from a workstation, or you can use EDIT.NLM from the server. To use EDIT.NLM, enter the command:

```
LOAD EDIT
```

Then specify the path and name of the desired log file.

Beyond the Basics

This chapter has described the simplest ways to install and upgrade your server. It also explained the basics of how to use the server's console commands and NLMs.

The following topics are addressed later in this book:

- For information on NDS, see Chapter 4.

- For instructions on installing workstations, see Chapter 3.

- For information on setting up or upgrading printing services, see Chapter 8.

The default installation options of the Simple Installation are adequate for many network setups, and many network administrators never need much more information than that in this book. However, once you're gotten comfortable with the intraNetWare server basics, you may want to learn more about the advanced features of intraNetWare servers. There is plenty to learn because intraNetWare is an incredibly powerful product, and in software lingo, "powerful" often goes hand-in-hand with "complex."

You can find more information about the following topics in Novell's online documentation (which came with your intraNetWare package) and in *Novell's IntranetWare Administrator's Handbook* (from Novell Press):

- Using the Custom Installation of intraNetWare

- Migrating previous NetWare data from an old server machine to a new one

- Understanding Ethernet frame types

- Managing the intraNetWare server once it's installed

TIP Another useful resource for server management information is the *Novell Application Notes*. Also called AppNotes for short, this is a monthly publication put out by the Novell Research Department, and each issue contains research reports and articles on a wide range of advanced topics. To order a subscription, call 800-377-4136 in the U.S., or 303-297-2725 worldwide.

CHAPTER 3

Installing Workstations

Instant *Access*

Installing a Workstation

▸ A workstation on an intraNetWare network can be running DOS, Windows 3.1, Windows 95, Windows NT, OS/2, or Mac OS.

▸ Install intraNetWare client software on a computer to turn it into a network workstation. The client software enables the workstation to communicate with the network.

▸ The latest client software can be found on Novell's Web site, at www.novell.com. (The client software on the intraNetWare CD-ROM is an older version, but is still adequate if you don't have Internet access.)

Logging In

▸ After the client software is installed, you can log in to the network from the workstation. The intraNetWare Login program is installed on the workstation as part of the client software.

▸ To log in, enter your username and password.

The Second Step — Installing the Workstations

Workstations are the computers that a company's employees use for their daily work — writing memos, creating spreadsheets, sending e-mail, and other normal computer-related activities. After you've installed a server, the next logical step is to install the workstations.

To users, working on a network workstation doesn't appear much different than using the computer by itself (often called a standalone computer). This is because intraNetWare takes care of the workstation's communications with the rest of the network without affecting how the computer's own operating system (such as Windows 95 or OS/2) functions. Therefore, users can work with files — open files, run applications, and save files — in the same way they would if the computer weren't attached to a network. What makes a network workstation different from a standalone computer is the fact that users can access files, applications, printers, and other resources stored on the network, in addition to the files stored on the computer's own disks. Workstation users can also share those applications, files, and printers with other users throughout the network.

Workstations on an intraNetWare network can be running any of the following operating systems:

- DOS
- Windows 3.1
- Windows 95
- OS/2
- Windows NT
- Mac OS (for Macintoshes)

You don't need to have all workstations running the same operating systems, either. You can have Windows 95, Windows 3.1, and Macintosh workstations all running on the same network, all accessing the same printers, files, and so on.

To make a workstation function on an intraNetWare network, you have to install a special set of intraNetWare workstation software. This software, called the intraNetWare client software, allows the workstation to communicate with the rest of the network. (On an intraNetWare network, workstations are often called *clients* because they request services from the network.)

Each type of workstation operating system requires a particular type of intraNetWare client software. (For example, a Windows 95 workstation uses a different set of client software than a Windows NT workstation.)This chapter explains how to obtain the latest version of client software. It also explains how to install intraNetWare client software on the most common types of workstations — Windows 3.1 and Windows 95.

If you have Macintosh, OS/2, or Windows NT workstations, see the Novell online documentation for more information about installing the necessary client software.

TIP

Getting the Latest Client Software

Most of the different types of client software are included on the intraNetWare CD-ROM that you purchased. However, Novell updates client software on a fairly regular basis (every few months or so). Therefore, the client software on your CD is older software, and newer versions of the client software exist on the World Wide Web.

If at all possible, you should try to use the updated client software from the Web. Generally, each new update of the client software includes both bug fixes and new features that make it easier to use, more efficient, or easier to install. In addition, new LAN drivers for newly created network boards may also be included.

To obtain the newest versions of client software, visit Novell's Web site, at www.novell.com. Periodically, Novell changes the organization of material on its Web site, but downloadable client files are usually located in the technical support section of the Web site.

When you locate the area of the Web site that contains the downloadable client files, select the link to the platform you want (such as Windows 95, Windows 3.1, or Windows NT). Follow the instructions on the screen for downloading your desired client files.

When downloading files, be sure you select the option to download a single ZIP file (a compressed file that contains all of the client software), rather than downloading the files individually. It is much faster to download a single ZIP file. If you are asked whether you want to open the file or save it to a disk, it's faster to save it to your hard disk and then unzip the file on that disk.

TIP

A single client ZIP file can be very large — up to 12MB or 13MB. It will unzip and extract hundreds of files, taking up as much as 60MB to 75MB of disk space. Therefore, make sure you save the ZIP file to a hard disk or other storage device that has plenty of disk space available.

You can unzip files by using commonly found ZIP programs such as those produced by PKWare. There are both shareware versions of ZIP programs that you can download for free and full-featured versions that you can purchase. For more information about ZIP programs, search the Web for zip programs, or see PKWare's Web site at www.pkware.com.

Once you've downloaded (and unzipped) the client files, you will see a set of executable files. Double-click each of these files to execute them. This will cause each of the files to decompress and extract dozens of additional files. When all those files are extracted, you're ready to run the intraNetWare Client installation program.

Installing intraNetWare Client Software

The installation program for the intraNetWare client software changes slightly with each new update of the software. In addition, the screens that appear during the installation program will vary from workstation to workstation, depending on the workstation's particular hardware setup, the operating system, any pre-existing client software already installed on it, and other such conditions.

The fundamental steps of the client installation are fairly consistent from version to version, however, and the typical installation is simple regardless of the version. The following instructions describe the basic flow of the installation program, along with explanations of the screens you will most likely see. Don't panic if your installation process doesn't show all of the same types of information described here. When asked to choose from multiple options, the default option is usually recommended, and you'll usually be safe selecting the default.

Remember that you can press the F1 key to read online help at any time during the client installation program.

TIP

The intraNetWare client installation program automatically copies all necessary intraNetWare files to the workstation. It also edits any DOS, Windows 3.1, or Windows 95 files that require modifications.

NOTE

If you're installing the client software that came in your intraNetWare CD-ROM package, the client software is called *NetWare Client 32 for Windows 95* (or Windows 3.1, depending on the flavor you're using). More recent updates of the client software are called *intraNetWare Client for Windows 95* (or Windows 3.1). In the following instructions, the newer name is used for consistency. If you're using the older version of the client software, your screens will say *NetWare Client 32* instead.

You can choose one of the following four methods to install the intraNetWare client on your workstation:

▶ You can download the latest client software from Novell's Web site. This is the recommended method because it ensures that you get the latest version with the most recent updates. You can download the files directly into a folder on the workstation, and run the installation program from there. You can also download the files onto one workstation, run a special program to make a set of installation diskettes, and then run the installation program from those diskettes. This is useful if you have several computers, not all of which are connected to the Internet.

▶ You can install the client directly from the *NetWare 4.11 Operating System* CD-ROM, if the workstation has a CD-ROM drive. This version of the intraNetWare client software is older than that available on the Web.

▶ You can install the client from installation diskettes you create from the CD-ROM. To create installation diskettes, load INSTALL.NLM on the server, choose Product Options, and then choose Make Diskettes. You'll need eight blank diskettes. Again, this version of the intraNetWare client software is older than that available on the Web.

▶ If you are upgrading an existing NetWare workstation to a newer version of the intraNetWare client, you can install the client from the CD-ROM, from diskettes, or from a network directory on the server. To use the network directory method, you must put the client installation files into a directory on the server. If you've downloaded the updated client files from the Internet, copy those files to a network directory on the server. If you're using the older client files from the CD-ROM, load INSTALL.NLM on the server, choose Product Options, and then choose Create Client Installation Directories on Server.

To install intraNetWare client software on a Windows 95 or Windows 3.1 workstation, complete the following steps:

1. Connect the workstation to the rest of the network by installing the network board in the workstation, and connecting a network cable from the network board to a hub or other network connection, as shown in Figure 3.1. See your hardware manufacturer's documentation for more information about limitations and guidelines for installing network hardware.

FIGURE 3.1 *Connecting the Workstation to the Network*

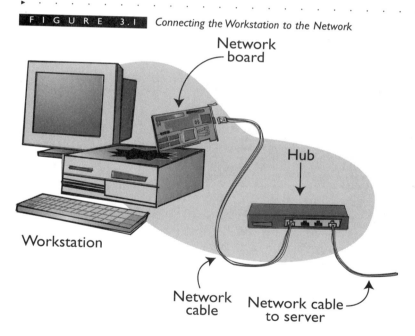

Network board

Hub

Workstation

Network cable

Network cable to server

2. If you're using Windows 95, click the Start button, and choose Run.

If you're using Windows 3.1, open the Windows Program Manager and select Run from the File menu.

3. Click Browse to locate the SETUP.EXE file in the client installation directory, as shown in Figure 3.2. Then click OK to begin the installation.

If you're installing from files you've downloaded from the Web, look for SETUP.EXE in the directory that contains the downloaded and extracted files.

If you're installing from a network directory, the path to the Windows 3.1 version of SETUP.EXE is generally PUBLIC\CLIENT\ DOSWIN32\IBM_6. The Windows 95 version is generally in PUBLIC\CLIENT\WIN95\IBM_ENU.

If you're installing from the CD-ROM, the Windows 3.1 directory is PRODUCTS\DOSWIN32\IBM_6. For Windows 95, look in PRODUCTS\WIN95\IBM_ENU.

F I G U R E   3 . 2   *Locating SETUP.EXE*

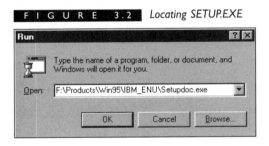

4. If prompted, select the language you want to install.

5. Choose Yes to accept the license agreement that appears. This agreement describes the terms and conditions for using this software.

6. If a screen similar to that shown in Figure 3.3 asks you to choose between the Typical installation and a Custom installation, choose Typical. This option will set up the client with the most common default settings, which should be adequate in most situations.

7. Choose Install (or Start or Next, in some versions), to begin the installation.

FIGURE 3.3 *Select Typical Installation*

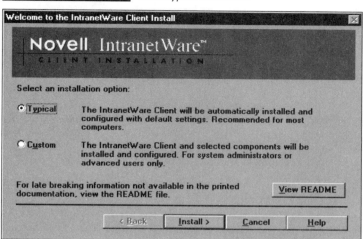

8. IntraNetWare client software detects and automatically loads many LAN drivers. If it cannot detect your network board, it will prompt to you select a board. You'll need to insert a diskette that contains your board's LAN driver. Most manufacturers include a LAN driver diskette with the network board they sell.

9. If asked whether you want the installation program to modify the workstation's AUTOEXEC.BAT file, select Yes. The installation program will modify this startup file so that the client software will execute properly whenever the workstation is rebooted. The original version of the file will be saved and renamed to AUTOEXEC.OLD so that you can retrieve it later if you want it.

10. If you are prompted to set a Preferred Tree and Name Context, as shown in Figure 3.4, you can enter the name of your tree (created when the server was installed in Chapter 2). If you only have one tree in your organization, this is not necessary, but it's still a safe thing to specify in case of future growth.

The name context is your location in the Directory tree. For example, if this workstation will be in the container called Sales, under the Organization object called BlueSky, the name context would be OU=Sales.O=BlueSky. Entering a name context during the installation distinguishes this workstation from others that may have the same name, but may be in different contexts. In this example, the context is O=BlueSky.

Enter Preferred Directory Tree and Name Context.

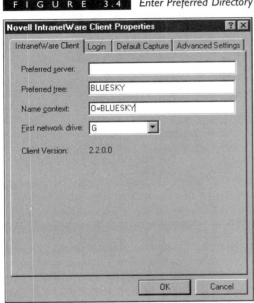

11. When the installation is complete, you'll be asked if you want to Reboot the computer, Return to Windows without rebooting, or Customize the installation (see Figure 3.5).

In most cases, you should choose Reboot, which will reboot the computer and make the settings you've just installed take effect.

FIGURE 3.5
Select Reboot.

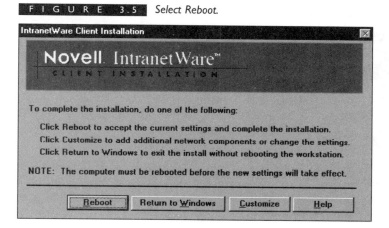

Now the intraNetWare client software is installed, and the workstation is ready to connect to the network.

Connecting to the Network and Logging In

When the workstation reboots after you install the client software, it automatically connects to the network. Now you can log in to the network. How you log in depends on the type of workstation you're using. The following sections describe the different ways you can log in.

LOGGING IN FROM WINDOWS 3.1

If you're using Windows 3.1, the intraNetWare Login (or NetWare Login) icon will appear in the intraNetWare Tools (or NetWare Tools) program group on your Windows desktop. (Whether the name NetWare or intraNetWare appears depends on the version of client software you installed.)

To log in to the network, double-click the Login icon, and then enter your login name and password when prompted (see Figure 3.6).

F I G U R E   3 . 6   *The Login Screen (on a Windows 3.1 Workstation)*

Novell NetWare Login

NetWare

Login	Connection

Logging into NetWare using:

🌳 OUTVIEW

N_ame: JSimon

P_assword: **********

OK

Cancel

Help

NOTE

You can't use a login name unless it has already been defined on the server. If this is the first workstation installed on the network, the only username available so far will be Admin. Chapter 5 explains how to create additional users on the network.

You can set up the Login program so that it executes automatically whenever you start up the intraNetWare client in Windows 3.1. This way, whenever you first load Windows, the Login screen will prompt you for your username and password.

To make the Login program execute automatically, double-click the NetWare User Tools icon on your desktop. Then click the Hot Key button (the button that shows a picture of a key with flames). Click the Startup tab to open the Startup page, then mark the Launch on Startup button under the Windows Login heading (see Figure 3.7). Under the Login tab, you can set whether the Login window, by default, logs you into a tree or into a server. When you're finished, close the User Tools.

Now, when you start Windows (which automatically launches the intraNetWare client software) the Login screen appears. Enter your name and password, then click OK. To change the server or tree you want to log in to, click the Connection tab to open that page, and enter your desired tree or server.

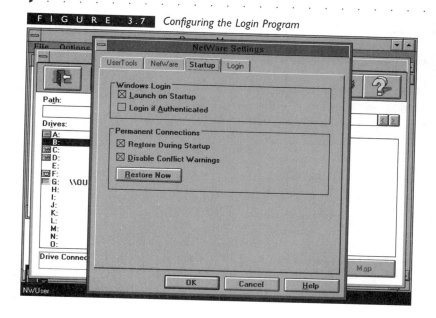

FIGURE 3.7 *Configuring the Login Program*

LOGGING IN FROM WINDOWS 95

When you reboot a Windows 95 workstation after installing the intraNetWare client software, the intraNetWare Login (or NetWare Login) screen appears. (Whether the name *NetWare* or *intraNetWare* appears depends on the version of client software you installed.)

When the Login screen appears, as shown in Figure 3.8, enter your login name and password.

By default, a screen will appear showing the results of the login request. When the login is completed, you can close this screen. You're now logged in to the network.

Windows 95 includes an icon on your desktop called Network Neighborhood. The intraNetWare client software modifies the information that this icon's program sees, so that the Network Neighborhood can recognize the intraNetWare tree and server.

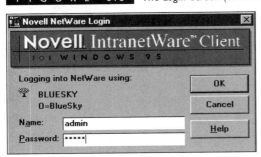

Double-click the Network Neighborhood icon to see what your intraNetWare network looks like from Windows 95. Figure 3.9 shows an example of a simple Network Neighborhood — you can see the BlueSky Directory tree and the server named Blue. You'll also see a file icon called BlueSky. This isn't really a file; it's the Organization object at the top of the Directory tree. Because Windows 95 doesn't recognize NDS objects, it displays the file icon by default.

F I G U R E   3 . 9   *The Network Neighborhood*

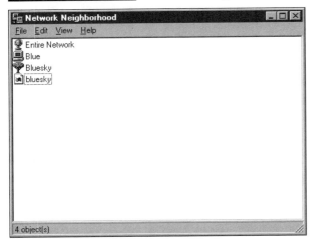

If you double-click the server's icon (called Blue in this example), you will see the server's volumes. In this case, server Blue has a single volume, called SYS. You can open the volume by double-clicking it, and see the folder and files it contains, just as if you were opening up folders on your own workstation (see Figure 3.10).

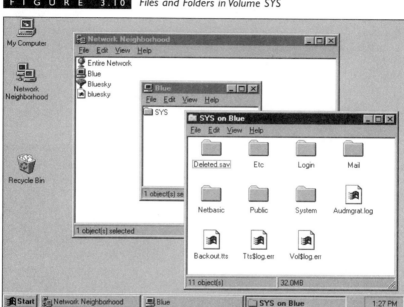

FIGURE 3.10 *Files and Folders in Volume SYS*

Beyond the Basics

In this chapter, you learned how to install workstations on the network. The following topics are addressed later in this book:

- ▶ For information on viewing and working with the objects in the Directory tree, see Chapter 4.

- ▶ For information on creating additional user accounts on the network, see Chapter 5.

- ▶ For information on working with network files and applications, see Chapter 7.

You can find more information about the following topics in Novell's online documentation (which came with your intraNetWare package) and in *Novell's IntranetWare Administrator's Handbook* (from Novell Press):

▸ Using the Custom Installation of intraNetWare client software

▸ Installing OS/2, Macintosh, or Windows NT workstations

CHAPTER 4

Managing Novell Directory Services

Instant Access

Understanding NDS

- Novell Directory Services (NDS) is a distributed database of information about every entity and resource on the network.

- Every entity (such as users and groups) and resource (such as servers, volumes, and printers) on the network must have an NDS object defined for it.

- To create or change NDS objects, use the NetWare Administrator utility.

- Your name context specifies your location in the NDS tree.

Planning an NDS Tree

- The NDS database organizes NDS objects into a tree-like structure, with the Root object at the top, and other objects fanning out below it in branches.

- You can use container objects, such as Organization objects and Organizational Unit objects, to subdivide the other objects (called *leaf objects*) into logical groupings, often based on your company's departments or its geographical location.

- If the NDS database is very large, you can divide the database into Directory partitions.

What Is Novell Directory Services?

Novell Directory Services (NDS), in simplest terms, is a database of network information. It contains information that defines every object on the intraNetWare network, such as users, groups, printers, print queues, servers, and volumes. For every NDS object, the NDS database describes the type of object it is, where it resides, what level of security the object can exercise, who can access it, and other similar types of information.

As discussed in Chapter 1, the NDS database is not confined to a single server. Instead, all the intraNetWare servers in a network tree share a single, distributed database. This greatly simplifies your network management life. For example, with NDS, you only have to create a user or other object once in the network tree, and every server will automatically recognize that same user or object. You can allow a user to access different servers simply by granting him or her the appropriate rights to the necessary volumes on each server.

Chapter 1 also explained that NDS uses a hierarchical database structure. With this type of structure, you can group objects together under categories and subcategories. This makes it easier to locate specific objects. It also allows you to control objects as a group, such as when you're modifying the security levels of those objects.

The NDS database is often referred to as the Directory tree. Figure 4.1 is a simple illustration of a Directory tree, showing how the tree begins with a Root object at the top. Beneath the root, objects are divided into branches and sub-branches that fan out beneath it.

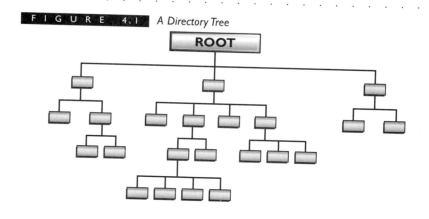

FIGURE 4.1 *A Directory Tree*

NDS Objects

For each type of network entity that will operate on the network, you will create an NDS object. This object may represent a real entity, such as a user, or it may represent a service, such as a print server.

Each NDS object contains several *properties,* which are the pieces of information that define the object. For example, a User object contains properties that define the user's full name, his or her ID number, an e-mail address, group memberships, and so on. (Properties are also called *attributes.*) Each type of object, such as a Server or Printer object, may have different properties than another type of object. Each type of object, such as User, Print Queue, or Server, is referred to as an *object class.*

CATEGORIES OF OBJECT CLASSES

Object classes fall into three basic categories, as follows:

▶ Root object — The Root object is unique and is situated at the very top of the Directory tree. Every other object in the tree is located beneath the Root object. When the first intraNetWare server is installed in a company, the installation program creates a new Directory tree with the Root object at the top. Subsequent servers will be installed underneath the original Root object.

▶ Container objects — Container objects are, simply put, objects that contain other objects. For example, a container object called Sales could contain all the users who work in the Sales department, their workstations, and their printers.

▶ Leaf objects — These objects represent the individual entities on the network. Leaf objects, such as users, servers, and volumes, cannot contain other objects.

You can use these three types of object classes to place your NDS objects into a manageable organization. The Root object resides at the top of the tree. The container objects form branches and subbranches. The leaf objects are the individual users, printers, servers, and so on, that populate those branches.

Figure 4.2 shows how these three categories of object classes appear in the Directory tree.

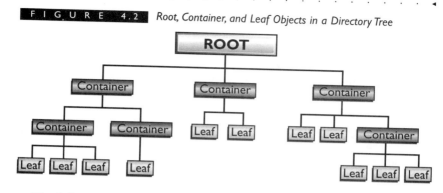

FIGURE 4.2 *Root, Container, and Leaf Objects in a Directory Tree*

The following four container object classes are available, though you will probably only use one or two of them:

▶ Country (seldom used in NDS trees)

▶ Locality (seldom used in NDS trees)

▶ Organization (always used in NDS trees)

▶ Organizational Unit (often used in NDS trees)

NOTE

Country and Locality objects are used primarily for compliance with X.500 naming specifications, but are seldom used in Novell Directory Services trees. The X.500 specifications, which were created by organizations seeking standards for Directory Services, include a standardized form of naming restrictions for all Directory Services applications. (Some intraNetWare utilities don't even recognize the Locality object. In most cases, Organization and Organizational Unit objects are all you will need to organize your NDS tree.)

You can have only one level of Country objects (if you use them at all), which fall immediately below the Root object. A Country object is often designated by the abbreviation "C," such as "C=US."

You can have only one level of Organization objects. This falls below the Country object if there is one specified, or the Root object if there isn't one. You need at least one Organization object. During the server installation, you're asked to specify an Organization name for this mandatory object. Organization objects are assigned the abbreviation "O," as in "O=BlueSky."

Finally, you can have multiple levels of Organizational Unit objects, which fall below the Organization objects. Organizational Unit objects have the abbreviation "OU," as in "OU=Sales."

The Locality object, if used, can be located under any of the other container objects. It is assigned the abbreviation "L."

Unlike container objects, all leaf objects use the same abbreviation, regardless of the type of objects they may be. All leaf objects use the abbreviation "CN," which stands for *"Common Name."* This designation is required by the X.500 specifications. Therefore, all leaf objects, such as printers, users, servers, and print queues, use the abbreviation CN, as in "CN=ServerA" or "CN=Fred."

Figure 4.3 shows the simplest form of Directory tree you can have. It has only one level of Organization objects (it is mandatory to have at least one Organization object — the example shows two), and all leaf objects (which use the abbreviation CN) reside immediately beneath it.

FIGURE 4.3 *The Simplest Directory Tree Format*

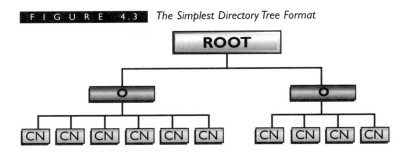

Figure 4.4 shows a tree that uses Organizational Unit objects to subdivide all of the objects.

Figure 4.5 shows a less-common tree format, which includes Country objects and Locality objects. (Remember, some intraNetWare utilities don't recognize Locality objects, so these are rarely used in intraNetWare networks.)

F I G U R E   4.4 A Common Directory Tree Format, Using Organizational Unit Objects

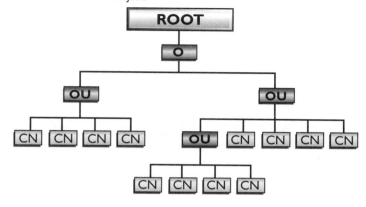

F I G U R E   4.5 A Complex Directory Tree Format, Using Country and Locality Objects

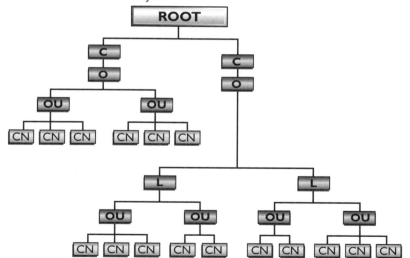

NDS OBJECT CLASSES

In intraNetWare, many different types of object classes are available. Table 4.1 lists all of the object classes. The table also indicates which objects are commonly used in the average intraNetWare network; some NDS objects exist for specific — but less common — needs, so it is likely that your network will not include many of these. These lesser-used NDS objects are generally aspects of some of the more advanced, specialized features of intraNetWare, so see the Novell online documentation if you'd like to learn more about them.

| T A B L E 4.1 | Object Classes Available in intraNetWare |

OBJECT CLASS	COMMONLY USED	DESCRIPTION
AFP Server		This object is an AppleTalk File Protocol (AFP) server that is a node on the network. (See the Novell documentation for more information about AFP servers.)
Alias		This object is a representation of another object that is really located in a different part of the Directory tree. Aliases let you place duplicate icons for an object in multiple locations in the tree. This enables users to get to it wherever they are in the tree. For example, if you want the Sales users to be able to access a printer in the Marketing office, you could put an Alias object for that printer in the Sales container, while the original printer object remains in the Marketing container. (See the Novell documentation for more information about Aliases.)

OBJECT CLASS	COMMONLY USED	DESCRIPTION
Application	X	This object is a pointer to an application installed on the network. There are different variations of this object, depending on the type of application: DOS, Windows 3.x, Windows 95, and Windows NT. An Application object can be "associated" with users or groups. Then that application can easily be executed from each user's NetWare Application Launcher. (See Chapter 7 for more information on using Application objects.)
Auditing File		This object manages an audit trail's configuration and access rights, and is used only if the auditing feature is used. (The auditing feature tracks various types of network usage, which can then be audited by an independent auditor, much like having your financial books audited. This feature is seldom used in ordinary situations. See the Novell documentation for more information about auditing.)
Bindery Object		This object represents an object that was upgraded from a bindery-based server, but which could not be converted into a corresponding NDS object. (See the Novell documentation for more information about Bindery objects.)
Bindery Queue		This object represents a print queue that exists outside the NDS tree (either on a NetWare 3.x server or in another NetWare 4 tree). This object lets you manage this queue, even though it's outside of your current NDS tree. (See the Novell documentation for more information about Bindery Queue objects.)

(continued)

	TABLE 4.1	*Object Classes Available in intraNetWare (continued)*
OBJECT CLASS	**COMMONLY USED**	**DESCRIPTION**
Computer		This object indicates any computer that exists on the network. It can be a server, workstation, or any other type of computer.
Country		This optional container object represents the country where a portion of your company is located.
Directory Map	X	This object is a representation of a directory path that typically points to an application or directory. (See Chapter 5 for more information about using Directory Map objects.)
Distribution List		This object contains a list of e-mail recipients; it is used if Message Handling Services (MHS) is installed. (MHS is a type of communications protocol that is used by some older e-mail packages. See the documentation on your e-mail package for more information.)
External Entity		This object stores information about non-NDS entities for other applications or services. It is used if Message Handling Services (MHS) is installed.
Group	X	This object contains a list of users who have at least some identical characteristics, such as the need for access rights to the same application. Users listed as group members receive a security equivalence to the group. (See Chapter 5 for more information about Group objects.)
Locality		This optional container object represents a location.

OBJECT CLASS	COMMONLY USED	DESCRIPTION
License Certificate		This object represents a product license certificate. When an application that uses NetWare Licensing Services is installed, that product's certificate is added as an object in the License Product container object. (See the Novell documentation for more information about NetWare Licensing Services.)
List		This object simply contains a list of other objects. Objects that are list members do not have a security equivalence to the List object. (For more information about security equivalences, see Chapter 6.)
LSP Server		This object represents a License Service Provider server. It is used only if NetWare Licensing Service is used.
Message Routing Group		This object represents a group of message servers. The individual servers are connected directly to each other so that e-mail messages can be routed between them. It is used if Message Handling Services (MHS) is installed.
Messaging Server		This object represents a server that receives and transfers e-mail messages.
NetWare Server	X	This object indicates a NetWare server installed on the network.
Organization	X	This object is simply an organization's name (such as a company name).
Organizational Role	X	This object is a position (such as director, project leader, or recreation coordinator) that various users can occupy. (It allows you to assign rights to the position rather than to specific users).

(continued)

T A B L E 4 . 1		*Object Classes Available in intraNetWare (continued)*

OBJECT CLASS	COMMONLY USED	DESCRIPTION
Organizational Unit	X	This container object can form a subdivision under an Organization. Examples of this include division, department, project team, or workgroup.
Print Server	X	This object is a NetWare print server that provides print services. (See Chapter 8 for more information about printing.)
Printer	X	This object is a printer attached to the network.
Profile	X	This object has the sole function of providing a login script. The script can be used by several users — not all of whom need to be in the same container. (See Chapter 5 for more information about login scripts.)
Queue	X	This object indicates a print queue. (See Chapter 8 for more information about printing.)
Root	X	This object is the highest point — the starting point — of the Directory tree. (It contains no information.)
Unknown		This represents an object that the server couldn't restore because the object's class is no longer defined in the current schema. (Schemas are explained later in this chapter.)
User	X	This object represents a network user. (See Chapter 5 for more information about users.)
Volume	X	This object indicates a network volume. (See Chapter 7 for more information about volumes.)

THE NDS SCHEMA

The overall plan that defines and describes the allowable types of NDS objects, their properties, and the rules that govern their creation and existence, is called the *NDS schema*. The schema also determines how objects can inherit properties and trustee rights of other container objects above it. In addition, the schema defines how the Directory tree is structured and how objects in it are named.

Software developers who create applications that work with NDS objects can expand or change the schema by identifying new classes of objects (say, for example, a database server). They can also add additional properties to existing object classes (such as adding a property called *Pager Number* to a User object).

NOTE

When you install or upgrade to intraNetWare, you may notice messages indicating that the NDS schema is being extended. This is done to support some of the features of intraNetWare that require additional object classes in the schema.

WORKING WITH NDS OBJECTS

Once you've installed a server and a workstation, you can log in to the intraNetWare network and look at the NDS tree you've created so far. As you create new users and groups, or install new printers or servers, you can see the tree grow.

The primary tool for looking at the Directory tree, and for creating or modifying NDS objects, is the NetWare utility called *NetWare Administrator*. The NetWare Administrator utility (sometimes referred to as NWAdmin) runs in Windows 3.1, OS/2, or Windows 95.

Typical tasks you can do with NetWare Administrator are as follows:

- ▶ Create new NDS objects, such as users, groups, or printers
- ▶ Delete objects
- ▶ Move objects to different parts of the Directory tree
- ▶ Search for objects by particular properties (such as all users in a given department)
- ▶ Change an object's properties
- ▶ Rename objects

The Windows 3.1 version of NetWare Administrator (which can also run on OS/2) is called NWADMN3X.EXE; it is located in the PUBLIC directory under the volume SYS.

The Windows 95 version is called NWADMN95.EXE. It can be found in the WIN95 folder, within the PUBLIC folder, under volume SYS.

NOTE

If you have upgraded your network from NetWare 4.1 to intraNetWare, you will discover that the old version of NetWare Administrator, called NWADMIN.EXE, is still in your PUBLIC directory.

If you want to use the new NetWare Administrator utility that comes with intraNetWare, you must first upgrade your workstation to the client software that comes with intraNetWare. The new version of NetWare Administrator requires new files that are contained in the new client software. If you don't upgrade your client software, you will have to continue using the older NetWare Administrator utility.

To use NetWare Administrator, you must install it on your workstation and add its program icon to your workstation's desktop, as explained in the following sections.

Setting Up the NetWare Administrator Utility for Windows 3.1

To set up NetWare Administrator on a Windows 3.1 workstation, complete the following steps:

1. From a Windows 3.1 workstation, start Windows and highlight the program group in which you want NetWare Administrator to appear. (The NetWare Tools program group was created during the workstation installation, so you can use that group.)

2. From the File menu, choose New, and then select Program Item.

3. For the Description, enter the name you want to use, such as NetWare Administrator or NWAdmin.

4. Use the Browse button to specify the location of the NWADMN3X.EXE file (SYS:\PUBLIC\NWADMN3X.EXE) and the working directory (SYS:\PUBLIC).

5. Click OK.

The NetWare Administrator icon will now appear on your desktop. To launch NetWare Administrator, double-click this icon.

Setting Up the NetWare Administrator Utility for Windows 95

To set up NetWare Administrator on a Windows 95 workstation, complete the following steps:

1. From the Windows 95 desktop, right-click your mouse and choose New.

2. Select Shortcut.

3. Choose Browse, open the SYS volume, and then the PUBLIC folder followed by the WIN95 folder. Select the file NWADMN95.EXE.

4. Choose Next.

5. Enter a name for the shortcut, or use the default name provided (NWADMN95.EXE).

6. Choose Finish.

NetWare Administrator will now appear as a shortcut icon on the desktop. Double-click the shortcut icon to launch NetWare Administrator.

Now you can use NetWare Administrator to create and manage all NDS objects, including users and groups.

NDS Replicas and Partitions

As explained earlier, the NDS database is common to all servers on the network. If the database was stored on only one server (with all other servers accessing it from that server), the entire network would be disabled if the server went down.

To prevent this single point of failure, intraNetWare can create *replicas* of the NDS database and store those replicas on different servers. Then, if one server goes down, all other servers can still access the NDS database from another replica.

If your NDS database is large enough, you may not want to store the entire database on each server. In this case, you can create Directory *partitions,* which are portions of the database that can be replicated on different servers. A Directory partition is a branch of the Directory tree, beginning with any container object you choose. Partitions can also hold subpartitions beneath them (called *child partitions*). If you have a smaller NDS database, the whole database can reside in a single partition. Using partitions can improve network performance, especially if the network spans across a wide-area network (WAN). Partitions can also make it easier to manage portions of the tree separately.

Figure 4.6 shows the same network that was illustrated in Figure 4.4. In this drawing, its NDS database is divided into two partitions.

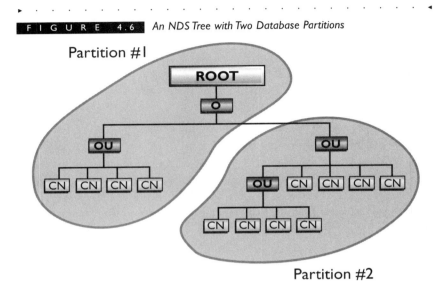

Partition #1

Partition #2

Managing NDS replicas and database partitions is an advanced feature of intraNetWare. In large, complex networks, administrators can create different types of replicas and partitions to better control the amount of information being updated and synchronized on the network. However, the intraNetWare installation program automatically detects and sets up replicas and partitions that work well for most networks. This is a feature that many network administrators of average networks do not need to change.

To create, delete, or merge Directory partitions, you can use a utility called *NDS Manager*. This utility can be executed by itself, or it can be added to the NetWare Administrator utility so it appears as an option under the NetWare Administrator's Tools menu. For more information about this utility, see the Novell online documentation.

Planning the NDS Directory Tree

To plan your Directory tree, you can take advantage of the Organization and Organizational Unit container objects. With them, you can make the tree resemble your company's organization — organized by departments, geography, or some other logical scheme.

The key to planning your Directory tree is to decide how best to group objects together so that:

▸ Users can quickly and easily find the resources they use most often.

▸ You can easily manage all the resources, including responding to changes in the corporation.

The following sections offer some tips for planning your Directory tree.

STARTING AT THE TOP

The Root object resides at the very top of the tree. Immediately beneath the Root object lies the first level of container objects — the Organization objects.

For most companies, having a single Organization object at the top of the tree is the most logical move, especially if users will need to have access to all parts of the tree. Under this single Organization object, you can use Organizational Unit objects (OU objects) to subdivide the tree into useful groupings, if necessary.

Deciding whether you need to use OU objects at all is the first decision. If your company is small, you may want to have a single Organization object (representing your company) with all leaf objects directly beneath that container. This is how the Simple Installation feature of the intraNetWare INSTALL utility sets up your tree by default. Figure 4.7 shows how a tree for a small company, named BlueSky Research, might look.

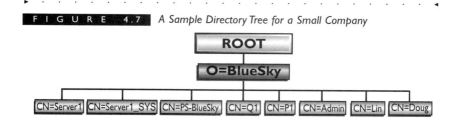

F I G U R E   4 . 7   *A Sample Directory Tree for a Small Company*

If your company is larger, you may want to use OU objects to divide the tree into more manageable chunks. (You can use multiple levels of OU objects if you need to.)

First, consider how many different locations you have that connect to each other across WAN (wide-area network) links (in other words, over phone lines). If you have sites across town from each other, or in different cities or countries, you should probably create an OU object to represent each site.

Because the NDS database resides on multiple servers in an intraNetWare network, changes made to the database must be synchronized across the network to all the affected servers. If you have servers at different geographical sites connected by phone lines, the data being transferred during synchronization can keep those phone lines very busy at times.

Using OU objects to divide the tree according to geographical sites helps cut down on the amount of synchronization traffic that goes across the phone lines. You can make each geographical site fall into its own OU object, and specify that a new partition of the database begin at that OU object. Then, when someone makes changes to an NDS object under that OU object, the changes only get synchronized with servers at the site containing replicas of that partition. The changes don't have to be synchronized to other sites immediately, cutting down on the amount of traffic across the phone lines.

Now you have planned the top of your NDS tree. You either have a single Organization object, or you have a layer of OU objects representing WAN sites. Next, you will plan where to put all of the leaf objects.

ORGANIZING BY DEPARTMENTS
VERSUS LOCATIONS

Your goal with the NDS tree is to make network objects easy for users to find, and easy for you to manage. The two most common ways to organize a tree are by department and by location.

For some companies, organizing by departments or divisions is the most logical way to set up the NDS tree. If all the Marketing users need access to completely different resources (such as servers, volumes, and printers)

Individual users, printers, and so on can be placed inside the OU object that corresponds to their department. (These individual objects are all leaf objects.) Figure 4.8 shows how a large company, called BigTime Engineering, might set up its Directory tree based on departments. Note the different levels of OU objects. The asterisks beneath the container objects represent various types of leaf objects (CN objects).

FIGURE 4.8 *A Sample Directory Tree for a Large Company Divided by Departments*

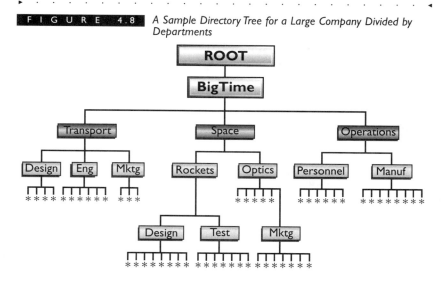

On the other hand, you may find that users access resources based more on where they're located, than on their department. For instance, suppose the second floor of your building contains the engineering department, the maintenance people, and your inside sales representatives. They all use the same three printers, access files and applications on the same server volumes, and so on. Dividing these users by department probably won't accomplish anything for you — you'll just have two or three unnecessary OU objects.

Instead, all those users and resources could be located under a single OU called Floor2. Then, they could easily locate resources they need, and you don't have to maintain three separate groups.

Figure 4.9 illustrates a Directory tree for a large company, called Yippy Skippy Toys, divided by location instead of departments.

You can, of course, mix the two methods, using both location and departmental OU objects, if that makes the most sense for your network.

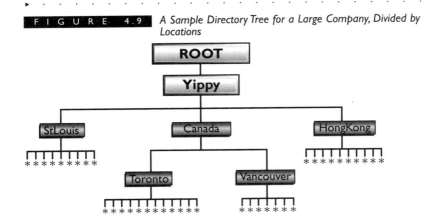

FIGURE 4.9 A Sample Directory Tree for a Large Company, Divided by Locations

TIP

When planning your NDS tree structure, try to make it flexible enough so that you can easily change it if your company makes organizational changes. Consider the type of organizational changes your company is most likely to make. Does it reorganize departments on a frequent basis? Are you expecting the company to move to a new location soon? Is the company expanding, adding on new buildings, or leasing new floors of an existing building? The answers to these questions may help you decide on the most efficient way to set up your NDS tree.

USING NAMING STANDARDS

Another planning aspect that can make your NDS tree management go more smoothly is to plan a standard way to name objects such as users, servers, and printers. By establishing some naming standards up front, you make it easier for users to locate the resources they need. The following suggestions and tips may help you decide how you want to standardize your naming guidelines:

> ► If several people will be responsible for creating and managing NDS objects, make sure they're all committed to using the same standards.

> ► Get naming standards approved by management, if necessary.

> ► In general, keep names as short as possible, to make it easier to type full names. It's easier to type "BigTime" (or even "BT") than "BigTimeEngineering."

▶ Decide on a standard for usernames, such as last names only, first name and last initial, first two initials and last name, or some other logical format for your situation. Many companies make their usernames conform to the restrictions specified by their e-mail package, so users only need to remember one username.

▶ Decide how you will handle objects with similar names. For instance, if you've settled on using the first initial and last name for usernames, how will you deal with John Smith and Jill Smith?

▶ Do you want to make some object names indicate the types of object they are, such as using SERV_xxx for all server names?

▶ Do you want the names of printers and similar objects to indicate information such as the type, location, or owner? For example, you could specify that a printer be named P1-HP3si-Mktg to indicate that it is Printer #1 in the marketing department, and that it is a particular type of Hewlett Packard laser printer.

Name Context — Your Location in the Tree

Each object in the Directory tree exists in a specific location of the tree. This location is called the object's *name context*.

A name context is really a sort of address for that object's location; it consists of the names of any container objects over that object. An object's *full name* (also called the *full distinguished name*) consists of the object's name, plus its name context. Each of the names in a name context is separated by periods.

For example, suppose user Doug is located under the Organization object called BlueSky. Knowing where Doug is located, you can determine the following information about him:

▶ His name context is BlueSky, because that's the only container object above him.

▶ His common name is Doug.

▶ His full name is Doug.BlueSky.

Figure 4.10 shows Doug's location in the Directory tree.

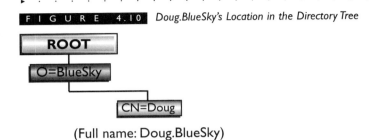

(Full name: Doug.BlueSky)

The name context of an object is useful because it lets you know exactly where that object is in the Directory tree. In addition, it lets you uniquely identify two objects that may have the same common name (such as "Doug"), but which reside in two different parts of the tree.

Within a single container, no two objects can have the same name. However, two objects can have the same name if they are in separate containers. This is because their name context is different, so each one has a unique full name.

For example, at BigTime Engineering, in the Transport Organizational Unit, there can be only one user with the common name Eric located within the container called Mktg. However, there can be other users named Eric in the tree if they are within other containers. Say there's an Eric in Mktg, and another Eric in Design, both of whom work in the Transport division of BigTime Engineering.

The Marketing Eric's full name would be Eric.Mktg.Transport.BigTime. Each container name is added to Eric's common name (separated by periods) to spell out his address in the Directory tree, clear back to the Organization's name. His name context, or location in the tree, is Mktg.Transport.BigTime.

The Design Eric's full name would be Eric.Design.Transport.BigTime. Because his full name is different from the other Eric's full name, NDS can keep them both straight.

Figure 4.11 shows where each Eric is located in the Directory tree at BigTime Engineering.

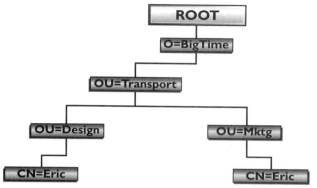

F I G U R E   4.11   *Two Users with the Same Common Name Can Reside in Different Containers in the Directory Tree.*

(Full name: Eric.Design.Transport.BigTime)   (Full name: Eric.Mktg.Transport.BigTime)

NOTE

In some cases, you may see a full name (or a name context) that includes the object abbreviations. For example, you may see CN=Eric.OU=Design.OU=Transport.O=BigTime. This is the official, formal way to show full names; however, most intraNetWare utilities let you eliminate the object abbreviations and use just the names instead.

Specifying objects in the Directory tree is similar to specifying subdirectories in a DOS file system. In the file system, if you are at the root of the volume or disk or in a completely separate directory path, you have to specify a full directory path to get to the subdirectory you want (such as D:\REPORTS\SALES\1998).

In the same way, if you are at the root of the Directory tree or in a completely different branch of the tree, you have to specify an object's full name to find it (such as Eric.Design.Transport.BigTime).

However, if you are already somewhere in the subdirectory's directory path, you only need to specify the portion of the path that will get you to the desired subdirectory (such as SALES\1998). You don't need to specify the subdirectory's full path.

Similarly, if you are already within a container over an object's location, you only need to specify the portion of the Directory tree address that exists between you and the object (such as Eric.Design). You don't need to specify the object's full name back to the root. This is called specifying a *partial name* (or a *relative distinguished name*).

If you do want to specify an object's full name back to the root, place a period at the beginning of the object's name (in any commands ßyou type).This indicates to the utility you're using that it is a full name and shouldn't be interpreted as a partial name. For example, you would type Eric.Design.Transport.BigTime to indicate that this is Eric's full name.

To move around in the Directory tree's context, moving up and down through containers, you will use the NetWare Administrator utility. You open and close containers in the NetWare Administrator just like you open and close folders in Windows.

Keeping Your NDS Software Up to Date

Periodically, Novell releases updated versions of DS.NLM (the NDS database program) and its management utilities on the Novell Web site (www.novell.com). These updates may add minor features or fix problems. You should try to keep your network updated with these new versions whenever possible.

If you obtain an updated version of DS.NLM, install it on all of the intraNetWare servers in your network. All servers must be running the same version of DS.NLM to use any new features of DS.NLM. Keeping all of your servers running the same version will help simplify your support of the Directory tree.

Beyond the Basics

This chapter explained the basics of NDS, and showed you how Directory trees are set up. The following topics are explained in other sections of this book:

► For instructions on creating NDS objects, such as User objects, using the NetWare Administrator utility, see Chapter 5.

► For information about NDS object security features, see Chapter 6.

► For instructions on installing NDS when you install a server, see Chapter 2.

NDS is another aspect of intraNetWare that has a number of advanced features that let you customize the network to fit your needs. After you've mastered the fundamentals of NDS, you may want to learn more. If so, some resources you can use include Novell's online documentation, *Novell's IntranetWare Administrator's Handbook* from Novell Press, or *Novell's Guide to intraNetWare Networks* by Jeff Hughes and Blair Thomas from Novell Press (which describes NDS design in detail). In these resources, you can learn more about the following topics:

- ► Understanding database replicas and partitions
- ► Using NDS Manager to work with replicas and partitions
- ► Using the SET NDS TRACE and DSREPAIR utilities to identify and fix NDS problems
- ► Using Bindery Services to allow bindery-based applications to use the objects in the NDS database
- ► Using NetSync to manage NetWare 3.1x servers from intraNetWare's NetWare Administrator utility on an intraNetWare server
- ► Working with multiple NDS trees
- ► Merging multiple NDS trees

TIP

As mentioned in Chapter 2, another useful resource for intraNetWare management information is the *Novell Application Notes.* This monthly publication contains research reports and articles on a wide range of advanced topics, including NDS management. To order a subscription, call 1-800-377-4136 in the U.S., or 1-303-297-2725 worldwide.

CHAPTER 5

Creating and Managing Users

Instant Access

Creating Users and Groups

► To work on the network, a user must have a valid user account (an NDS object); rights to work with necessary files, directories, and NDS objects; a home directory (optional); and a login script to set up the user's work environment (optional).

► To create a user, use the NetWare Administrator utility.

► To create a group, use NetWare Administrator to create the Group object, then open its Members page to assign users to the group.

Logging In and Out

► To log in, users can type **LOGIN** at the DOS prompt, or they can use the Login program that was installed as part of the intraNetWare client software. Users must specify a valid username and password.

► To keep from having to type their full names every time they log in, users can specify their name context in the NET.CFG file (for DOS and Windows 3.1 workstations), or in the Network Neighborhood properties (for Windows 95 workstations).

► Users should log out of the network whenever they leave their workstation to prevent someone else from unauthorized access.

► To log out, DOS and Windows 3.1 users can type **LOGOUT** at the DOS prompt, Windows 3.1 users can use the NetWare User Tools utility, and Windows 95 users can use the Network Neighborhood.

► Users can use the NetWare User Tools utility on Windows 3.1 workstations to accomplish basic network tasks.

Automating the User's Work Environment

► Use the NetWare Application Launcher to put icons for applications on users' workstations (so they don't have to know where the applications are located).

► Use login scripts to automate the process of setting up the workstation environment, mapping drives, capturing printer ports, and so on.

Populating Your Network

Even if all the hardware and software is set up for your network, a new user can't just log in and begin using the network. He or she must first obtain a user account on the network.

Each person who will use the network should have his or her own user account. That way, each user can log in using his or her own name. (Although users can share a login name, this is generally not as safe, and can cause unnecessary confusion.)

Of course, after a brand-new installation, the only User object that will exist in the tree is the ADMIN User object.

 NOTE If you have upgraded your server from NetWare 3.1x, one more User object exists: Supervisor. The Supervisor User object can only be accessed from NetWare 3.1x or 2.x utilities, and is only used for compatibility with older versions of NetWare.

Therefore, before the users can begin using the network, you (as the network administrator) must create user accounts for each of them. In addition, there are several other tasks you can perform to make life easier for the users:

► You may want to create some Group objects, and organize the users into those groups. Groups allow you to manage security, printer assignments, and other issues that may affect many (or all) of the users in the same way.

► To make the network easier to use for DOS or Windows 3.1 users, you can create login scripts. Login scripts automatically set up the users' workstation environments with necessary drive mappings and other types of useful environmental settings. (Windows 95 users can use the Network Neighborhood to modify their environments, instead.)

► You can use the NetWare Application Launcher to set up an icon on users' desktops that points directly to network applications. Then, the users can simply launch the application from their desktops without having to know where the application is located, which drives to map, and so on.

What Do Users Need?

Creating a user's account means creating a new object for the user in the NDS tree. However, it also involves more than that.

Before a user can really work on the network, you need to set up many of the following tools or characteristics (some are optional, depending on your situation):

- The user's account (which is an NDS object for the user with its associated properties filled in, such as the user's last name, full name, telephone number, and so on)

- The user's group memberships

- A home directory (folder) for the user's work files

- A login script (for DOS and Windows 3.1 users) that maps drives to the directories and applications to which the user will need access

- NDS security (rights that control how the user can see and use other NDS objects in the tree)

- File system security (rights that regulate a user's access to files and directories the user needs to work with)

- Account restrictions, if necessary, to control when the user logs in, how often the user must change passwords, and so on

- Access to the network printers

- An e-mail account, if necessary

The following sections of this chapter describe how to create user and group accounts on the network, how to create user home directories, and how users can log in and log out. It also explains the basics of login scripts.

NOTE

NDS security, file system security, and account restrictions are explained in Chapter 6.

Chapter 8 explains how to give users access to network printers.

For information on creating an e-mail account for a user, see the documentation that came with your e-mail program.

Creating Users and Groups

Users are the individuals who have accounts on the network. Each real-life user has a specific User object defined in the NDS Directory tree. This User object is the account that defines when the user can log in, what rights the user has to work on the network, what the user's full name is, and other types of information. Each piece of information that defines the User object is called a *property*.

A Group object is a single object that is assigned a list of users. Whenever one of the Group object's properties is changed (such as a new security assignment), every user in the Group's list is suddenly changed the same way.

Using Group objects is a fast, efficient way to assign security levels to groups of users who have the same needs, but who may not be in the same container object. You can also use Group objects when some — but not all — of the users in a container have similar needs.

TIP

If all users in container object (such as an Organization) have the same needs, you probably don't need to use a Group object. Just change the container object's properties to affect all of the users in the container.

Because you can use container objects to assign rights and login scripts to all the users in those containers, you may find that you don't need to use as many groups as you may have in NetWare 3.1x or earlier versions.

To create a new user or group on the network, you use the NetWare Administrator utility from a workstation. The NetWare Administrator is an intraNetWare utility that can run on Windows 3.1, OS/2, or Windows 95. (If you have not yet installed the NetWare Administrator on your workstation, see Chapter 4 for instructions.)

NOTE

To create any new NDS object, including users and groups, you have to be logged in as the Admin user, or as another user that has been given the rights necessary for creating or changing objects. See Chapter 6 for more information about security rights.

CREATING A USER

Before creating a new User object for a user, answer the following questions:

- ▶ Under which container will the user's object be placed?
- ▶ Where will the user's home directory (folder) be placed?

NOTE

In many cases, network administrators create a directory, called USERS, on a server's volume. Then, the administrator creates a home directory for each user underneath USERS. Users have all rights to their home directory, so they can store applications, work files, or personal files there. Users can create additional directories underneath their home directory — it's just like any other directory or folder on their workstation's hard disk. You can specify whether to create a home directory automatically, and where to put it, when you create a new user.

To create a new User object, complete the following steps:

1. Create a directory for all users' home directories. For example, you might want to create a network directory called USERS on volume SYS.

2. Start up the NetWare Administrator utility by double-clicking its icon. The NetWare Administrator's Browser window should appear, as shown in Figure 5.1. (If the Browser window doesn't appear, choose NDS Browser from the Tools menu.)

F I G U R E   5.1   *The NetWare Administrator's Browser Window*

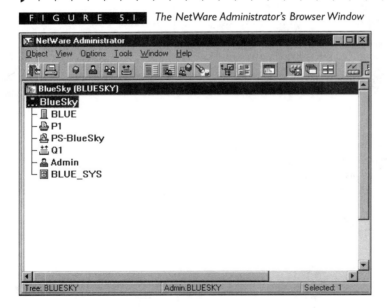

3. Select the container object (an Organization or Organizational Unit object) that will hold the new user.

4. From the Object menu, choose Create.

5. From the New Object dialog box that appears (see Figure 5.2), choose User, and then choose OK.

FIGURE 5.2 *Creating a New User Object in the New Object Dialog Box*

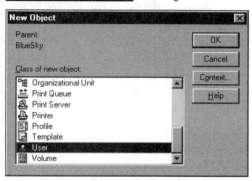

6. In the Create User dialog box, enter the user's login name and last name (see Figure 5.3). The login name is the name you want this user to type when he or she logs in.

FIGURE 5.3 *Enter the User's Login Name and Last Name.*

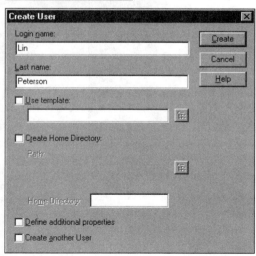

7. Create a home directory for this user.

   a. Mark the check box next to Create Home Directory.

   b. Click the Browse button to specify a path to the home directory. (The button isn't actually labeled "Browse," but it has an icon resembling a directory structure on it. The button is located to the right of the Home Directory and Path area on the screen.)

   c. From the Directory Contents panel on the right, double-click the container and then the volume that will hold the user directories.

   d. When the directory you created in Step 1 appears in the left panel (under Files and Directories), select that directory and click OK (see Figure 5.4). The path to that directory should now appear in the Create User dialog box.

F I G U R E   5 . 4   *Select the Path to the Home Directory.*

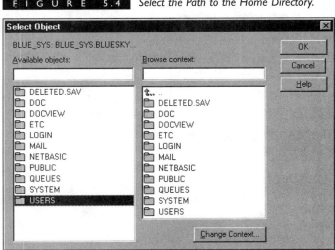

8. Mark the Define Additional Properties check box. (This will allow you to see more information about the User object after you create it in the next step.)

9. Choose Create.

10. The user's Identification page appears, as shown in Figure 5.5. The Identification page will appear every time you use the NetWare Administrator utility to look at this object in the future. Along the right side of the screen are large rectangular buttons with turned-down corners. Each of these buttons represents a different page of information about the user. You can fill in some, none, or all of the information on these pages depending on your needs. If you have entered new information in one of these pages that needs to be saved, the turned-down corner will appear black. Choose OK when finished.

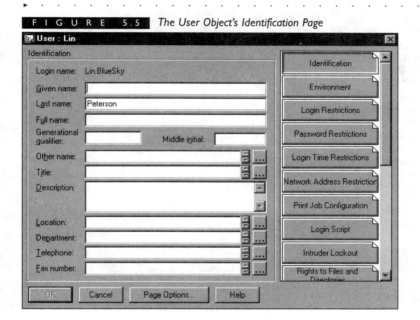

FIGURE 5.5 *The User Object's Identification Page*

11. Create another user by following the same steps.

After you've created a new User object, that User object will appear in the Directory tree. You can use the NetWare Administrator's Browser to see where the object is in the tree and to see, or change, the User object's information.

CREATING GROUPS AND ASSIGNING GROUP MEMBERSHIP TO USERS

Creating a Group object is similar to creating a user. The following steps show how to create a Group object and assign group membership to a user:

1. Start up the NetWare Administrator utility by double-clicking its icon. The NetWare Administrator's Browser window should appear, as shown in Figure 5.6. (If the Browser window doesn't appear, choose NDS Browser from the Tools menu.)

FIGURE 5.6 *The NetWare Administrator's Browser Window*

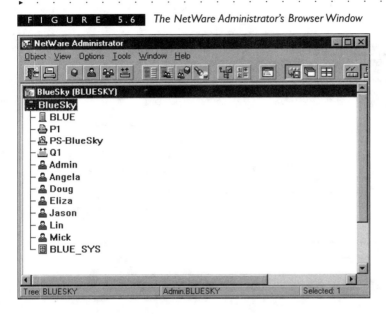

2. Select the container object that will hold the new group.

3. From the Object menu, choose Create.

4. From the New Object dialog box that appears (see Figure 5.7), choose Group, and then choose OK.

5. In the Create Group dialog box, enter the Group object's name, as shown in Figure 5.8.

6. Mark the check box next to Define Other Properties.

7. Choose Create.

8. The group's Identification page appears. Enter any information you desire on the Identification page, such as a description of the Group object (see Figure 5.9).

F I G U R E   5.7   *Creating a New Group Object in the New Object Dialog Box*

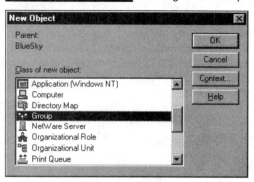

F I G U R E   5.8   *Enter the Group Object's Name.*

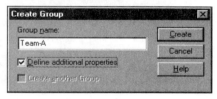

F I G U R E   5.9   *The Group Object's Identification Page*

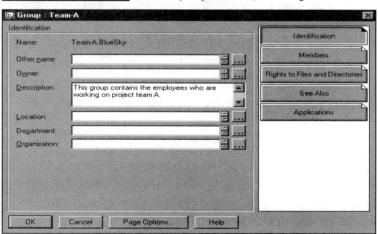

9. Choose the Members page and click Add.

10. From the screen that appears (see Figure 5.10), specify any existing users who should be members of this group. From the right panel, open the container that holds the user you want. From the left panel, select the user, and then choose OK. The user's name now appears as a member of the group. (To select multiple users, use Shift-Click or Ctrl-Click.)

► . . . . ◄

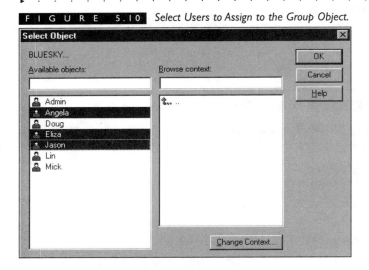

F I G U R E   5 . 1 0   *Select Users to Assign to the Group Object.*

TIP

If the group already exists, you can also assign a user to that group by selecting the User object, opening the user's Group Membership page, and adding the group.

OPENING AN OBJECT'S INFORMATION PAGES

There are three ways to open an object's information pages in NetWare Administrator:

► If the object is a leaf object (such as a user or group), double-click the object's icon.

► Highlight the object, and then choose Details from the Object menu (which appears in the menu bar across the top of the NetWare Administrator's window). Figure 5.11 shows the Object menu.

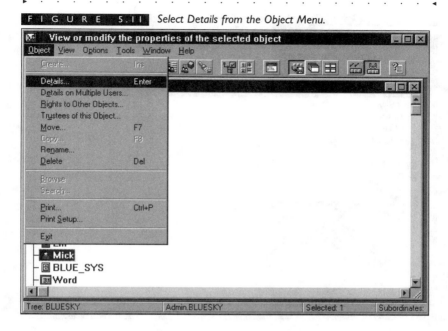

▶ Right-click the object, then choose Details from the menu that appears, as shown in Figure 5.12.

Double-clicking a container object won't show you the container's detail pages. Instead, double-clicking the icon will just open the object in the Browser, showing the objects underneath it. Therefore, to see a container object's detail pages, you must choose the Details option from either the Object menu, or the right-click menu.

User Network Activities

Once users have been created, they can begin working on the network. In most cases, users on a network will notice very little difference from working on a standalone computer. They still use the applications they were used to before. They still open, save, and delete files the same way. They can still play the same games — if they can get away with it.

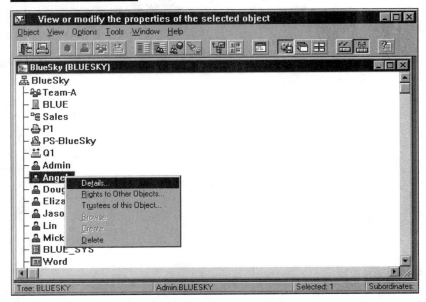

Most users will only notice the following primary differences:

► They have to enter a login name and password.

► They have more drives and directories available to them.

► They are restricted from accessing some files.

► Their print jobs go to the same printer as everyone else's.

Whether you want them to be able to control most of these network activities themselves is up to you.

For most Windows 3.1 and DOS users, the following three intraNetWare utilities will take care of their networking tasks:

► The Login utility (from either the DOS command line or from Windows)

► The Logout utility (from either the DOS command line or from Windows)

► The NetWare User Tools utility

Windows 95 users will use Windows Explorer and Network Neighborhood to perform network tasks.

LOGGING IN

To log in to the network, the user must use intraNetWare's Login program to enter a login name and a password. The network verifies the name and password. If the name and password match, the network lets the user in to the network. If the name and password don't match, the network prevents the user from logging in.

How you log in to the network depends on what operating system you're running on your workstation:

▸ DOS users type the following command at the DOS prompt, substituting their login name for *name* (and entering a password when prompted):

```
LOGIN name
```

▸ Windows 3.1 or Windows 95 users can use the Login program that is installed as part of the intraNetWare client software. It automatically runs whenever the workstation is rebooted. When the Login window appears, as shown in Figure 5.13, they enter a login name and password.

▸ Windows 95 users can also double-click the Network Neighborhood icon on their desktop. They can then right-click the desired NDS tree, click Log In To NDS Tree, as shown in Figure 5.14, and enter a login name and password.

F I G U R E   5.13   *The Login Program*

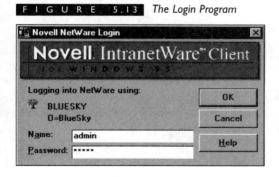

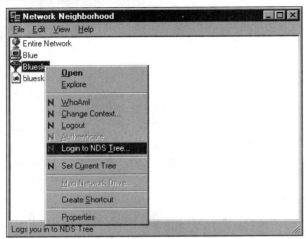

By default, users must enter their full names when they log in. For example, Eric's full name might be Eric.Design.Transport.BigTime; he would have to enter that name every time he logged in.

This occurs because the Login utility doesn't know the NDS name context in which the user was created. It assumes the default context is at the root of the Directory tree. If you've created the user in a container beneath the root (which is sometimes the case), Login won't find the user in the tree if the user enters only his or her common name. If Login can't find the user, the user can't log in to the network.

However, there is an easy way to store the user's name context (location in the tree) on the workstation, so that the user can simply enter his or her short name (such as Eric) instead:

▶ DOS and Windows 3.1 users can add a command to a file on their workstation named NET.CFG.

▶ Windows 95 users can configure the intraNetWare client software to store the user's name context in the client software.

The following sections explain how to set the name context.

Specifying a Name Context for DOS and Windows 3.1 Workstations

On DOS and Windows 3.1 workstations, the intraNetWare client software creates a file called NET.CFG. You can use any text editor (such as Windows' NotePad) to edit this file.

Locate the file by opening first the Novell directory, and then the Client32 directory. When you've opened the NET.CFG file in the text editor, scroll down through the file until you see the heading, "NetWare DOS Requester." Under this heading, type the following command, substituting the user's name context for *context*:

```
NAME CONTEXT="context"
```

For example, to specify Eric's context, enter the following command in the NET.CFG file:

```
NAME CONTEXT="Design.Transport.BigTime"
```

Then, save the file. You will have to reboot the workstation to make this new command take effect. After you've rebooted the workstation, Eric can just log in using his common name, Eric, which is obviously going to be easier for him to remember.

To simplify the user's life even more, you may also want to put the Login command in the user's AUTOEXEC.BAT file so that it executes every time the user boots the workstation.

Specifying a Name Context for Windows 95 Workstations

When you installed the intraNetWare client software on a Windows 95 workstation, you may have taken the opportunity to specify a name context during the installation.

If you didn't specify a name context during the installation, or if you want to change the name context to something different, you can easily specify a new name context by completing the following steps:

1. Right-click the Network Neighborhood icon on your Windows 95 desktop.

2. Choose Properties.

3. From the list that appears (see Figure 5.15), highlight Novell intraNetWare Client (or Novell NetWare Client32, if you're using an older version of the client software), then click Properties.

FIGURE 5.15
Highlight Novell intraNetWare Client, and Then Click Properties.

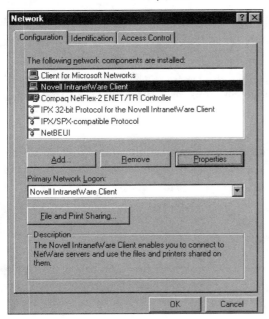

4. The screen that now appears (see Figure 5.16) lets you specify a preferred server, a preferred tree, and a name context. In the Name Context field, enter the context for this user. (If your network has more than one tree, you can also enter a preferred tree, to indicate which one you want to log in to on a regular basis. In most cases, you don't need to indicate a preferred server, because intraNetWare lets you log into the entire tree — not to a specific server, like earlier versions of NetWare required.)

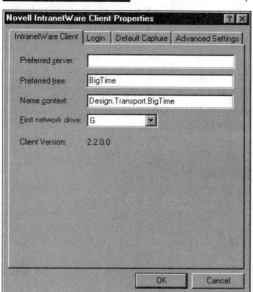

Enter a Name Context for the User.

5. Click OK to save the name context information.

6. Exit the Network Neighborhood properties.

After the workstation is rebooted, Eric will be able to log in using just his common name, Eric, instead of his full name.

LOGGING OUT

When you finish working on the network, you should log out of it to make sure no one else accesses the network using your account. Always ensure that you log out before you leave your desk, even if you leave your computer turned on. How you log out depends on the operating system you're using on your workstation, for example:

▶ If you're using a DOS workstation, simply type the following command at the DOS prompt:

```
LOGOUT
```

▶ If you're using a Windows 3.1 workstation, you can either go to DOS and type **LOGOUT** at the DOS prompt, or you can use the NetWare User Tools utility to log out. Double-click NetWare User Tools, select NetWare Connections, choose the server or tree from which you want to log out, and choose Logout. (The NetWare User Tools utility is explained in the following section.)

▶ If you're using a Windows 95 workstation, double-click the Network Neighborhood icon, right-click the NDS tree, and choose Logout, as shown in Figure 5.17.

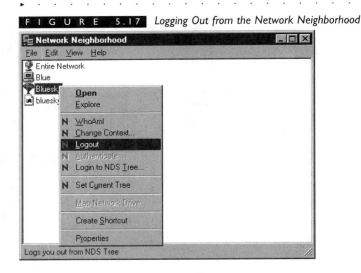

F I G U R E   5.17   *Logging Out from the Network Neighborhood*

USING NETWARE USER TOOLS

Novell's intraNetWare includes a utility, called NetWare User Tools, that allows Windows 3.1 users to perform their most common network tasks. The intraNetWare client installation program automatically places the icon for NetWare User Tools in the NetWare Tools program group on your Windows 3.1 desktop.

TIP

Windows 95 users will use the Windows Explorer and Network Neighborhood instead of the NetWare User Tools to complete network tasks.

With NetWare User Tools, users can do the following:

▶ Set up print queues and control how their print jobs are printed on the network. (See Chapter 8 for more information about printing.)

▶ Send short messages to other network users.

▶ Map drive letters to network directories. (Drive mappings are explained later in this chapter.)

▶ Change passwords.

▶ Log in to and out of Directory trees and network servers.

▶ Change their own name contexts in the Directory tree.

To use NetWare User Tools, double-click the NetWare User Tools icon. Use the icons along the top of the utility to perform different network tasks.

When you make changes in NetWare User Tools (such as mapping drives to directories, or changing your printer port to point to a print queue), you can click the Permanent button. This will make those assignments permanent; if you don't make the changes permanent, they will be erased when you log out.

Use the Help button to read about the tasks you can do with this utility.

Making Applications Easy to Access

One of the best new features of intraNetWare, as far as users are concerned, is the NetWare Application Launcher. Once you have the NetWare Application Launcher set up on each user's workstation, you can use NetWare Administrator to make an application become an object in the NDS tree. Then, the icon for the Application object will appear automatically in the NetWare Application Launcher window on the desktop of each user you assign to that application.

Figure 5.18 shows what the NetWare Application Launcher window might look like with a couple of applications assigned to user Admin.

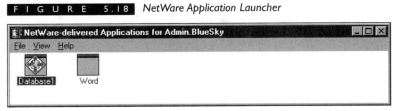

The users don't need to know where the application is, they don't need to map drives or enter launch parameters, and you don't need to update login scripts. When you update the application, the icons in all of the desktops will continue to point to the new application.

INSTALLING THE NETWARE APPLICATION LAUNCHER ON WINDOWS 3.1 WORKSTATIONS

To set up the NetWare Application Launcher on a Windows 3.1 workstation, complete the following steps:

1. Start Windows and highlight the program group in which you want NetWare Application Launcher to appear. The NetWare Tools program group was already created during the workstation installation, so you can use that group.

2. From the File menu, choose New, and then select Program Item.

3. For the Description, enter the name you want to use (such as *NetWare App Launcher* or *NAL*).

4. Use the Browse button to specify the location of the NALW31.EXE file (SYS:\PUBLIC\NALW31.EXE) and the working directory (SYS:\PUBLIC).

5. Click OK. The NetWare Application Launcher icon appears on the desktop.

Now, any Application object you create and associate with this user will automatically appear in this user's Application Launcher window. To create an Application object, skip to the section entitled "Creating an Application Object" later in this chapter.

INSTALLING THE NETWARE APPLICATION LAUNCHER ON WINDOWS 95 WORKSTATIONS

To set up the NetWare Application Launcher on a Windows 95 workstation, complete the following steps:

1. Right-click anywhere on the Windows 95 desktop, and then choose New.

2. Select Shortcut.

3. Choose Browse, locate the PUBLIC directory under volume SYS, and choose NALW95.EXE.

4. Choose Open, and then Finish.

The NetWare Application Launcher appears as a shortcut icon on the desktop. Double-clicking the icon will start the NetWare Application Launcher. Any Application object you create and associate with this user will automatically appear in this user's Application Launcher window. The following section explains how to create an Application object.

CREATING AN APPLICATION OBJECT

To make a network application appear in users' NetWare Application Launchers, you must create an Application object in the NDS tree for that application.

To create an Application object for a network application, complete the following steps:

1. Start NetWare Administrator.

2. Select the container object that will hold the Application object.

3. From the Object menu, choose Create.

4. From the New Object dialog box that appears, choose the Application object for the appropriate operating system (DOS, Windows 3.x, Windows 95, or Windows NT), and then choose OK.

5. When the Application object's dialog box appears, as shown in Figure 5.19, enter its name and path.

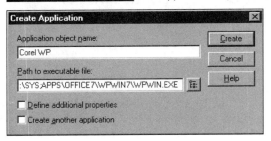

6. Check the Define Additional Properties box, and then click Create. The new object's information page appears, as shown in Figure 5.20.

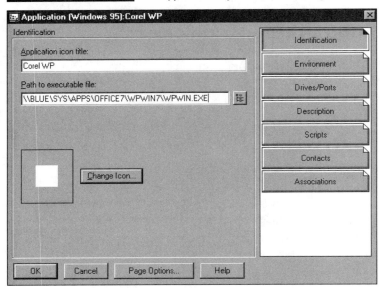

7. In the information page, enter any additional information necessary for this application, such as its command line parameters, working directory, drives or ports, a description of the application, and so on.

8. In the Associations page, add the users or groups who should be able to use this application.

9. Click OK when you're finished.

Login Scripts

Login scripts are tools similar to batch files that you can use to set up users' workstation environments automatically. Each time a user logs in, the Login utility executes the login scripts. These can set up frequently used drive mappings, capture the workstation's printer port to a network print queue, display connection information or messages on the screen, or do other types of tasks for the user.

NOTE

In intraNetWare, you can assign a drive letter (such as G or H) to point to a specific network directory. This works the same way as making drive C point to your hard disk, or drive E point to a CD-ROM. When you assign a drive letter to a directory, it's called a *mapping a drive*. The resulting drive assignment is called a *drive mapping*.

When you log in, you see a series of commands scroll by automatically. Those are the commands being executed by your login script.

Login scripts are a fairly advanced feature of intraNetWare. However, this chapter will explore the basics of login scripts and the most common commands used in those scripts.

A default login script is set up when intraNetWare is installed. This script contains some very basic drive mappings, so you can get to the intraNetWare utilities on the server. However, you can create your own login scripts if you'd like to set up more drive mappings for your workstation.

TIP

Login scripts are primarily for users of DOS and Windows 3.1 workstations. Windows 95 users can use the desktop features on their own workstations to set up many of the things login scripts set up. For example, Windows 95 users can set up short-cuts to their applications or frequently used folders. Therefore, if you use Windows 95, you may not want — or need — to use more than the default login script.

In intraNetWare, there are three types of login scripts:

▶ Container Login Scripts — The container login script (also called the system login script) is a property of a container object. All of the commands in the container login script execute for every user within that container who logs in. Therefore, this is a good place to put commands that are common to all users within the container.

▶ Profile Login Scripts — With a profile script, you can create a script that will apply to several users who don't necessarily have to be in the same container. It's kind of a group login script. The profile login script is a property of a Profile object, which defines a list of users who belong to the Profile. (A Profile object exists soley to support these profile login scripts. If you don't want to use a profile login script, you don't need to create any Profile objects.) A user can have only one profile login script execute upon login.

▶ User Login Scripts — A user's login script is a property of his or her User object. If there are specific drive mappings or other commands that this particular user needs (but others don't), you can store those commands in the user login script. If the user does not have a specific user login script, the default login script will execute instead, setting up the most basic drive mappings.

These three types of login scripts work together to set up each user's environment upon login. They execute in the following order:

1. Container login script

2. Profile login script

3. User login script (or default login script, if a user login script doesn't exist)

All three are optional. If you don't create one of them, the Login program will skip to the next in the list. If no login scripts exist, the default script will be the only one that runs when a user logs in. Figure 5.21 shows three different users in the BlueSky tree, and the objects in the tree that contain login scripts.

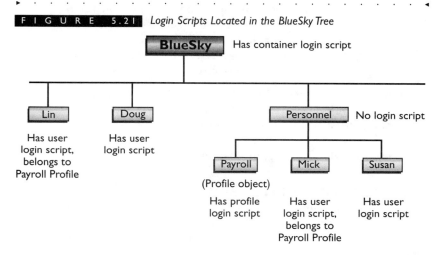

FIGURE 5.21 *Login Scripts Located in the BlueSky Tree*

When user Lin logs in, three login scripts will execute for her. First, the container login script that belongs to the container immediately above her (BlueSky) executes, followed by a profile script (because she belongs to the Payroll Profile object) and then her own user login script.

When user Doug logs in, two login scripts execute for him. First, the container login script that belongs to his container (BlueSky) executes, followed by his own user login script.

When user Mick logs in, two login scripts execute for him. A profile login script executes first (because he belongs to the profile Payroll); then his own user login script executes. The container immediately above him (Personnel) does not have a login script, so no container script will execute for Mick.

When user Susan logs in, only one script executes for her: her own user login script. She doesn't belong to the profile Payroll, and her container doesn't have a login script, so neither a profile nor container script will execute for her.

Because up to three different login scripts can execute for a given user, conflicts between the login scripts may occur. If they do, the final login script to execute wins. Therefore, if the container login script maps a directory to drive letter G, and then the user script maps a different directory to drive letter G, the user script's mapping overwrites the container script's mapping.

NOTE

Container login scripts only apply to the users immediately within that container. They don't apply to users in a sub-container. If the container that holds user Andrea doesn't have a login script, no container login script will execute when Andrea logs in, even if a container higher up in the tree has a login script.

To simplify the administration of your network's login scripts, try to put as much common information as possible (such as drive mappings to application directories) in the container and profile login scripts. It's much easier to change a drive mapping in one script and have it apply to all your users than to make the same change dozens or hundreds of times for every user script.

CREATING A LOGIN SCRIPT

You use the NetWare Administrator utility to create login scripts just as you assign any other properties to NDS objects. Open the object's Details page (choose Details from the Object menu), and then click the button for the Login Script page.

When you open up the Login Script property for a User, Profile, or container object, you are presented with a blank screen (or the previous login script, if one already exists). In this screen, shown in Figure 5.22, type any commands you want the login script to hold: drive mappings, printer port captures, messages, environment settings, and so on.

In general, you can only change your own login script if you're an ordinary user. If you're the Admin user, you can change login scripts for other users and for containers. (Even if you aren't the Admin user, you can be given rights to modify other objects' login scripts, if necessary. For more information about the rights you need to change other objects' properties, see Chapter 6.)

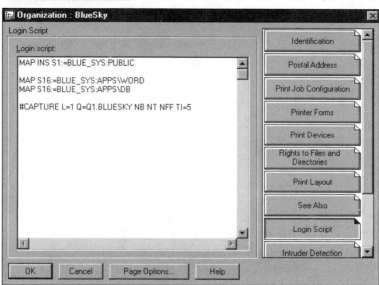

FIGURE 5.22 *The Login Script Page for a Container Object*

ASSIGNING PROFILE LOGIN SCRIPTS TO USERS

To create a profile login script, you create a Profile object just as you create any other NDS object. Create its script in the Profile object's Login Script property. After you've created the script, you must assign it to individual users. To do this, complete the following steps:

1. Use the Browser to select a User object.

2. Choose Details from the Object menu, and then open the Login Script page.

3. Enter the name of the Profile object in the Profile field beneath the login script text window, as shown in Figure 5.23.

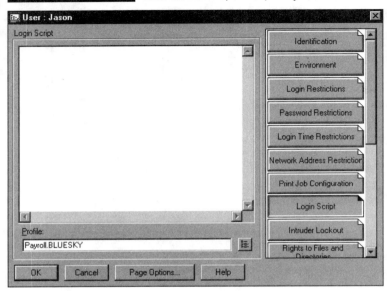

FIGURE 5.23 *Enter the Name of the Profile Object.*

4. Save the information and return to the Browser.

5. From the Browser, select the Profile object.

6. From the Object menu, choose Trustees of This Object.

7. In the Trustees window that appears (see Figure 5.24), click the Add Trustee button and then enter the name of the user who will use this profile login script.

8. Make sure the Browse object right and Read property right are checked, and then choose OK to assign those rights to the user.

THE MOST COMMON LOGIN SCRIPT COMMANDS

There are more than 30 commands you can use in login scripts. However, the two main reasons people use login scripts are to redirect parallel ports to print queues and to map drives to network directories. Therefore, it's likely that you will only see, or use, two different login script commands. These two commonly used commands are:

- ► #CAPTURE
- ► MAP

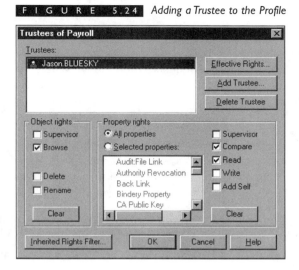

FIGURE 5.24 *Adding a Trustee to the Profile*

The #CAPTURE Login Script Command

This command redirects the workstation's parallel port, so that it points to a network print queue instead of to a printer attached directly to the workstation. (This concept is explained more fully in Chapter 8.)

To execute the CAPTURE program, remember to put the pound (#) symbol at the beginning of the command. When the CAPTURE program is finished executing, the login script will take over again and continue running, executing other commands as necessary.

For example, to capture a user's LPT1 port to use a network print queue named LaserQ, you might put the following command in the login script:

```
#CAPTURE L=1 Q=.LaserQ.Sales.BlueSky NB NT NFF TI=5
```

The MAP Login Script Command

Use this command to map drive letters to network directories. When you put a MAP command in a login script, a drive letter will be mapped to the specified network directory every time the user logs in.

To map a drive letter to a directory in a login script, type the MAP command using the following format:

```
MAP letter:=path
```

For example, to map drive L to SYS:APPS\WP, the command would be as follows:

```
MAP L:=SYS:APPS\WP
```

You can also use MAP to map search drives. Search drives are special types of drive mappings that act like DOS path commands. Search drives are used to indicate directories that contain applications or utilities. A search drive lets users execute an application without having to know where the application is located. The network searches through all of the available search drives for the application so the user doesn't have to search for it.

To map a search drive, you don't designate a specific drive letter. Instead, you use the letter S, followed by a number. Novell's intraNetWare will assign search drives their own letters in reverse order, starting with the letter Z. (You can have up to 16 search drives mapped, so those drives would be letters Z through K.) For example, if you already have one search drive mapped, and you want to map the second search drive to the SYS:MSWORD directory, enter the following line in the login script:

```
MAP S2:=SYS:MSWORD
```

TIP

Search drive mappings are added to the workstation's DOS PATH environment variable. This means that if you specify that a search drive is S1, that search drive mapping will overwrite the first DOS path that had already been set. To avoid overwriting a path setting, use the INS option (which stands for "insert"). For example, you can type:

```
MAP INS S1:=SYS:PUBLIC
```

instead of:

```
MAP S1:=SYS:PUBLIC
```

By using the INS option, the search drive mapping for the SYS:PUBLIC directory will be inserted at the beginning of the DOS path settings. This moves the original first path setting to the second position.

In login scripts, the first search drive should be mapped to the PUBLIC directory. This directory contains the intraNetWare utilities and other files that users need.

To map the first search drive to the PUBLIC directory (which is in the SYS volume), use the following command:

```
MAP INS S1:=SYS:PUBLIC
```

Because intraNetWare assigns drive letters for search drives starting at the end of the alphabet, this command will assign the drive letter Z to the SYS:PUBLIC directory. If you go to the Z drive, you'll see the PUBLIC files listed.

TIP

Instead of mapping search drives in order (S3, S4, S5, and so on), you can use MAP S16 for all subsequent mappings that don't require an exact position or a specific drive letter. Each MAP S16 command will insert its drive mapping at the end of the list, pushing up the previous mappings.

This just makes the list of search drives more flexible. For example, if you delete one, the others will reorder themselves automatically. Also, you don't run the risk of overwriting a search drive that may have been specified in another login script.

There are several variations of the MAP command you can use to accomplish different tasks, as shown in Table 5.1.

T A B L E 5 . I	MAP Command Options
TASK	**DESCRIPTION**
Map drives in order, without specifying drive letters	If you don't want to specify exact drive letters, you can map each available drive, in order. This is useful if you don't know what drive letters have already been mapped in a system or profile login script. To assign drive letters this way, use an asterisk, followed by a number. For example, to get the first and second available drives, you could use the following commands: MAP *1:=VOL1:APPS\WP MAP *2:=VOL1:DATA\REPORTS

(continued)

T A B L E 5 . 1	*MAP Command Options (continued)*
TASK	DESCRIPTION
Map the next available drive	To map the next available drive, use the letter N (without a colon), as in the following command: `MAP N=VOL1:APPS\WP`
Delete a drive mapping	To delete a mapping for drive G, for example, use the following command: `MAP DEL G`
Turn off MAP's display	Whenever a MAP command is executed in the login script, it will display the new drive mapping on the workstation screen unless you specify otherwise. To turn off this display, use the following command: `MAP DISPLAY OFF`
Turn on MAP's display	At the end of the login script, you may want to turn MAP's display back on and show a listing of all the completed drive mappings. To do this, put the following commands at, or near, the end of the login script: `MAP DISPLAY ON` `MAP`
Map a fake root	Some applications must be installed at the root of a volume or hard disk. If you would rather install the application in a subdirectory, you can do that, and then map a fake root to the application's subdirectory. A *fake root* mapping makes a subdirectory appear to be a volume, so that the application runs correctly. (See Chapter 7 for more information about fake roots.) You can map a fake root in a regular drive mapping or in a search drive mapping. To map drive H as a fake root to the VOL1:APPS\CAD subdirectory, use the following command: `MAP ROOT H:=VOL1:APPS\CAD`

TASK	DESCRIPTION
Map a drive to a Directory Map object	You can create an NDS object, called a Directory Map object, that points to a particular directory. Then you can map drives to that object instead of to the actual directory path. This way, if you later move the directory to another part of the file system, you can just change the Directory Map object's description instead of updating all the affected login scripts. Preferably, use Directory Map objects in the user's current context. If the Directory Map object is in another part of the NDS tree, create an Alias object for the Directory Map object in the user's current context. To map a search drive to a Directory Map object named Database, use the following command:

MAP S16:=DATABASE |

Beyond the Basics

This chapter explained how to create users and groups, how to log in and out of the network, and how to use the NetWare Application Launcher.

The following topics, mentioned in this chapter, will be explained more fully in other chapters in this book:

▸ To install NetWare Administrator on your workstation, see Chapter 4.

▸ For more information about NDS objects and name contexts, see Chapter 4.

▸ For information about NDS security, file system security, see Chapter 6.

▸ To set up passwords and account restrictions, see Chapter 6.

▸ To give users access to network printing, see Chapter 8.

For more information on the following topics, refer to Novell's online documentation or *Novell's IntranetWare Administrator's Handbook* (from Novell Press):

▸ Using login scripts and their commands

▸ Using the NET.CFG file

Managing Network Security

Instant Access

Login Security

▸ Each user on the network must have a valid user account (NDS User object), and should have a valid password.

▸ To set or change passwords, use the NetWare Administrator utility, the Login program, or the SETPASS utility.

▸ To change account restrictions, which limit how and when a user can log in, use the NetWare Administrator utility.

▸ To turn on intruder detection, which locks an account after repeated, failed login attempts, use the NetWare Administrator utility.

NDS Security

▸ NDS trustee rights control what an object can do to other objects, such as read object information, change object information, delete objects, and so on.

▸ To view or change NDS trustee rights, use the NetWare Administrator utility.

File System Security

▸ File system trustee rights are assigned to users, and control what those users can do to specific files and directories, such as opening, changing, or deleting them.

▸ To view or change file system trustee rights, use the NetWare Administrator utility.

▸ File and directory attributes are assigned to files or directories, and control what users or applications can do with those files or directories.

▸ To view or change file and directory attributes, use the NetWare Administrator utility.

How Does intraNetWare Manage Security?

One of the aspects of NetWare that sets it apart from other network operating systems is its high level of security. How you implement this security is up to you. You can make your intraNetWare network as open as you need, or as secure as Fort Knox.

Some people may not think they need to worry about network security. It's easy to think that only banks and government agencies need to worry about network security. However, network security doesn't just mean preventing spies and hackers from breaking into your network. For example, network security can:

- Prevent employees from seeing each other's personnel or salary files
- Keep employees from accidentally erasing each other's files
- Keep viruses from spreading
- Let other users see some of your personal files, without letting them see the files you'd rather they didn't
- Prevent users from changing other users' security levels
- Protect applications from being inadvertently deleted or copied over
- Allow certain users to manage printers and print queues, while preventing other users from messing with them at all
- Allow users to read public documents without letting them modify or erase them
- Let key people have rights to manage certain groups of users, portions of the Directory tree, or all the files on a volume or in a directory, so that you can distribute the workload of network management.

These are only a few of the ways network security can protect and simplify your network. If you think about your network situation for a while, you may come up with additional ways that network security can benefit you and your users.

Novell's intraNetWare uses three basic security features to allow you to control your network's security:

- Login security, which ensures that only authorized users can log in to the network
- NDS security, which controls whether NDS objects (such as users) can see or manipulate other NDS objects and their properties

▶ File system security, which controls whether users can see and work with files and directories

Each of these types of security is described later in this chapter.

Login Security

Login security is intraNetWare's first line of defense, ensuring that only authorized users can get into the network.

The three main aspects of login security are:

▶ Ensuring that all users have valid user accounts and valid passwords (required)

▶ Using account restrictions (optional) to limit the times that users can log in, the workstations they can use, and such things as the length of their passwords and how frequently they must change their passwords

▶ Using intruder-detection features (optional) to recognize when someone may be trying to break into the network by guessing passwords.

USER ACCOUNTS AND PASSWORDS

Everyone who accesses the network should have his or her own user account. While it may seem convenient to have several people use a single user account, or to allow someone else to log in using your account, this can be a potential security problem. For example, you may not want all those users to have rights to access all of the same files. If they are all using the same account, you cannot control their individual access, you cannot control the password they are using, and you may end up with unexpected conflicts.

It's a much better plan to give users their own, individual user accounts. Then, once users have their own accounts, they each have their own passwords as well.

If passwords are to be a useful form of security, you should ensure that they are being used, that users are changing them frequently, and that users aren't choosing passwords that can be guessed easily.

You can set these types of password restrictions by using the NetWare Administrator utility. (For instructions on setting up the NetWare Administrator utility on a workstation, see Chapter 4.) To set password restrictions for a user, open the NetWare Administrator's Browser and select the User object. Then, from the Object menu, choose Details, select the Password Restrictions page, and enter the restrictions you want to apply to the user. Figure 6.1 shows the Password Restrictions page for a User object.

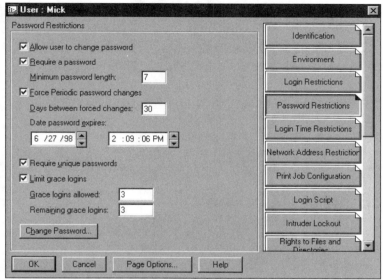

F I G U R E   6 . 1   *A User Object's Password Restrictions Page in NetWare Administrator*

TIP

The following tips can help preserve password security (and you can enforce most of them by using password restrictions):

► Require passwords to be at least five characters long (seven or eight are better). The default minimum is five characters.

► Require that passwords be changed every 30 days or less.

► Require unique passwords so that users can't reuse a password they've used before.

► Do not allow unlimited grace logins. Limit the number of grace logins to three. (A grace login allows you to log in using an expired password.)

> ► Remind users not to tell others about their passwords or allow others to use their accounts.

> ► Tell users to avoid choosing passwords that can be guessed easily, such as birthdays, favorite hobbies or sports, family member names, pet names, and so on. Instead, tell users to mix words and numbers together to form words that can't be found in a dictionary, such as BRAVO42 or ST66CL.

Users can change their own passwords in any of the following ways:

► Type the command **SETPASS** at the DOS prompt, and enter the new password when prompted for it.

► Open the Password Restrictions page in the NetWare Administrator utility, and specify a new password there.

► Specify a new password while logging in. If the password has expired, the Login utility will tell the user, and allow him or her to type in a new password right then.

ACCOUNT RESTRICTIONS

With user account restrictions, you can limit how a user can log in to the network.

Password restrictions, as explained in the previous section, are one form of account restriction. You can also implement the following three additional types of account restrictions:

► Login Restrictions specify whether the account has an expiration date (which might be useful in situations such as schools, where the authorized users will change with each semester), and whether the user can be logged in from multiple workstations simultaneously.

► Login Time Restrictions dictate the times of day that users must be logged out of the network. (By default, users can be logged in at any time — there are no restrictions.)

► Network Address Restrictions specify which network addresses (workstations) a user can use to log in. (By default, there are no restrictions on addresses.)

To set any of these account restrictions, you use the NetWare Administrator utility. (For instructions on setting up the NetWare Administrator utility on a workstation, see Chapter 4.)

To set account restrictions for a user, use the NetWare Administrator utility and select the User object. Then, choose Details from the Object menu. You'll see an Information page for each type of account restriction listed along the right side of the Details screen. Open the Information page for the type of restriction you want to set, and specify the limits you want.

As an example, Figure 6.2 shows the Login Time Restrictions page for a user named Mick. By default, users are not restricted from logging in at any time. However, in Mick's case, the network administrator has restricted Mick's account so that he cannot log in at all on Saturdays or Sundays. (Gray cells in the grid indicate times that the user cannot be logged in. To change a cell from gray to blank, simply click the cell.)

FIGURE 6.2 *A User Object's Login Time Restrictions Page in NetWare Administrator*

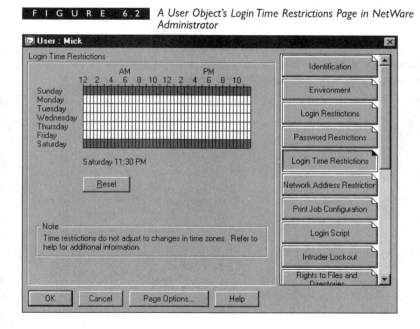

INTRUDER DETECTION

Enforcing account restrictions and passwords can keep unauthorized users from breaking into the network. However, we've all seen movies where the bad guys (and sometimes the good guys) hack into a computer by repeatedly guessing at passwords. Novell's intraNetWare provides a feature that can keep such hackers from trying over and over again until they guess correctly. This feature is called *intruder detection*.

With intraNetWare, you can set the network so that users are locked out after a given number of failed login attempts. This helps ensure that users don't try to break into the network by simply guessing another user's password, or by using programs that automatically generate passwords.

To set up intruder detection, you use the NetWare Administrator utility and assign intruder detection for a container. Then, any user account within that container is subject to being locked if a set number of login attempts fail.

To enable intruder detection, complete the following steps:

1. From the NetWare Administrator's Browser, select the container for which you want to set up intruder detection, and then choose Details from the Object menu.

2. Open the Intruder Detection page shown in Figure 6.3.

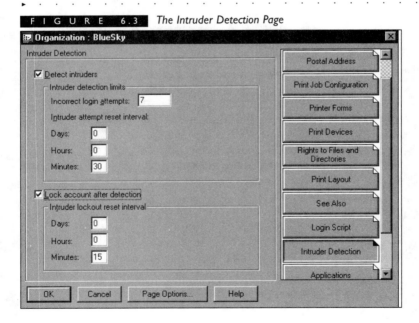

FIGURE 6.3 *The Intruder Detection Page*

3. To detect intruders, mark the Detect Intruders check box. Then, specify the intruder detection limits. The Incorrect Login Attempts and Intruder Attempt Reset Interval allow you to specify how many incorrect login attempts will be allowed in a given time. If you mark the Detect Intruders check box, the default values that appear allow seven incorrect attempts within a 30-minute interval. You may want to reduce the number of attempts to four or five, depending on how likely your network is to have such an intruder.

4. If you want the user's account to be locked after an intruder is detected, mark the Lock Account After Detection check box. Then, specify how long you want the account to remain locked. The default locks the account for 15 minutes after the given number of failed login attempts. After 15 minutes, the account will be reopened automatically (intruder detection for that account will be reset). You may want to increase this time if you are concerned about intruders.

To see if a user's account has been locked, use the NetWare Administrator and select the user in question. Choose Details from the Object menu, and then open the user's Intruder Lockout page. This page shows whether the account is locked, as shown in Figure 6.4. If the Account Locked check box is marked, the account is locked. To unlock it, click the check box to clear it.

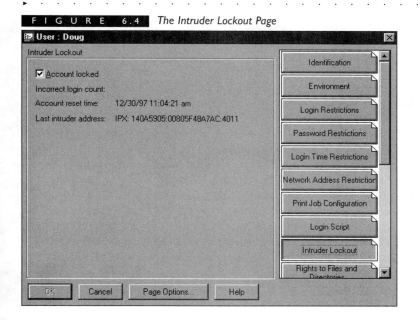

FIGURE   6.4   *The Intruder Lockout Page*

This page also shows when the user's account was locked. In addition, it shows the address of the workstation from which the failed login attempts were tried.

NDS Security

Once you've created your NDS Directory tree, you've probably invested a fair amount of time ensuring that the objects you've created contain all the right information in their properties. Now you can decide who gets to see that information and who can change it.

To make the information about the objects in your tree secure, you can use NDS trustee rights to control how objects in the tree can work with other objects and their properties. *NDS trustee rights* are permissions that allow users or objects to perform tasks such as viewing other objects, changing their properties, deleting them, and so on.

When you assign a user enough NDS trustee rights to work with another object, you've made that user a *trustee* of the object. Each object contains a property called the *Access Control List* (ACL), which is a list of all the trustees of this particular object.

When the network is first installed, the user Admin has all NDS trustee rights to all objects in the tree. This means that when you log in as user Admin, Admin's NDS trustee rights let you create and delete other objects, see them, read and modify all their properties, and so on. Admin is the only user who has full NDS rights to everything in the network immediately after installation.

By default, when all others users are created, they are granted only a subset of NDS rights, so they have limited abilities to work with other NDS objects. However, while logged in as Admin, you can add to or remove these NDS rights to customize your users' abilities. You can even grant other users the same NDS rights as the Admin user, so that they can have the same control over all other objects.

For security reasons, you should be frugal with NDS rights. NDS rights are a tool to protect your network objects from both accidental and intentional tampering. You may want to assign two users full NDS rights to the network, such as Admin and another user account that only you can use. This way, there is a backup account you can use if, for example, you forget the Admin's password or delete the Admin user.

NDS RIGHTS

There are two types of NDS trustee rights. *Object rights* control how the user works with the object (see Table 6.1). *Property rights* control whether the user can see and work with an object's properties (Table 6.2). (As explained in Chapter 4, an NDS object's properties are the defined characteristics of the object. For example, a User object's properties might include the user's full name, telephone number, trustee rights to other objects, login script, and title.)

| TABLE 6.1 | NDS Object Rights |

NDS OBJECT RIGHT	DESCRIPTION
Supervisor	Grants the trustee all NDS rights to the object and all of its properties. If a trustee has the Supervisor right, the trustee can create, change, or delete any aspect of the object. The Supervisor right can be blocked by the Inherited Rights Filter (explained in the next section).
Browse	Allows the trustee to see the object in the NDS tree. If you don't have this right to an object, that object won't appear in the NetWare Administrator's Browser screen when you look at it.
Create	Allows the trustee to create a new object in this container. (This right only appears if you're looking at the trustee assignments for a container object.)
Delete	Allows the trustee to delete an object.
Rename	Allows the trustee to change the object's name.

TABLE 6.2	NDS Property Rights
NDS PROPERTY RIGHT	**DESCRIPTION**
Supervisor	Grants the trustee all NDS rights to the property. It can be blocked by the Inherited Rights Filter (explained in the following section).
Compare	Allows the trustee to compare the value of this property to a value the user specifies in a search. (For example, with the Compare right to the Department property, a user can search the tree for any object that has Marketing listed in its Department property.)
Read	Allows the trustee to see the value of this property. (The Read right automatically grants the Compare right, as well.)
Write	Allows the trustee to add, modify, or delete the value of this property. (The Write right automatically grants the Add or Delete Self right, as well.)
Add or Delete Self	Allows trustees to add or remove themselves as a value of this property. This right only applies to properties that list User objects as values, such as group membership lists or the Access Control List. (While this right is officially called the Add or Delete Self right, it usually appears on the screen as simply the "Add Self" right.)

To change object or property rights, refer to "Seeing and Changing an Object's NDS Rights" section later in this chapter.

INHERITING NDS RIGHTS

NDS object and property rights can be inherited. This means that if you have NDS rights to a parent container, you can inherit those rights and exercise them in an object within that container, too. Inheritance keeps you from having to grant users NDS rights at every level of the Directory tree.

However, it is sometimes desirable to block inheritance. For example, you may want to allow a user to delete objects in a parent container, but not let that user delete any objects in a particular subcontainer. Inheritance can be blocked in two ways:

► By granting a new set of NDS rights to an object within the container. Any new assignment will cause the inherited NDS rights from a parent container to be ignored. You can grant a new set of rights using the NetWare Administrator utility, as explained later in this chapter.

- By removing the right from an object's Inherited Rights Filter (IRF). Every object has a property called an *Inherited Rights Filter*, which specifies which NDS rights can be inherited from a parent container. By default, an object's IRF allows all NDS rights to be inherited. You can change the IRF, however, to revoke one or more NDS rights. Any rights that are revoked from the IRF cannot be inherited.

You can only inherit an NDS right if you've been assigned that right at a higher level. If you don't have the Supervisor right in the parent container, for example, you can't inherit it and use it in another object even though that right is allowed in the IRF. The IRF doesn't grant NDS rights; it just allows you to inherit them if they've already been assigned to you.

Figure 6.5 shows the NDS rights that Angela can inherit. In the container called Space, Angela has four trustee rights: Browse, Create, Delete, and Rename. Ordinarily, she would inherit all four of those rights in the subcontainer called Rockets. However, the administrator has changed Rocket's IRF, and removed the Rename right. That means Angela cannot inherit that right, even though she has it at a higher level in the tree. Therefore, in the Rockets container, Angela only inherited three rights: Browse, Create, and Delete.

One of Angela's Inherited Rights Is Blocked by the IRF.

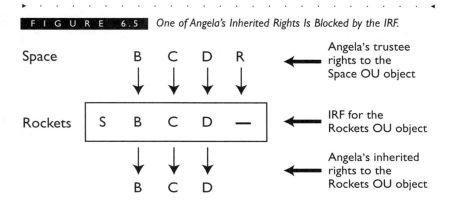

The NetWare Administrator utility prevents a user from cutting off all supervisor access to a branch of the NDS tree by searching for an object with supervisor rights to the given container. If an object with supervisor rights isn't found, NetWare Administrator warns you and prevents you from blocking rights.

NDS SECURITY EQUIVALENCE

Sometimes, you may decide you want to give one object exactly the same NDS trustee rights as another object. You can do this easily by assigning the first object a *security equivalence* to the second object.

You assign a security equivalence by using the Security Equal To property. With security equivalence, you can make user Jason have the same NDS rights to the same NDS objects as user Erica, for example. (In fact, a security equivalence will give Jason the same file system rights as Erica, too. File system rights are explained later in this chapter.)

When you add a user to a Group object's membership list or to an Organizational Role object's list, the user really becomes security equivalent to that Group or Organizational Role object. Then, when you grant a right to the Group object, for example, all of the users who belong to the Group get that same right because of their security equivalences.

When you are given security equivalence to another user, you only receive the same NDS rights (and file system rights) that the other user was explicitly granted. You do not get equivalences to that other user's equivalences. In other words, security equivalence doesn't travel. If Jason is equivalent to Erica, and Erica is equivalent to Mick, Jason doesn't end up being equivalent to Mick, too. Jason only receives whatever rights Erica received explicitly.

EFFECTIVE NDS RIGHTS

Because a user can be given NDS rights to an object and its properties through a variety of methods (explicit assignment, security equivalence, and inheritance), it can be confusing to determine exactly what NDS rights the user can really use. A user's *effective NDS rights* are the combination of NDS rights that the user can ultimately exercise. The user's effective rights to an object are determined in one of the following two ways:

▶ The user's inherited NDS rights from a parent container, minus any rights blocked by the object's IRF.

▶ The sum of all NDS rights granted to the user for that object through direct trustee assignments and security equivalences to other objects. The IRF does not affect direct trustee assignments and security equivalences.

For example, suppose user Joanna has been given the Browse right to a container object. Joanna has also been given a security equivalence to user Mick, who has Create, Delete, and Rename rights to the same container. This means Joanna's effective NDS rights to this container are now Browse, Create, Delete, and Rename, as illustrated in Figure 6.6.

FIGURE 6.6 *Joanna's Effective NDS Rights Are Her Explicit Trustee Assignment Plus Her Security Equivalence.*

Mick's assignment	=	C D R

Joanna's assignment   =   B
                              + C D R (security equivalence to Mick)

Joanna's effective rights	=	B C D R

Even if the container's IRF blocks the Delete right, Joanna still has that right. This is because the IRF only affects inherited rights, and inherited rights are completely ignored if the user has explicit trustee assignments to an object or a security equivalence that gives her NDS rights to that object.

SEEING AND CHANGING AN OBJECT'S NDS RIGHTS

To work with the trustees of an object, and to see or change NDS trustee rights, use the NetWare Administrator utility, which runs in Windows 3.1 or Windows 95. (To set up NetWare Administrator on your workstation, see Chapter 4.)

Seeing an Object's Trustees, and Modifying the Trustees' Rights

From the NetWare Administrator's Browser, select the object whose list of trustees you want to see, and then choose Trustees of This Object from the Object menu. (You can also click the right mouse button to bring up a menu that contains some of the more frequently used tasks, and select Trustees of This Object from that menu.)

Figure 6.7 shows the Trustees of This Object screen for a printer named P1. Notice that the Admin user, the Print Server, and the Root object are all listed as trustees of this printer.

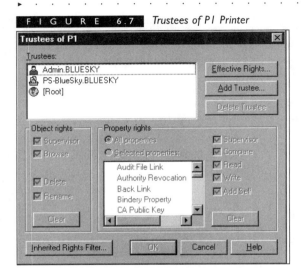

F I G U R E   6 . 7   *Trustees of P1 Printer*

You can add or delete trustees by clicking the Add Trustee or Delete Trustee buttons and selecting the trustees you want.

If you click each trustee in the list, you can see the specific NDS object and property rights belonging to that trustee. (You can also see a trustee's effective rights by clicking the Effective Rights button.) Figure 6.8 shows the rights that the print server has to this printer.

To add or delete NDS rights from a trustee, mark or unmark the check boxes next to each right you want to change. If the box is marked, that right is assigned to the trustee.

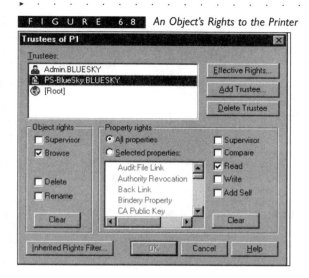

FIGURE 6.8 *An Object's Rights to the Printer*

Seeing and Changing the Inherited Rights Filter

From the NetWare Administrator's Browser, select the object whose IRF you want to see, and then choose Trustees of This Object from the Object menu. (You can also click the right mouse button and choose the same option from that menu.)

On the Trustees of This Object screen, click the Inherited Rights Filter button to bring up the IRF information, as shown in Figure 6.9.

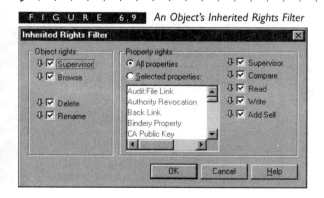

FIGURE 6.9 *An Object's Inherited Rights Filter*

By default, any object or property rights can be inherited from the parent object. If you want to block an NDS right from being inherited, unmark the check box located beside that particular right. (Click a check box to mark or unmark it.)

Assigning Property Rights to an Object

To grant a user property rights to an NDS object's properties, select the NDS object, and then choose Trustees of This Object from the Object menu. (You can also click the right mouse button and choose the same option from that menu.)

On the Trustees of This Object screen, click the trustee to which you want to grant property rights. Once you've clicked the trustee you want, you can choose one of two ways to assign property rights:

▶ You can click the All Properties button, which is a quick way to give the user the same property rights to all the properties of that object. If you select All Properties, those property rights can be inherited.

▶ You can click Selected Properties and give the user different property rights to each individual property. Property rights assigned only to specific properties cannot be inherited.

Figure 6.10 shows the property rights that user Jason has been assigned for a print server object. His property rights apply for all of the print server's properties.

Seeing the List of NDS Objects to Which an Object Has Rights

To see all the objects to which a particular object has NDS rights, select the object. Then, from the Object menu, choose Rights to Other Objects (or click the right mouse button and select the same option from the menu that appears).

Specify the name context (location in the NDS tree) where you want to search for objects to which your selected object has rights. Then, the Rights to Other Objects screen appears. Figure 6.11 shows the Rights to Other Objects screen for the Admin user. The list of objects that Admin has rights to in this example includes print servers, print queues, other users, and so on.

FIGURE 6.10 A User's Property Rights

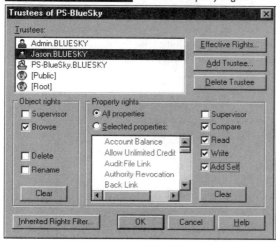

FIGURE 6.11 Rights to Other Objects Screen for Admin User

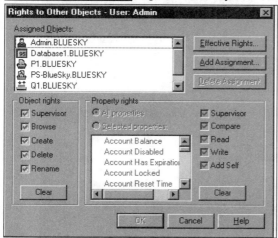

To change the rights this object has to another object, first click the name of the second object in the list. Then, to grant a right, click the check box beside the right to mark it. To remove a right, click the check box again to unmark it. (A marked checkbox indicates that the right is granted. A blank checkbox means the object cannot exercise that right.)

You can also give this object new trustee assignments to additional objects, by clicking the Add Assignment button. Likewise, you can delete trustee assignments by choosing Delete Assignment.

Seeing and Changing Security Equivalences

To see or change a user's security equivalence, select the user, and then choose Details from the Object menu (or right-click the user and select Details). Then open the Security Equal To page.

From this page, you can add or delete other objects to which this user has a security equivalence. See Figure 6.12 for an example of the Security Equal To page for a user named Lin. You can add or delete security equivalences by clicking the Add or Delete buttons.

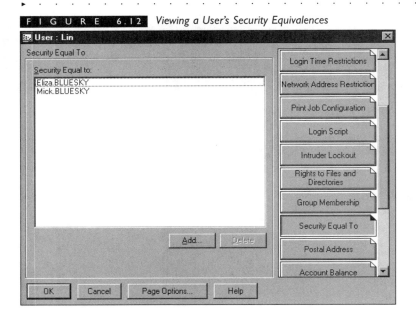

F I G U R E   6.12   *Viewing a User's Security Equivalences*

File System Security

File system security ensures that users can only access and use the files and directories you want them to see and use. The two different types of security tools that you can implement in the file system, either together or separately, to protect your files are:

- ▸ File system trustee rights, which you assign to users and groups. Just as NDS object rights and NDS property rights control what users can do with other objects, file system trustee rights control what each user or group can do with the file or directory.

- ▸ Attributes, which you can assign directly to files and directories. Unlike file system rights, which are specific to different users and groups, attributes belong to the file or directory, and they control the activities of all users, regardless of those users' file trustee rights.

The next few sections explain file system trustee rights. File and directory attributes are explained later in this chapter, in the "File and Directory Attributes" section.

File System Trustee Rights

File system trustee rights allow users and groups to work with files and directories (folders) in specific ways. Each right determines whether a user can do things such as see, read, change, rename, or delete the file or directory.

When a user is given a file system right for a particular file, the right affects the user's allowable actions in that file only. When a user is given a file system right for a directory, the right affects the user's allowable actions on that particular directory, as well as on all the files within that directory.

As with NDS rights, when a user is given rights to a file or directory, the user is called a *trustee* of that file or directory.

NOTE

Although file system rights are similar in nature to the NDS rights for objects and properties (described earlier in this chapter), they are not the same. File system rights are separate from NDS rights. They affect only how users work with files and directories. NDS rights affect how users work with other NDS objects.

The only place where NDS rights and file system rights overlap is at the NetWare Server object. If a user is granted the Supervisor object right to a Server object, that user is also granted the Supervisor file system right to any volumes attached to that server. Because user Admin has full NDS rights to all objects in the tree after the installation (although you can limit Admin's rights later), user Admin has the Supervisor file system right to the entire file system, too.

There are eight different file system trustee rights. You can assign any combination of those file system rights to a user or group, depending on how you want that user, or group, to work with files and directories.

Table 6.3 lists the available file system rights. Because a trustee right may act a little differently when assigned for a file than when it is assigned for a directory, Table 6.3 also explains the difference.

TABLE 6.3 *File System Trustee Rights*

FILE SYSTEM RIGHT	ABBREVIATION	DESCRIPTION
Read	R	*Directory:* Enables the trustee to open and read files in the directory. *File:* Enables the trustee to open and read the file.
Write	W	*Directory:* Enables the trustee to open and write to (change) files in the directory. *File:* Enables the trustee to open and write to the file.
Create	C	*Directory:* Enables the trustee to create subdirectories and files in the directory. *File:* Enables the trustee to salvage the file if it was deleted.

FILE SYSTEM RIGHT	ABBREVIATION	DESCRIPTION
Erase	E	*Directory:* Enables the trustee to delete the directory and its files and subdirectories. *File:* Enables the trustee to delete the file.
Modify	M	*Directory:* Enables the trustee to change the name, directory attributes, and file attributes of the directory and its files and subdirectories. *File:* Enables the trustee to change the file's name or file attributes.
File Scan	F	*Directory:* Enables the trustee to see the names of the files and subdirectories within the directory. File: Enables the trustee to see the name of the file.
Access Control	A	*Directory:* Enables the trustee to change the directory's IRF and trustee assignments. *File:* Enables the trustee to change the file's IRF and trustee assignments.
Supervisor	S	*Directory:* Grants the trustee all rights to the directory, its files, and its subdirectories. It cannot be blocked by an IRF. *File:* Grants the trustee all rights to the file. It cannot be blocked by an IRF.

INHERITING FILE SYSTEM RIGHTS

Just like NDS rights, file system rights can be inherited. This means that if you have file system rights to a parent directory, you can inherit those rights and exercise them in any file and subdirectory within that directory, too.

Inheritance is a handy feature that keeps you from having to grant users new file system rights at every level of the file system. There are two ways to block inheritance:

► You can grant the user a new set of file system rights to a subdirectory or file within the parent directory. Any new assignment will cause the inherited rights from a parent directory to be ignored.

► You can remove the right from a file's or a subdirectory's Inherited Rights Filter (IRF).

Every directory and file has an Inherited Rights Filter that specifies which file system rights can be inherited from a parent directory. By default, a file's or directory's IRF allows all rights to be inherited. You can change the IRF, however, to revoke one or more rights. Any file system rights that are revoked from the IRF cannot be inherited.

You can only inherit a file system right if you've been assigned that right at a higher level. If you don't have the Create right in the parent directory, for example, you can't inherit it and use it in another subdirectory — even though that right is allowed in the IRF. The IRF doesn't grant rights; it just allows you to inherit file system rights if they've already been assigned to you at a higher level.

For instructions on assigning file system rights or changing the IRF, see the "Seeing and Changing a User's File System Rights" section later in this chapter.

FILE SYSTEM SECURITY EQUIVALENCE

Security equivalence for file system rights works the same way as security equivalence for NDS rights (explained earlier in this chapter). You can assign one user the same NDS rights and file system rights as another user by using the Security Equal To property. With security equivalence, you can make user Lin have the same rights to the same NDS objects, files, and directories as user Erica.

When you add a user to a Group object's membership list, or to an Organizational Role object's list, the user then becomes security equivalent to that Group or Organizational Role object. Then, when you grant a right to the Group object, for example, all of the users who belong to the Group get that same right because of their security equivalences.

NOTE

Remember, when you are given security equivalence to another user, you only receive the same rights that the other user was explicitly granted. You do not get equivalences to that user's other equivalences.

For example, assume Don has explicit rights to folder A, and a security equivalence to Janet that gives him rights to folder B. If another user, Anthony, is security equivalent to Don, Anthony will automatically get Don's rights to A. However, Anthony won't get rights to folder B, because Don's security equivalence to Janet cannot be transferred to Anthony.

EFFECTIVE FILE SYSTEM RIGHTS

Just as with NDS rights, determining which file system rights a user can actually exercise in a file or directory can be confusing at first. A user's effective file system rights are the file system rights that the user can ultimately execute in a given directory or file. The user's effective rights to a directory or file are determined in one of two ways:

- The user's inherited rights from a parent directory, minus any rights blocked by the subdirectory's (or file's) IRF.

- The sum of all rights granted to the user for that directory or file, through both direct trustee assignment and security equivalences to other users.

A file's or directory's IRF does not affect direct trustee assignments and security equivalences. Therefore, if you have been given an explicit trustee assignment in a file or directory, any rights you might have inherited from a parent directory will be completely ignored.

On the other hand, if you have not been given an explicit trustee assignment or security equivalence that specifically gives you rights in a file or directory, then you can use inherited rights in that file or directory. You will automatically inherit any rights you had in a parent directory, minus any rights blocked by the current file's or directory's IRF.

SEEING AND CHANGING A USER'S
FILE SYSTEM RIGHTS

To see a user's file system rights, use the NetWare Administrator utility (which runs in Windows 3.1 and Windows 95). To use the NetWare Administrator utility, you can either select a user and see the user's trustee assignments (a list of the files and directories of which that user is a trustee), or you can select a file or directory and see a list of all its trustees.

Seeing and Changing a User's Trustee Assignments

To see or change a user's trustee assignments, complete the following steps:

1. From the NetWare Administrator's Browser, select the user and choose Details from the Object menu.

2. Open the Rights to Files and Directories page.

3. To see the user's current file system rights, you must first select a volume that contains directories to which the user has rights. To do this, click the Show button. Then, in the Browse Context panel on the right side, navigate through the Directory tree to locate the desired volume, as shown in Figure 6.13. Select the volume from the Available Objects panel on the left side, and then click OK.

4. Now, under the Files and Directories panel, a list appears showing all of the files and directories of which the user is currently a trustee (see Figure 6.14).

F I G U R E   6.13   *Selecting a Volume*

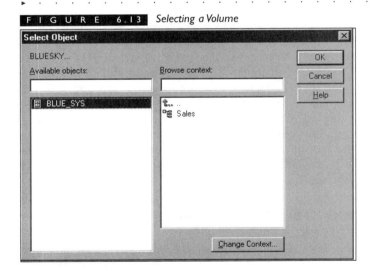

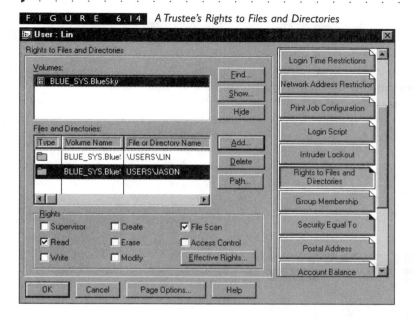

FIGURE 6.14 *A Trustee's Rights to Files and Directories*

5. To see the user's assigned file system rights to one of these directories or files, select the directory or file, and then look at the list of rights below. A mark in the check box next to each right means that the user has rights to the given file or directory. To change the user's rights, click each desired check box to either mark it or clear it.

6. To see the user's effective file system rights to this file or directory, click the Effective Rights button.

7. To assign the user file system rights to a new file or directory, click the Add button. In the Directory Context panel on the right side, navigate through the Directory tree to locate the desired volume or directory. Then, select the volume, directory, or file from the left panel, and click OK. Now the newly selected file, directory, or volume appears under the Files and Directories panel. Make sure the new file, directory, or volume is selected, and then assign the appropriate file system rights by marking each desired check box.

8. To see or change a user's security equivalence, open the user's Security Equal To page. There, you can add or delete other objects to which this user has a security equivalence. Remember that security equivalence affects both NDS and file system rights.

Seeing and Changing a Directory's List of Trustees

To use the NetWare Administrator utility to see all the trustees of a directory (or a file or volume), complete the following steps:

1. From the NetWare Administrator's Browser, select the directory and choose Details from the Object menu.

2. Open the Trustees of this Directory page. This page shows the containers and users that have trustee rights to this directory (see Figure 6.15). This page also shows the directory's IRF. By default, the IRF allows any file system rights to be inherited from the parent directory.

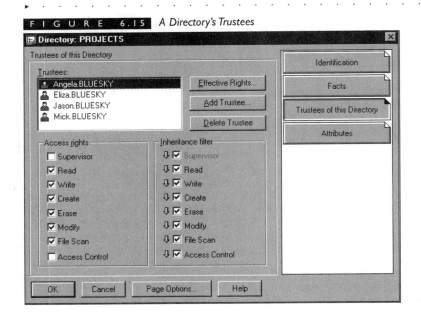

FIGURE   6.15   *A Directory's Trustees*

3. To change the IRF to block a file system right from being inherited, click the check box next to that right to clear its box.

4. To see a particular trustee's effective file system rights to the directory, click the Effective Rights button, and then select the trustee. (You can either type in the trustee's name or click the Browse button next to the Trustee field to navigate the NDS tree and select the trustee that way.) That trustee's effective rights will appear in boldface type.

5. To add a trustee to the directory, click the Add Trustee button. Navigate through the Directory tree in the right panel, and then select the user you want from the Objects panel on the left side. That user now appears in the Trustees list. Select that user, and then mark the check boxes next to the file system rights you want the user to have.

File and Directory Attributes

Another important NetWare security tool for securing files and directories is attributes. *Attributes* are properties of files and directories that control what can happen to those files or directories. Attributes, which are also called *flags,* are different from trustee rights in several ways, including:

▶ Attributes are assigned directly to files and directories, while rights are assigned to users.

▶ Attributes override rights. In other words, if a directory has the Delete Inhibit attribute, you can't delete the directory even if you've been granted the Erase right.

▶ Attributes don't grant rights. Just because a file has the Read-Write attribute doesn't mean you can write to it if you don't have the Write right.

▶ Attributes affect all users, including the Admin user.

▶ Attributes affect some aspects of the file that rights do not, such as determining whether or not the files in a directory can be purged immediately upon deletion. (Purging is explained in Chapter 7.)

File and directory attributes are a very powerful security feature of intraNetWare. They are explained here in this chapter so you can understand them should the need arise. However, you will probably find that you seldom need to change or even be aware of attributes.

In some cases, applications will automatically set attributes needed to protect their executable files from being erased accidentally. This is often the only time you may encounter these attributes.

> Some available attributes are used by the more advanced features of intraNetWare that aren't explained in this book, such as file compression, file migration, or block suballocation (advanced features used for maximizing the usage of disk space on a server). Should you decide to implement these advanced features in the future, you will need to use some of these attributes. See the Novell online documentation for more information about these features.

TYPES OF FILE AND DIRECTORY ATTRIBUTES

There are eight attributes that apply to both files and directories. An additional eight apply only to files. All of the attributes are listed in Table 6.4. The table also shows the abbreviations used for each attribute, and whether the attribute applies to both directories and files or only to files.

T A B L E 6.4 File and Directory Attributes

ATTRIBUTE	ABBREVIATION	FILE	DIRECTORY	DESCRIPTION
Delete Inhibit	Di	X	X	Prevents users from deleting the file or directory.
Hidden	H	X	X	Hides the file or directory so it isn't listed by the DOS DIR command or in the Windows File Manager, and can't be copied or deleted.
Purge Immediate	P	X	X	Purges the file or directory immediately upon deletion. Purged files can't be salvaged. (Purging is explained in Chapter 7.)
Rename Inhibit	Ri	X	X	Prevents users from renaming the file or directory.
System	Sy	X	X	Indicates a system directory that may contain system files (such as DOS files). Prevents users from seeing, copying, or deleting the directory (however, does not assign the System attribute to the files in the directory).
Don't Migrate	Dm	X	X	Prevents a file or directory from being migrated to another storage device. (See the Novell documentation for information about file migration.)
Immediate Compress	Ic	X	X	Compresses the file or directory immediately. (See the Novell documentation for information about file compression.)

(continued)

TABLE 6.4 *File and Directory Attributes*

ATTRIBUTE	ABBREVIATION	FILE	DIRECTORY	DESCRIPTION
Don't Compress	Dc	X	X	Prevents the file or directory from being compressed.
Archive Needed	A	X		Indicates that the file has been changed since the last time it was backed up. (See Chapter 7 for more information about backing up files.)
Execute Only	X	X		Prevents an executable file from being copied, modified, or deleted. Use with caution! Once assigned, it cannot be removed, so assign it only if you have a backup copy of the file. You may prefer to assign the Read-Only attribute instead of the Executable Only attribute.
Read-Write	Rw	X		Allows the file to be opened and modified. Most files are set to Read-Write by default.
Read-Only	Ro	X		Allows the file to be opened and read, but not modified. All NetWare files in SYS:SYSTEM, SYS:PUBLIC, and SYS:LOGIN are Read-Only. Assigning the Read-Only attribute automatically assigns Delete Inhibit and Rename Inhibit.
Shareable	Sh	X		Allows the file to be used by more than one user simultaneously. Useful for utilities, commands, applications, and some database files. All NetWare files in SYS:SYSTEM, SYS:PUBLIC, and SYS:LOGIN are Shareable. Most data and work files should not be Shareable, so that users' changes do not conflict.

ATTRIBUTE	ABBREVIATION	FILE	DIRECTORY	DESCRIPTION
Transactional	T	X		When used on database files, allows NetWare's Transactional Tracking System (TTS) to protect the files from being corrupted if the transaction is interrupted. (See the Novell documentation for more information about TTS.)
Copy Inhibit	Ci	X		Prevents Macintosh files from being copied. (Does not apply to DOS files.)
Don't Suballocate	Ds	X		Prevents a file from being suballocated. Use on files, such as some database files, that may need to be enlarged or appended to frequently. (See the Novell documentation for more information about suballocation.)

ASSIGNING FILE AND DIRECTORY ATTRIBUTES

To assign attributes to a file or directory, use the NetWare Administrator utility (which runs in Windows 3.1 and Windows 95).

To use NetWare Administrator, select the file or directory and choose Details from the Object menu. Then select the Attributes page. The marked check boxes show which attributes have been assigned to the file or directory. To change the attributes, click the check boxes to mark or unmark them.

Figure 6.16 shows a file's attributes as displayed in the NetWare Administrator utility. Figure 6.17 shows a directory's attributes.

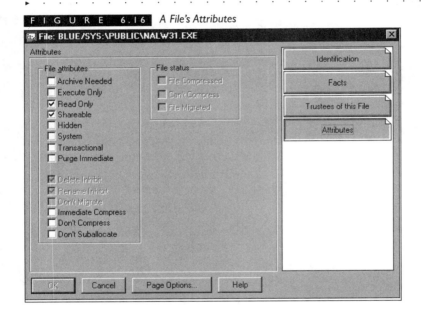

F I G U R E   6.16   *A File's Attributes*

FIGURE 6.17
A Directory's Attributes

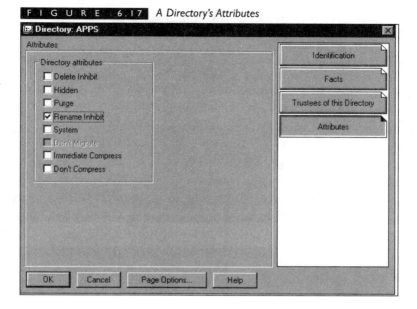

Beyond the Basics

This chapter explained the fundamentals of intraNetWare security. The following topics, mentioned in this chapter, are explained more fully in other chapters in this book:

- For more information on NDS objects, see Chapter 4.
- For more information on creating and managing users, see Chapter 5.
- For information on managing files and directories (such as purging and salvaging files), see Chapter 7.

Some of the topics mentioned in this chapter deal with advanced features of intraNetWare. For more information on the following topics, refer to Novell's online documentation or to *Novell's IntranetWare Administrator's Handbook* from Novell Press:

- Advanced file management features, such as block suballocation, file migration, and file compression

- ▶ Additional utilities you can use to work with rights and attributes
- ▶ Additional security features, such as NCP packet signing

CHAPTER 7

Managing Network Files

Server Volumes

▸ Server volumes are similar to a root directory. Volume SYS contains all intraNetWare files, plus any additional network files you add.

Managing Files and Directories

▸ To perform normal tasks with files and directories, you can use your normal operating system's tools, such as the File Manager (in Windows 3.1), Windows Explorer (in Windows 95), or DOS commands such as COPY and MD.

▸ To manage network characteristics of files and directories, such as trustee assignments and Inherited Rights Filters, use the NetWare Administrator utility.

Purging and Salvaging Files

▸ When files are deleted from the network, they are retained in a salvageable state so that you can retrieve them if necessary.

▸ To remove files completely, purge them by using the NetWare Administrator utility.

▸ To salvage deleted files, use the NetWare Administrator utility.

Backing Up and Restoring Files

▸ To back up files so that you have an archived copy in case the original becomes lost or corrupted, use the intraNetWare SBACKUP utility, or use a third-party backup product.

The Advantages of Storing Files on the Network

One of the most visible characteristics of a network that network users can take advantage of, is the ability to access files and applications that aren't located on their own workstations. Having network applications and files stored in a central location also makes life easier for the network administrator.

The following are just a few of the benefits of storing applications and files on the network. You can probably think of additional benefits for your particular situation:

▶ Many of today's applications have multiuser licenses available, which makes it much easier to install and update applications for all the users on a network. Instead of installing the application on every user's workstation, you can install it once on a server, and let each user access the application there.

▶ Users can share files and folders with each other, without having to trade diskettes or e-mail them to each other.

▶ If users store all of their files on the network instead of on their workstations, the network administrator can make sure all files get backed up (archived) on a regular basis, without depending on each individual user to back up his or her own files each night.

▶ The network administrator can implement file system security features that protect the network files and applications. (Files stored on a local workstation hard disk cannot be protected by intraNetWare security.)

This chapter explains how the intraNetWare file system can work for you, and the tools you can use to manage your network files.

Understanding Server Volumes

To understand and plan your network file system, begin at the top — with volumes. A *volume* is the highest level in the file system hierarchy, and it contains directories and files. An intraNetWare volume is just like a root directory on a floppy diskette or a hard disk.

Each intraNetWare server has at least one volume, SYS, which contains all the intraNetWare files and utilities. The intraNetWare Simple Installation creates a single SYS volume that contains all of the disk space on the server's first hard disk. Subsequent hard disks get their own volumes, named VOL1, VOL2, and so on (up to 64 volumes), as shown in Figure 7.1. If your server has only one hard disk, your server will have only the SYS volume if you used the Simple Installation. (If you use the Custom option of the intraNetWare installation program, you can specify different sizes or names for your volumes.)

F I G U R E   7 . 1   *Each Hard Disk Will Have Its Own Volume.*

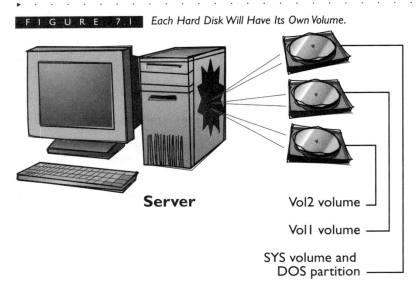

Server

Vol2 volume

Vol1 volume

SYS volume and
DOS partition

When you create a server volume using the intraNetWare installation program (INSTALL.NLM), a Volume object is automatically created in the NDS tree at the same time. The Volume object is placed in the NDS tree in the same context as the server. By default, the Volume object is named with the server's name as a prefix. For example, if the server's name is Sales, the Volume object for volume SYS is named Sales_SYS.

If you double-click a volume's icon in the NetWare Administrator Browser, the files and directories within the volume will appear, as shown in Figure 7.2. If you choose Details from the Object menu, you can see the Volume object's NDS information, as shown in Figure 7.3.

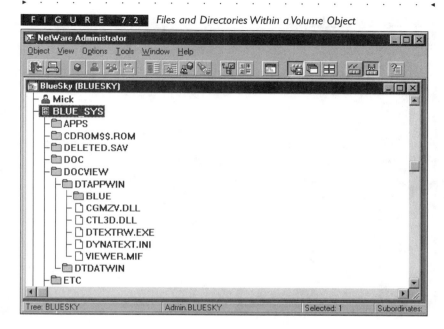

FIGURE 7.2 *Files and Directories Within a Volume Object*

You can also open the volume from within your workstation's Windows File Manager (in Windows 3.1) or Windows Explorer (in Windows 95) to see the files and directories within it, just as you open any other directory (folder). Your Windows utilities won't display the Volume object's NDS information, however.

Planning Network Directories

On your network, you have at least one default volume, named SYS. You also will discover that several directories were created automatically within SYS.

You can create additional directories within SYS to hold all of your applications and regular working files. You can also create directories within other volumes (if other volumes exist on your server).

Before you begin adding directories to your network file system, you may want to plan your directory organization. You will need to decide which types of files you want to reside on the server, which ones should stay on workstations, and so on.

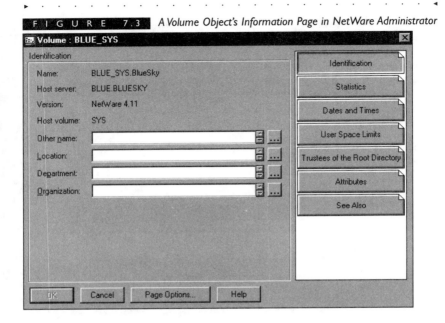

A Volume Object's Information Page in NetWare Administrator

WHAT GOES ON THE SERVER?

The types of files and directories that should be stored on the server can vary, depending on how much control you want your users to have over those files. In many cases, the difference between storing files in network directories and storing them on workstations is the amount of work you have to depend on the users to do, and the amount of work you have to do yourself. For example, if you let users store their working files on their workstations, then you have to depend on the users to back up their own files on a regular basis. (Depending on users to do routine maintenance tasks is never a safe bet, even if they have the best intentions.) If they store the same files on the network, you can back the files up for them automatically. That way, you know you've archived all the necessary work files, and the users didn't even have to worry about them.

As another example, if you keep applications stored on the server, you can easily update the application for all your users *once*. If the application is stored on every workstation, you have to update the application multiple times instead of just once.

Another consideration when deciding where to store files is disk space. If your server disk space is limited, you'll probably want to limit the types of files that are stored on the network and tell users to store their files on their workstations.

If, however, you can install adequate storage space on the server, you'll probably want to encourage users to store everything on the server instead, for security and backup purposes. The following sections describe some of the types of network directories and files you can have on your server.

Directories Created Automatically

When you first install intraNetWare on the server, some directories are created automatically in the SYS volume. These directories contain the files needed to run and manage intraNetWare. You can create additional directories and subdirectories in volume SYS or, if you created additional volumes during installation, you can create directories for your users in the other volumes.

The following directories are created automatically on volume SYS:

▶ LOGIN contains a few files and utilities that will let users change their name context (location) in the NDS tree and log in to the network.

▶ SYSTEM contains NetWare Loadable Modules (NLMs) — programs that the network administrator can load to configure, manage, monitor, and add services on the NetWare server. It also contains LAN drivers, disk drivers, and other files needed for the server installation program (INSTALL.NLM).

▶ PUBLIC contains all the intraNetWare utilities and related files. It also contains .PDF files (printer definition files) if you choose to install them on the server. In addition, PUBLIC contains the client subdirectories, which contain the files required for installing intraNetWare client software on workstations.

▶ MAIL is empty when it is first created. It may be used by e-mail programs that are compatible with NetWare. In NetWare 3.1x and NetWare 2.x, the MAIL directory contained subdirectories for each individual user. Each of these subdirectories, named with the user's object ID number, contained the user's login script file. If you upgrade a NetWare 3.1x or 2.x server to intraNetWare, those existing users will retain their MAIL subdirectories in intraNetWare, but the login scripts will become properties of their User objects instead.

▶ ETC contains files used for managing protocols and routers.

▶ DELETED.SAV is empty when it is first created. It will store directories that are deleted from the network, along with their files, until those directories are either salvaged (restored to the network) or purged (completely erased). Salvaging and purging are explained later in this chapter.

▶ NETBASIC contains files for a scripting program that software developers can use on the server. This is an advanced feature of intraNetWare that isn't discussed in this book.

▶ DOCVIEW contains the DynaText viewers, which are used for reading the online documentation. (This directory is only created if you install the online documentation on the server.)

▶ DOC contains the actual online documentation. (This directory is only created if you install the online documentation on the server.)

These directories contain the files required for running and managing your NetWare network. Be careful not to rename or delete any of them without making absolutely sure they're unnecessary in your particular network's situation.

Application Directories

Many of today's applications have been designed to work on networks and support multiple users. When you buy or upgrade an application, try to purchase a multiple user license for it, as those are sometimes less expensive than buying multiple copies of single-user programs.

It may be easier to assign file system trustee rights if you group all multi-user applications on the network under a single volume or parent directory. For example, by installing your word-processing, spreadsheet, and other programs into their own subdirectories under a parent directory named APPS, you can assign all users the minimum necessary rights to APPS. Then, the users will inherit those rights in each application's subdirectory. (For more information about file system rights, see Chapter 6.)

If different applications will be available to different groups of users, try to organize the applications' directory structures so you can assign comprehensive rights in a parent directory. This will eliminate the need to create multiple individual rights assignments at lower-level subdirectories.

If you install applications into subdirectories under a common parent directory, you can usually designate that daily work files of users be stored in their own home directories elsewhere on the network. This will allow you to grant more restrictive rights to the application directory (so that users can't accidentally delete any necessary application files). At the same time, it lets you grant broader rights to users in their own directories so that they can create, change, or delete the work files created from the application.

When planning network subdirectories for your applications, follow any special instructions from the manufacturer for installing the application on a network. Some applications can be run either from a local hard disk on the workstation or from a network directory. Be sure to follow the instructions supplied by the manufacturer.

In some cases, the instructions may indicate that the application has to be installed at the root of a volume. If your application requires this, you can still install it in a subdirectory under the APPS directory if you want, and then map a fake root to the application's subdirectory. A *fake root* mapping makes a subdirectory appear to be a volume, so that the application runs correctly.

For example, suppose you want to install an application called YOYO into a subdirectory under a directory called APPS on the volume called VOL1. However, the application's instructions say that YOYO must be installed at the root of the volume. Create a subdirectory called YOYO under VOL1:APPS, and install the application into YOYO. Then, you can map a fake root to the YOYO subdirectory and assign it to be a search drive at the same time by using the command:

```
MAP ROOT S16:=VOL1:APPS\YOYO
```

You can type this command at the workstation's DOS prompt if you only need the mapping to be in effect until the user logs out. If you want it to be in effect each time the user logs in, put the command in a login script. (For more information about mapping drives in login scripts, see Chapter 5.)

When you install an application, you may want to flag the application's executable files (usually files with the extension .COM or .EXE) with the Shareable and Read Only file attributes. This will allow users to simultaneously use the applications, but will prevent users from deleting or modifying them. (This is more typically controlled by assigning restrictive trustee rights to users in those applications' directories, however.) You can use the NetWare Administrator utility to assign file attributes. File and directory attributes are covered in Chapter 6.

Work Directories

When planning your network file system, decide where you want users' daily work files to reside. They can be stored in personal directories, in project-specific directories, or in some other type of directory structure.

All files related to Project Ace, for example, could be stored under a directory named ACE. Subdirectories could then be created for project-related files, such as status reports, billing information, and marketing publications. Project Zeus could have a parallel structure. Figure 7.4 shows a simple example of a directory structure for Project Ace.

FIGURE 7.4 *File System Structured by Projects*

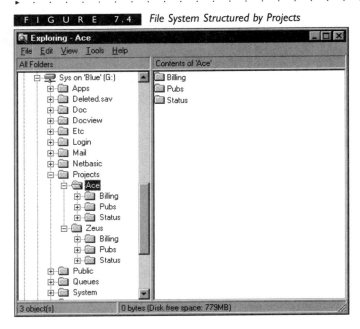

Allow ample network directory space for users to store their daily work files. Encourage your users to store their files on the network. This way those files can be backed up regularly by the network backup process, and they can be protected by intraNetWare security.

Home Directories

You must decide if you want users to have their own individual home directories. Users can store their work files in their home directories, as well as any other types of personal files (status reports, annual reviews, memos, and so on.)

In general, you can allow users full control over their own home directories. If you let them keep a full set of rights to their home directories, they can create new subdirectories within them, delete and salvage files in them, give other users access rights to their files, and so forth.

You can create home directories automatically when you create new users, as explained in Chapter 5.

WHAT GOES ON THE WORKSTATION?

Again, the types of files that can be stored on users' workstations depend on how you want to manage your network. The following sections offer you some explanations and suggestions.

Directories Created Automatically

Many of the directories that exist on a workstation were created automatically by the workstation's own operating system (such as Windows or DOS).

When you install the intraNetWare client software on a workstation, another directory (plus its related subdirectories) is added to the workstation. This directory is called NOVELL, and it contains all the necessary client files for that workstation to run. (The client installation program also modifies and installs various files in other pre-existing directories on the workstation.)

Application Directories

If you like, you can let users have their own copies of applications running locally on their workstations' hard disks. You might choose to install an application directly on a workstation instead of on the network, if you have one of the following situations:

▶ If your user has a laptop computer and needs to run the application when away from the network

▶ If you want your user to be able to run the application if the network is down

▶ If the application is not network-aware, and needs to be installed on a single computer

▶ If the application is used by only one user (especially if it requires access to a local device such as a CD-ROM)

Personal Directories

Many times, users store their personal files on their workstation's hard disk. Remind users that the network will not back up files stored on workstations, so that any files on the workstation are at risk unless the users are diligent about making their own backups.

Managing Files and Directories

Many of the tasks you perform on network files and directories will be the same types of tasks you do on a standalone computer — copying files, deleting them, renaming them, creating new ones, and so on. Not surprisingly, you can use the same tools to do these tasks as you would with files on your workstation's hard disk — such as the File Manager (in Windows 3.1), Windows Explorer (in Windows 95), or DOS commands such as COPY and MD.

Of course, network files and directories have additional characteristics with which you can work, such as trustee assignments and Inherited Rights Filters. To work with these aspects of network files and directories, you can use the NetWare Administrator utility.

Use the NetWare Administrator's Browser to select files and directories and view information about them. Select a file or directory and choose Details from the Object menu. From the Details screen that appears, you can open the Facts page, Trustees page, or Attributes page. Some of the types of information you can see about network files and directories include the following:

- ► Name spaces (explained in Chapter 2)
- ► Size restrictions of directories
- ► Creation dates and times
- ► Trustees
- ► Effective rights
- ► Inherited Rights Filters
- ► File and directory attributes
- ► File owners (the users who created the files)

Figure 7.5 shows the Facts page of information for a directory.

Purging and Salvaging Files

In intraNetWare, when files are deleted, they are not actually removed from the server's hard disk. Instead, they are retained in a salvageable state. Although you won't see a deleted file listed when you look at the file's directory (or folder), the file is really stored in a hidden state, in case you need to retrieve it later.

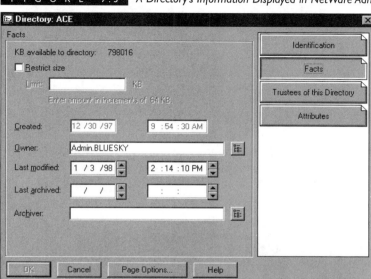

A Directory's Information Displayed in NetWare Administrator

Deleted files are usually stored in the same directory from which they were originally deleted. If, however, the directory itself was also deleted, the deleted files are stored in a special directory called DELETED.SAV at the volume's root.

Deleted files are stored in this salvageable state until one of four things happens:

- ► The file is salvaged, restoring it to its original form.

- ► The server runs out of free space on the disk and begins to overwrite deleted files. The oldest deleted files are overwritten first.

- ► The file is purged by the administrator or user. (When purged, a file is completely removed from the disk and cannot be recovered.) You can purge a file either manually, by using the NetWare Administrator utility, or you can use the Purge Immediate directory and file attributes to mark a file or directory to be purged immediately upon deletion.

- ► Assign the Purge Immediately directory attribute to the volume that contains files you want purged as soon as they are deleted. If you use this attribute, you cannot salvage files you delete from that volume.

You can only salvage or purge files to which you have adequate trustee rights. This prevents unauthorized users from salvaging files that they shouldn't see.

To use the NetWare Administrator utility to either purge or salvage a deleted file or directory, complete the following steps:

1. From the NetWare Administrator's Browser, select the directory containing the files or directories you want to salvage or purge.

2. From the Tools menu, select Salvage. (This option will let you both salvage and purge files.)

3. In the Include field of the Salvage dialog box that appears, as shown in Figure 7.6, indicate which files you want to see displayed. Specify a file name or use wildcards to indicate several files. A blank line or the wildcard symbols *.* will display all the deleted files in the selected directory.

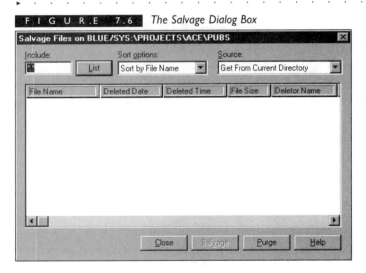

F I G U R E   7.6   *The Salvage Dialog Box*

4. From the Sort Options drop box, specify how you want the displayed files to be sorted — by Deletion Date, Deletor Name, File Name, File Size, or File Type.

5. From the Source drop box, choose whether you want to see deleted files in your current directory or in a deleted directory.

6. Click the List button to display the files you've specified. Figure 7.7 shows an example of the Salvage dialog box with deleted files listed.

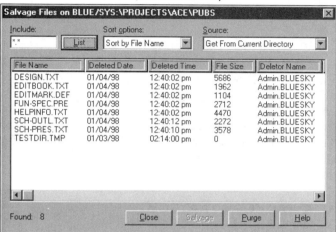

F I G U R E   7 . 7 *The Salvage Dialog Box Shows Files That Have Been Deleted from This Directory.*

7. From the displayed list, select the files you want to purge or salvage.

8. Click either the Salvage button or the Purge button, depending on what you want to do. If you salvage files from an existing directory, the files are restored to that directory. If you salvage files from a deleted directory, the files are restored at the root directory.

9. When finished, click the Close button.

Backing Up and Restoring Files

Files can be lost or damaged in a variety of ways. They can be corrupted by viruses, accidentally deleted by users, overwritten by other applications, or destroyed when a hard disk fails. Despite all the best precautions, you can't always prevent files from being lost.

What you can do, however, is make sure that you always have current backup copies of your network data so you can restore files. If you have a carefully planned and executed backup strategy, you can minimize the amount of work that will be lost if you have to restore a file from your archives.

TIP Encourage your users to store their critical files in network directories so you can be sure the files are backed up on a regular basis.

There are many different backup products available on the market. IntraNetWare includes a basic backup solution, called SBACKUP, that you can use. If you prefer, you can purchase a third-party product that may provide additional features you need.

Backing up network files involves more than just making a copy of the files. It's important to use a backup product, such as SBACKUP, that backs up not just the files themselves, but also the intraNetWare information associated with those files, such as trustee rights, Inherited Rights Filters, and file and directory attributes.

PLANNING A BACKUP STRATEGY

Planning an efficient backup strategy is one of the most beneficial tasks you can do as part of network management. With a good backup strategy, you can limit the time it takes to do backups, ensure that the least amount of working time is lost by your users, and avoid unnecessary headaches from searching for lost files.

Backup strategies can be different for every network. What works for someone else may not work well for you, and vice versa. When planning a backup strategy, you'll need to consider the following questions:

- ▶ What type of backup media do you need to use?
- ▶ What backup schedule should you follow?
- ▶ How frequently should you rotate your backup media?
- ▶ Where should the backups be stored?
- ▶ How often will you test the restore procedure?

The tips and suggestions in the next few sections can help you decide on your own backup strategy.

Choosing Your Backup Media

Before purchasing a backup device, you must decide what kind of backup media you want to use, such as tapes or optical disks. Many manufacturer's backup products can back up data onto a variety of storage media, but it's a good idea to know what you want before you buy something that limits your choices. The media you choose will probably depend upon the following factors:

- ► How much you're willing to spend
- ► How large your network is
- ► How long you need to retain your backed up data (Some media deteriorates after a few years; other media may have a 100-year guarantee.)

Tape is probably the most common backup media in use today, especially in small- to medium-sized businesses. Tapes are relatively easy to use, can be used in any size network, and are fairly inexpensive.

TIP

One of the downsides of tape is that backup manufacturers tend to use different, proprietary tape formats that aren't compatible with each other. Two tape standards have been established (one from Novell, and another from Microsoft), so some efforts have been made to standardize on one or the other, but there are still differences between manufacturers. Be sure any backup product you buy will be compatible with any other system with which you may need to share tapes.

Currently, the two most affordable and popular tape formats used in smaller businesses are:

- ► DAT (Digital Audio Tape)
- ► QIC (Quarter-Inch Cartridge)

A newer tape format, called Digital Linear Tape (DLT), has much higher performance and capacity than DAT or QIC, but it is also much more expensive. Its higher, more expensive performance makes it better suited for large networks. Another tape format, 8mm, is also faster and has more capacity than DAT and QIC, but isn't quite as expensive as DLT.

Tape, while easy to use and relatively affordable, is not necessarily suited to long-term storage of data. Like any magnetic medium, tape can oxidize or otherwise deteriorate over time; therefore, for long-term storage, you may want to consider some of the different types of optical disks. Some optical disks that are currently available include: CD-R (Compact Disk-Recordable), DVD, magneto-optical, and floptical disks.

These technologies are constantly being improved with innovative features and compatibility with earlier or existing products. Talk to your reseller about your network's specific needs, and choose the media that best suits your network.

Planning a Backup Schedule

A good way to determine how often to back up critical data is to calculate how long you could afford to spend re-creating the information if it was lost. If you can't afford to lose more than a day's worth of work, you should perform daily backups of that information. If losing a week's worth of work is more of a nuisance than a devastating blow, perhaps you don't need to do daily backups and can rely on weekly backups instead.

Most backup products, including intraNetWare's SBACKUP, will let you determine not only when you back up your network, but also what types of information you back up each time. In many cases, you'll find that there's no point in backing up your entire network every night if only a few of the files change during the day.

With most products, you can choose between doing a full backup and an *incremental* backup. In an incremental backup, only the files that have been changed are detected and backed up. With a little careful planning, you can create a schedule that staggers complete backups with incremental backups, so you still get full coverage without spending more time and money than necessary.

For example, you can do a full backup of the network once a week. Then, once a day, do incremental backups of only those files that have changed (the backup product can usually detect changed files for you). In the event of a total loss of files, you can restore all the files from the weekly backup, and then restore each of the daily tapes to update those files that changed during that week. In this way, you can cover all of your files while minimizing the time each backup session takes during the week. Figure 7.8 illustrates how you can use full and incremental backups during the week to ensure total coverage.

TIP

Any good backup product can detect changed files when doing an incremental backup. It does this by looking for a special file attribute called the *Archive Needed* attribute (also called the Modify bit). When a file is changed, this attribute is assigned to it. Then, the backup product detects this attribute and knows to back up this file.

In many cases, you can specify whether the backup product should then remove the attribute. (This is done so the file isn't backed up unnecessarily during the next incremental backup.) You can also choose to leave the attribute set so it still appears to be a changed file.

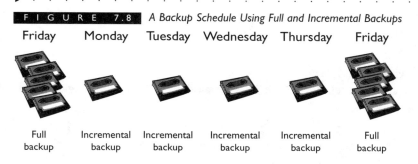

FIGURE 7.8 *A Backup Schedule Using Full and Incremental Backups*

Friday	Monday	Tuesday	Wednesday	Thursday	Friday
Full backup	Incremental backup	Incremental backup	Incremental backup	Incremental backup	Full backup

Another tip for minimizing backup time is to organize your directory (folder) structure so that often-changed files are separate from seldom-changed files. For example, there is no point in wasting your time by frequently backing up files such as applications and utilities. If you put applications in one directory, and work files in another, you can skip the application directory completely during incremental backups, making the process go faster.

Finally, be sure to document your backup schedule and keep a backup log. A written record of all backups and your backup strategy can help someone else restore the files if you aren't there.

Planning the Media Rotation

It's important to plan a rotation schedule for your backup media. You should decide how long you will retain old files, and how often you will reuse the same tapes or disks in advance.

Assume you're using tapes (although any rewriteable media gives you the same situation). If you have only one backup tape that you use every week, you could unknowingly back up corrupted files onto your single tape each time you replace the previous week's backup with the new one. In short, you're replacing your last good copy with a corrupted one.

To prevent this type of problem, plan to keep older backup tapes or disks on hand at all times. Many network administrators will use four or more tapes or disks for the same set of files—cycling through them one at a time. Each week, the most outdated tape or disk is used for the new backup. This way, three or more versions of backups are available at any given time. How many tape or disk sets you'll need depends on your rotation schedule. If you want to keep four weeks' worth of daily and weekly backups, you'll need at least 20 sets of tapes or disks—five for each week. Figure 7.9 shows a possible media rotation schedule.

► · ◄

F I G U R E   7 . 9 *An Example of a Media Rotation Schedule*

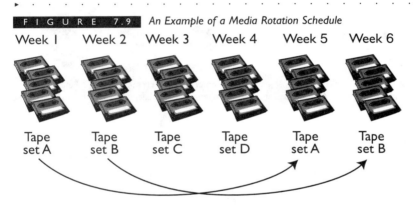

| Week 1 | Week 2 | Week 3 | Week 4 | Week 5 | Week 6 |

| Tape set A | Tape set B | Tape set C | Tape set D | Tape set A | Tape set B |

Some backup products offer preset rotation schedules for you. They will automatically prompt you for the right set of media and keep track of the schedule. (SBACKUP, being a very basic backup product, doesn't include this feature.)

Decide Where to Store the Backups

Another important aspect of your backup strategy is to plan where to store your backups. If you have backups of noncritical data, you may be comfortable keeping them onsite. However, when storing backups onsite, you should at least store them in a room separate from the server's room. If an electrical fire breaks out in the server room, your backup tapes won't do you much good if they burn right beside the server.

For mission-critical data, you may need to keep backups in an offsite location. That way, if there is a physical disaster (such as a fire, flood, or earthquake) they'll be safe. If the data is critical enough to store offsite, but you also want to have immediate access to it, consider making two backups, and storing one offsite and the other onsite.

Test the Restore Process

A final tip: Make sure your backups can be restored! A backup is only useful if the data in it can be restored successfully. Too many people discover a problem with their backups when they're in the middle of an important restoration process. Practice restoring files before you need to do so. By practicing, you may identify problems you didn't realize you had. Don't wait until it is too late.

USING SBACKUP

SBACKUP.NLM is the backup product that ships in intraNetWare. With SBACKUP, you can back up all the different types of files that can be stored on your server: DOS, Macintosh, OS/2, Windows NT, Windows 95, and UNIX.

As mentioned earlier, most backup products let you choose between at least two types of backups: full and incremental. SBACKUP actually gives you four choices:

- ▶ Full backup — This option backs up all network files. It removes the Archive Needed file attribute from all files and directories.

- ▶ Differential backup — This option backs up only files that were modified since the last full backup. It does not remove the Archive Needed attribute from these files, however, so the next time you run a backup, these files will still look like they were changed (and they'll be backed up again).

- ▶ Incremental backup — This option backs up only files that were modified since the last full or incremental backup. It removes the Archive Needed attribute from these files, so they won't be backed up the next time you run an incremental backup.

- ▶ Custom backup — This option lets you specify particular directories to back up or restore. You can specify whether or not to remove the Archive Needed attribute from those files.

Backing Up Files with SBACKUP

To use SBACKUP.NLM to back up files, you will load SBACKUP.NLM and device drivers for the backup device (tape or disk drive) on a server, as explained in this section. This server is called the *host server.*

Then you will load a NetWare Loadable Module called a Target Service Agent (TSA) — which also comes in intraNetWare — on any server containing the files you want to back up. This server is called a *target server.* (A TSA simply allows the target server to communicate with the host server.) You do not need to run SBACKUP on the target server — as long as it can communicate with a server that *is* running SBACKUP, the TSA is all the target server needs.

To back up the host server itself, you must load both SBACKUP and a TSA on that server. Complete the following steps to use SBACKUP to back up your network files:

1. Attach the backup device (tape or disk drive) to the host server. (Follow the manufacturer's installation instructions for that backup device.)

2. Load the necessary backup device drivers on the host server. Again, see the manufacturer's instructions to find out which drivers you need, and for instructions on installing the device drivers.

TIP

You can place the commands that load the backup device drivers in the server's STARTUP.NCF file if you want them to load automatically when the server is rebooted. To edit the STARTUP.NCF file, type LOAD EDIT STARTUP.NCF at the server's console. The text of the STARTUP.NCF file will appear, in a text editor. Add the commands you want, and then save the file by choosing Save from the File menu. The commands you enter in this file will be executed whenever the server is rebooted.

3. At the host server's console, type the following command to register the device with the server:

SCAN FOR NEW DEVICES

4. On each target server you want to back up, load the appropriate TSA, as explained in the following bullet list. Don't forget to load a TSA on the host server that's running SBACKUP if you want to back up the host server itself. Use one of the following commands to load the correct TSA:

   ► For NetWare 4.1 and intraNetWare target servers, type **LOAD TSA410.NLM**

   ► For NetWare 4.0 target servers, type **LOAD TSA400.NLM**

   ► For NetWare 3.12 target servers, type **LOAD TSA312.NLM**

   ► For NetWare 3.11 target servers, type **LOAD TSA311.NLM**

5. Load SBACKUP on the host server by typing **LOAD SBACKUP**.

6. From SBACKUP's main menu, choose Backup, as shown in Figure 7.10.

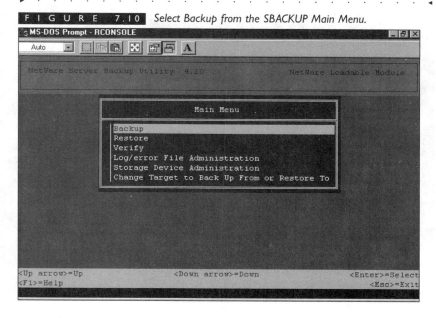

F I G U R E   7 . 1 0   *Select Backup from the SBACKUP Main Menu.*

7. If multiple servers have TSAs loaded, choose the target server that you want to back up.

8. When prompted, enter a user name and password for the target server (see Figure 7.11). The user must be Admin or a user with equivalent rights to this server. You may need to enter the user's full context name.

9. If more than one storage device is available, select the backup device you want to use.

10. Specify a location for both the session log and error files. The session log helps SBACKUP locate the backed up files for later restorations. The error files track any errors that may occur. Either press Enter to accept the default, or press Insert to navigate through the file system and select another location.

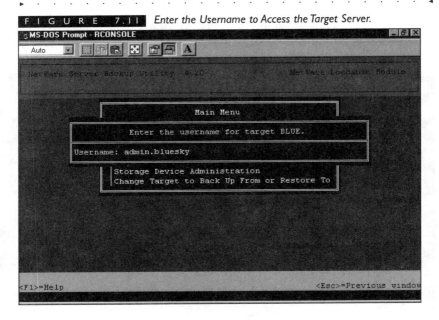

FIGURE 7.11 *Enter the Username to Access the Target Server.*

MS-DOS Prompt - RCONSOLE

Auto

NetWare Server Backup Utility 4.20   NetWare Loadable Module

```
                    Main Menu

        Enter the username for target BLUE.

Username: admin.bluesky

        Storage Device Administration
        Change Target to Back Up From or Restore To
```

<F1>=Help   <Esc>=Previous window

11. Select the type of backup you want to do (full, differential, incremental, or custom).

12. **(This step is for custom backup only.)** If you choose to do a custom backup, several screens appear that allow you to enter information about what you want to back up. You can select specific volumes, directories, and files to be included or excluded from the backup. Use *exclude* options when you want to back up most of the file system while omitting only a small part. Everything that you don't specifically exclude is backed up. Use *include* options when you want to back up only a small portion of the file system. Everything you don't specifically include is excluded. (When specifying subsets to back up, two options allow you to exclude or include Major TSA resources. A *Major TSA resource* is simply a volume. You can choose to include or exclude volumes, directories, or files.)

13. Enter a description for this backup session, so you can recognize it later.

14. If your backup device can append (add) data to previous sessions on the same media, specify whether you want this session to be appended to the same media as another session or not. If you choose not to append, existing data on the media will be erased and replaced with the new backup session's data.

15. Press F10 and choose whether to start the backup now or later. If you choose to start the backup later, enter the time and date you want it to begin.

Restoring Files with SBACKUP

To use SBACKUP.NLM to restore files, you load SBACKUP and device drivers for the backup device on the host server just as you did when preparing to back up the files. Then load TSAs on any target servers whose files you want to restore.

To restore files with SBACKUP, complete the following steps:

1. From SBACKUP's main menu, choose Restore, as shown in Figure 7.12.

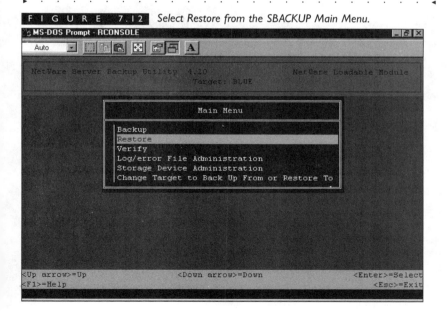

FIGURE 7.12 *Select Restore from the SBACKUP Main Menu.*

2. If multiple servers have TSAs loaded, choose the target server to which you want to restore files.

3. When prompted, enter a user name and password for the target server. (The user must be Admin or a user with equivalent rights to this server.) You may need to enter the user's full context name.

4. If you are restoring files from a session (and you know where its session files are), select Choose a Session to Restore. Then enter the path to the session files, as shown in Figure 7.13.

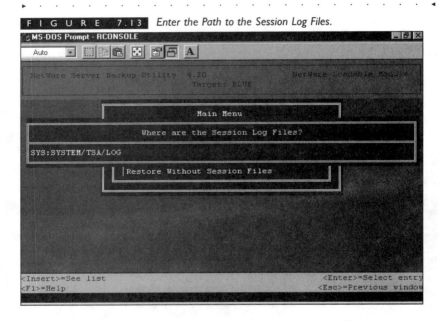

F I G U R E   7.13   *Enter the Path to the Session Log Files.*

5. From the list of sessions that appears, select the session you want to restore.

6. If the session files have been corrupted or deleted (and you want to restore the files directly from a backup media), choose Restore Without Session Files. Then specify a location for the new session log and error files for the restoration session.

7. Select the type of backup device and media from which you want to restore.

8. Choose whether you want to restore a single file or directory, an entire session, or do a custom restore. Then fill in any information about the files that you want to restore.

9. Press Enter to begin the restoration.

Beyond the Basics

This chapter explained the most common aspects of managing network files on an intraNetWare network.

The following topics, mentioned in this chapter, are explained more fully in other chapters in this book:

- ▶ For instructions on installing the NetWare Administrator utility on your workstation, see Chapter 4.

- ▶ For information about login scripts, see Chapter 5.

- ▶ For information about file system trustee rights and Inherited Rights Filters, see Chapter 6.

- ▶ For more information about installing Novell's online documentation, see Chapter 9.

There are many advanced intraNetWare features you can use to further manage network directories and files if your network situation requires it, once you're comfortable with the basics. For more information about the following topics, refer to the Novell online documentation, or to *Novell's IntranetWare Administrator's Handbook* from Novell Press:

- ▶ File compression (which compresses less frequently used files)

- ▶ Block suballocation (which allows several files to share a single block to avoid wasting space unnecessarily)

- ▶ Data migration (which lets you automatically move less frequently used files to an alternate storage device, such as an optical jukebox system)

- ▶ Additional intraNetWare utilities, such as RENDIR, NCOPY, NDIR, PURGE, and FILER, that allow you to work with file and directory information

- ▶ Restricting the amount of network disk space that users can access

- ▶ Purging and salvaging files

- ▶ Managing volumes (creating, deleting, and repairing them)

CHAPTER 8

Setting Up Printers

Instant Access

Installing Print Services

▸ To install print services using default options (the quick-and-easy way), use the Print Services Quick Setup feature of the NetWare Administrator utility, and then load PSERVER.NLM on the intraNetWare server.

▸ To connect a network printer to a DOS or Windows 3.1 workstation, load NPRINTER.EXE on the workstation.

▸ To connect a network printer to a Windows 95 workstation, load NPTWIN95.EXE on the workstation.

▸ To connect a network printer to an intraNetWare server, load NPRINTER.NLM on the server.

Printing

▸ To redirect LPT1 to a print queue, put a CAPTURE command in a login script, use NetWare User Tools (which runs in Windows 3.1), or configure the application for network printing.

▸ To print files from within an application, simply follow the application's normal printing procedures (ensure that the application is configured to print to a network printer).

The Advantages of Network Printing

IntraNetWare print services allow your network users to share printers connected to the network. With intraNetWare print services loaded, you can gain benefits such as:

- Increasing productivity and saving on hardware expenses by allowing users to share a smaller number of printers instead of buying each user a standalone printer. (You may also be able to buy a single, more sophisticated printer instead of multiple lesser-quality printers.)

- Letting users send their print jobs to different printers for different purposes, all from a single workstation.

- Prioritizing print jobs so that important print jobs are sent to the printer ahead of less important print jobs.

How intraNetWare Printing Works

In standalone printing, a printer is connected directly to the serial or parallel port (usually LPT1) on the workstation. When the user prints a file, the print job goes from the application to the print driver, which formats the job for the specific printer. (The print driver is software that converts the print job into a format that the printer can understand.) Next the print job goes to the parallel port, and then directly to the printer. Often, the application has to wait until the print job is finished before it can resume working. Figure 8.1 illustrates the path a print job takes when a printer is attached directly to a workstation.

With intraNetWare print services, the print job goes to the network instead of directly to the printer, though this process is transparent to users. Then the network takes care of sending the print job to the correct printer.

To accomplish this, intraNetWare print services employ two features, called *print queues* and *print servers*.

- The print queue is a special network directory (folder) that stores print jobs temporarily before they are printed. Multiple network users can have their jobs stored in the same print queue. The print queue receives all incoming print jobs from various users, and stores them in a first-come, first-served order.

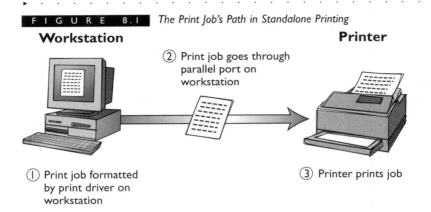

The Print Job's Path in Standalone Printing

Workstation   **Printer**

② Print job goes through parallel port on workstation

① Print job formatted by print driver on workstation

③ Printer prints job

▶ The print server is a software program, called PSERVER.NLM, that runs on the intraNetWare server. The print server controls how the print queues and printers work together. The print server takes the jobs from the print queue, one at a time, and forwards them on to the printer when the printer is available.

TIP

You can have more than one print queue on a network. Furthermore, you can set up one print queue so it services several printers (although this can be confusing because you never know which printer will print the job you send). You can also set up a single printer so it services several print queues.

However, it generally simplifies your administration tasks and reduces your users' confusion if you use a one-to-one correspondence between print queues and printers, so that each print queue sends jobs to its own printer.

When you set up intraNetWare print services, you assign a printer, a print server, and a print queue to each other so all three work together. Then you tell the workstation's parallel port to point to a network print queue instead of a directly attached printer. (This is called *redirection*.)

You can attach printers on an intraNetWare network to any of the following three different places:

▶ Directly to the server

▶ To a workstation on the network

▶ Directly to the network cabling

If you attach printers directly to the intraNetWare server, the server must run an NLM called NPRINTER.NLM. This NLM is a port driver, which is software that routes jobs out of the print queue, through the correct port on the server, to the printer.

If you attach a printer to a workstation on the network, that workstation must also be running a port driver. (This port driver is called NPRINTER.EXE for DOS and Windows 3.1, and NPTWIN95 for Windows 95.) The workstation's version of NPRINTER or NPTWIN95 works the same way as the server's version, sending print jobs through the port on the workstation to the printer.

To attach the printer directly to the network cabling, you must use a network-direct printer (see the sidebar, "Using Network-Direct Printers") that contains its own printer port driver (like NPRINTER). Figure 8.2 shows the various places printers can exist on a network.

FIGURE 8.2 *Printers Can Be Attached to Servers, Workstations, the Network Cabling, or Any Combination of the Three.*

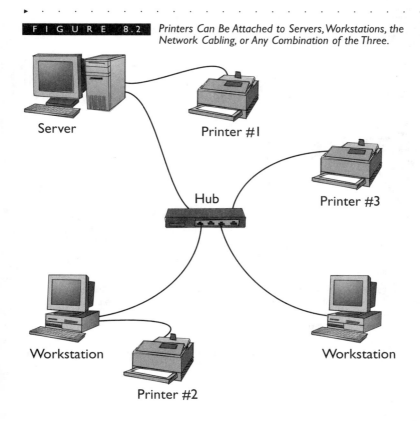

If you prefer, you can connect printers to a third-party print server that attaches directly to the network cabling. This type of print server acts like an intraNetWare print server, but is a separate device that connects to the network (unlike an intraNetWare print server, which runs within a server). For example, Hewlett Packard makes JetDirect print servers that can support printers on an intraNetWare network.

Figure 8.3 illustrates the path a print job takes through the network. In this particular example, the printer is attached to a workstation that is running NPRINTER.EXE.

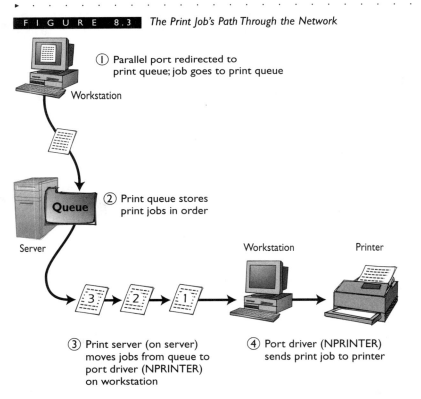

FIGURE 8.3 *The Print Job's Path Through the Network*

Workstation

① Parallel port redirected to print queue; job goes to print queue

Queue

② Print queue stores print jobs in order

Server

Workstation

Printer

③ Print server (on server) moves jobs from queue to port driver (NPRINTER) on workstation

④ Port driver (NPRINTER) sends print job to printer

With intraNetWare print services, the journey of a print job follows this path:

▶ The application works with the print driver to format the print job, just as it does in standalone mode.

▶ Instead of the parallel port pointing directly to a printer, the parallel port is redirected to a print queue. If you specify that one print job goes to one printer and another job goes to a second printer, they will both be redirected from the same parallel port to the correct print queues.

▶ When the printer is available, the print server takes the print job from the print queue and sends it to the port driver (such as NPRINTER.EXE or NPRINTER.NLM) running wherever the printer is connected.

▶ The port driver then sends the print job to the printer, and the job is printed.

Even if a workstation has a printer attached to it, it can still be used as a regular workstation. The workstation simply acts as a connection to the network for that printer.

TIP

The workstation attached to the printer should still redirect its own parallel port to the network. This way, the workstation uses network printing services like all the other workstations, instead of printing directly to the printer.

Even if a printer is attached directly to the workstation, it is usually more efficient to send the print job from the workstation to a network print queue, and then back to the printer. This also allows other workstations to use the printer.

Planning intraNetWare Print Services

Setting up printing services correctly can intimidate a lot of people. However, if your printing needs are straightforward, using Novell's Quick Setup program can greatly simplify the process. (The Quick Setup program is part of the NetWare Administrator utility.) After you install intraNetWare printing services, the printers, print queues, and print servers will all appear as NDS objects in the Directory tree. You can use the NetWare Administrator utility to manage those objects whenever you need to, just as you use it to manage other types of NDS objects.

USING NETWORK-DIRECT PRINTERS

Currently, a common type of printing connection is to use printers that connect directly to the network cabling, rather than to a server or a workstation. These types of printers, often called *network-direct printers*, may run in either remote printer mode or queue server mode.

Remote printer mode lets the printer function as if it were running its own NPRINTER port driver. It doesn't need to be connected to a workstation; its internal NPRINTER-like software lets it be controlled by the intraNetWare print server and allows it to take advantage of NDS functionality.

Queue server mode is bindery-based, and is used when the printer device has not been designed to work with NDS. (As mentioned in Chapter 2, the bindery is a simple form of network database used in NetWare 3.1x and earlier forms of NetWare. NDS replaced the bindery in intraNetWare.)

Be sure to read the manufacturer's documentation for more information about installing these types of printers, as there are usually restrictions on how they can be installed.

As you plan your printing setup, decide how many printers you need and where you want to locate them. If you will be attaching printers to workstations, you may want to choose workstations that aren't as heavily used as others. In addition, it will be important for the users of those workstations to remember not to turn off the workstation when other users are using the network. Instead, those users should just log out of the network when they are finished using the workstation.

TIP

When you plan how to set up intraNetWare print services, you may want to keep the following guidelines and restrictions in mind:

▸ In general, PSERVER.NLM uses about 27K of server RAM for each configured printer.

▸ PSERVER.NLM can service PC-based, UNIX, and Apple printers.

▸ A single print server can service up to 255 printers, although performance begins to degrade after about 60 printers or so.

▸ If you need more than one print server in your network, you can load PSERVER.NLM on additional intraNetWare servers, and those print servers can service more network printers.

Setting Up intraNetWare Print Services

The Print Services Quick Setup option in the NetWare Administrator utility is the quickest, easiest way to set up print services. If you want to set up each printer to service a single print queue — which greatly simplifies printing administration — this is the installation option to use. This option also assigns printers, print servers, and print queues to each other automatically so there is no chance for you to miss a connection and end up with a broken link somewhere in the print communication chain. After you've set up printing using this quick option, you can modify the setup later if needed.

NOTE

The NetWare Administrator utility runs under Windows 3.1, OS/2, or Windows 95. For instructions on setting up the NetWare Administrator utility on a workstation, see Chapter 4.

To set up print services using the Quick Setup option, complete the following steps:

1. Decide where you want to locate your printer and attach it to the server, workstation, or network cabling. See the printer manufacturer's instructions for installing the printer.

2. Log in to the network from any workstation as user Admin.

3. Launch the NetWare Administrator utility on the workstation.

4. Select the container object that will contain the print server, printer, and print queue. Quick Setup will put them all in the same container.

5. From the NetWare Administrator's Tools menu, select the Print Services Quick Setup option. The screen that appears shows the default names and information that NetWare Administrator will assign to the print server, printer, and print queue. See Figure 8.4 for an example of the Quick Setup screen.

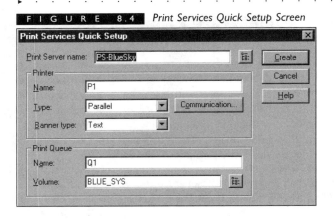

F I G U R E   8.4   *Print Services Quick Setup Screen*

6. If necessary, change the name of the print server, printer, or print queue to something you prefer.

7. Choose the printer type you are using (parallel, serial, UNIX, AppleTalk, or AIO) and fill in any necessary information about that printer type. Refer to the printer manufacturer's documentation for specific information about your printer.

8. If necessary, choose a different volume in which to store the print queue. (If you only have one volume, skip this step. If you have more

than one volume, you should put the print queues in a volume other than SYS. This will allow you to preserve SYS just for intraNetWare files, and give the print queues more room on another volume.)

9. Click Create. The Quick Setup program will take just a moment to create the necessary printing objects in NDS. When the NetWare Administrator utility displays the Directory tree's objects now (see Figure 8.5), you'll see the new printer (P1 in this example), the print server (PS-BlueSky), and the print queue (Q1).

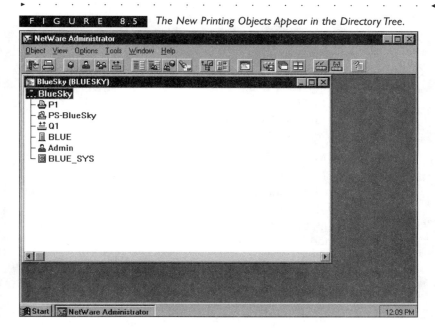

FIGURE   8.5   *The New Printing Objects Appear in the Directory Tree.*

10. Install a print server, if necessary. (If there's already a server on the network running a print server (PSERVER.NLM), skip to Step 11. Because a single print server can service up to 255 printers, you probably need only one print server running on the network.)

If you need to install a print server, go to the network server that will run the print server (or use Remote Console to access that server's console) and load the print server software using the following command:

```
LOAD PSERVER printserver
```

where *printserver* is the name of the newly created print server. For example, you might type:

```
LOAD PSERVER PS-BLUESKY
```

11. If the printer is attached to a network server that is not running PSERVER, load the NPRINTER.NLM on the network server, specifying the print server name and printer number in the NPRINTER command.

To find the printer's number, double-click the print server object's icon in NetWare Administrator, then click the Assignments page. This page lists all the printers associated with this print server, and indicates each printer's number.

For example, to load NPRINTER for printer P1 (printer number 0), which uses print server PS-BlueSky, use the following command:

```
LOAD NPRINTER PS-BLUESKY 0
```

If you have more than one printer attached to this server, load NPRINTER multiple times, specifying a different printer number (and print server if necessary) for each printer

12. If the printer is attached to a workstation, run NPRINTER.EXE (for DOS and Windows 3.1) or NPTWIN95.EXE (for Windows 95) on that workstation.

a. *For DOS and Windows 3.1,* type NPRINTER, followed by the print server name and printer number in the command. (You can include this command in the workstation's AUTOEXEC.BAT file.) For example, to load NPRINTER for printer number 0, which uses print server PS-BlueSky, use the following command:

```
NPRINTER PS-BLUESKY 0
```

b. *For Windows 95,* start up the intraNetWare Client software on the workstation. From the Network Neighborhood, locate the NPTWIN95.EXE file in SYS:PUBLIC\WIN95, and double-click it to launch it. Fill in the Add Network Printer dialog box. (To ensure that NPTWIN95 loads every time the workstation reboots, add this file to the Startup folder. Choose Start, then Settings, then

Taskbar, and then select the Start Menu Programs tab. Choose Add, and then Browse to find NPTWIN95.EXE. Choose Next, and then Startup. Enter a name for the icon, such as NPRINTER, and choose Finish.)

13. If you want to modify any information for the printing objects you've created, simply select the object from the NetWare Administrator Browser, choose Details from the Object menu, and edit the fields you want to change.

14. Configure your applications so that they send print jobs to the correct printer. Follow the manufacturer's instructions for setting up the application for network printing. In most cases, applications are network-aware. This means that you can simply supply the application with the printer's name, and the port redirection will be taken care of automatically.

15. If you have applications that may not redirect workstation ports to a print queue automatically, you'll have to tell the workstation to redirect its parallel port to a print queue. To do this, see the section "Redirecting Parallel Port to a Print Queue" later in this chapter.

Now your intraNetWare printing services are ready to use.

TIP

Server commands, such as those you used to load the print server and the server's NPRINTER, can be added to the intraNetWare server's AUTOEXEC.NCF file. This way, they automatically load whenever the server is rebooted.

To add these commands to this file, go to the server's console and type:

```
LOAD EDIT AUTOEXEC.NCF
```

This will bring up the file in a simple text editor. When the file appears, type in the server commands you want. (Put the commands to load the print server and NPRINTER, if necessary, toward the end of the AUOTEXEC.NCF file, after the command "MOUNT ALL.") When finished, press Esc to save the file and exit the EDIT program.

Upgrading NetWare 3.1*x* Print Services

If you want to upgrade NetWare 3.1*x* printing objects to NDS objects on an intraNetWare tree, you must use a utility called PUPGRADE.NLM. If you aren't upgrading from a NetWare 3.1*x* server, skip this section.

Ensure that you have upgraded the server before you try to upgrade the printing objects.

TIP

To upgrade your NetWare 3.1*x* printing objects, complete the following steps:

1. Copy the file PUPGRADE.NLM from the intraNetWare server's SYS:SYSTEM directory into the NetWare 3.1*x* server's SYS:SYSTEM directory.

2. Load PUPGRADE.NLM on the NetWare 3.1*x* server by typing the following command at the 3.1*x* server's keyboard:

   ```
   LOAD PUPGRADE
   ```

3. Enter the ADMIN user name and password.

4. Select Upgrade PRINTCON Database. This will upgrade any existing database of print job configurations. The print job configurations feature is an advanced feature of intraNetWare printing that tells the printer unique ways to print different jobs. Print job configurations specify printing instructions, such as which queue the job should be sent to and what kind of paper to use. By selecting this option, you'll ensure that any configurations that may have been set up earlier are upgraded.

5. Select Upgrade PRINTDEF Database if you want to upgrade the PRINTDEF database of printer definitions. You only need to do this if your printer isn't recognized by your applications, and you had to set up a special printer definition for that printer. This is an advanced feature of intraNetWare printing. You probably don't need to do this, but you can select this option anyway just to be safe. After selecting this option, specify the context in the NDS tree where you want this database to reside.

6. To upgrade your print server and printers from bindery objects to NDS objects in the NDS tree, select Upgrade Print Server and Printers.

From the list of NetWare 3.1*x* print servers that appears, select the print server you want to upgrade.

7. When the upgrade is finished, exit PUPGRADE.

8. Using the NetWare Administrator utility from a workstation logged into the intraNetWare server, add user Admin as an authorized user and operator of the upgraded print queues and print server. Because user Admin doesn't exist in NetWare 3.1*x*, it isn't added to these newly upgraded print objects automatically. (From the NetWare Administrator utility, double-click each print queue and print server icon to bring up their page of information. Then enter the Admin's name as an authorized user and operator.) Now your printing services have been upgraded.

Redirecting a Parallel Port to a Print Queue

After installing print services on your network, you must ensure that the applications your workstation uses can find the right printers. To do this, you must ensure that the workstation's parallel port is redirected to a print queue.

There are several methods for redirecting the workstation's parallel port, such as the following:

- ► Let the application redirect the parallel port.
- ► Use the intraNetWare CAPTURE utility or the NetWare User Tools utility on a Windows 3.1 or DOS workstation.
- ► Use the Network Neighborhood on a Windows 95 workstation.

The method you choose depends on your needs and on how your workstation is set up, as explained in the following sections.

LETTING THE APPLICATION REDIRECT THE PORT

In most cases, you can configure your applications so that they send print jobs to the correct printer. Most network-aware applications let you set them up so they redirect print jobs to a print queue by themselves. In many cases, you can simply specify a printer in the application. Because the printer, print queue, and print server are all assigned to each other, the job is sent to the correct print queue automatically. Follow the application manufacturer's instructions for setting up the application for network printing.

While you're setting up your application, you'll probably be asked for the printer's driver. If the printer uses a print driver that the application already has pre-installed, you can select that driver and continue the printer setup. If the application doesn't have the driver you need, you'll have to supply it (printer manufacturers usually supply the necessary print driver on a diskette).

REDIRECTING THE PORT ON A DOS OR WINDOWS 3.1 WORKSTATION

If you have applications that do not redirect workstation ports to a print queue automatically, you will have to use other methods to redirect the port. On a DOS or Windows 3.1 workstation, you can use the intraNetWare utility called CAPTURE.

When typing a CAPTURE command, you may need to specify the queue's full name. For example, to redirect users' LPT1 ports to the queue named Q1, with no banner page, no tabs, no form feed, and a five-second timeout interval, type the following command at the workstation's DOS prompt:

```
CAPTURE L=1 Q=.Q1.Sales.Satellite.RedHawk NB NT NFF
TI=5
```

TIP You can place the CAPTURE command in a login script so that it executes automatically. See the Novell documentation for more information about using login scripts for DOS or Windows 3.1 workstations.

You can also use the NetWare User Tools utility to assign the parallel port to a print queue. See Chapter 5 for more information about using the NetWare User Tools utility. See the Appendix for more information about the options you can use with the CAPTURE utility.

REDIRECTING THE PORT ON A WINDOWS 95 WORKSTATION

On a Windows 95 workstation, use the Network Neighborhood to select a printer and redirect its port. Open the Network Neighborhood, then double-click the printer you want to use. Windows 95 will then ask you to select the printer you want to use. If the printer uses a print driver that Windows 95 already has preinstalled, you can select that driver and continue the printer setup. If Windows 95 doesn't have the driver you need, you'll have to supply it (printer manufacturers usually supply the necessary print driver on a diskette).

Answer the remaining setup questions and specify that you want to capture the port.

Verifying Your Printing Setup

After you've set up your printing services, you can use the NetWare Administrator utility to see a graphical representation of your printing setup. Using this feature, you can see if all your printing objects are assigned to each other correctly.

To see this printing layout diagram, select the print server you're interested in. Double-click the print server's icon (or choose Details from the Object menu), and then open the Print Layout page. Figure 8.6 shows an example print layout diagram.

F I G U R E   8 . 6   *The Print Layout Page in NetWare Administrator*

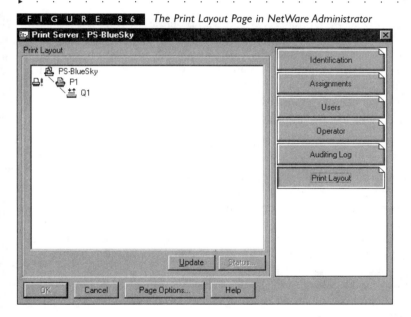

If all you see is a list of print servers, click a print server to expand the view to show its assigned printers and queues. Lines connecting the printing objects indicate that the objects are assigned to each other correctly. A dashed line connecting them indicates that the connection is only good for this session. When the server is rebooted, the connections will be removed.

If any printing object has an icon with an exclamation mark (!) beside it, there's a problem with that object. (Notice the print server object in Figure 8.6 has an exclamation mark.) Go back through the instructions and see if you missed any steps when assigning print queues, print servers, and printers to each other.

You can also right-click any of the objects to see more information about that particular object. In addition, you can see the print jobs in a queue by double-clicking the queue object. However, you cannot modify the print jobs from this screen. To modify the print jobs, you have to go back to the NetWare Administrator Browser, select a print queue, and open its Print Jobs page.

Handling Print Jobs

After intraNetWare print services are set up on the network, users can send their jobs to network print queues as long as they have access to those printers.

A user has access to a queue if he or she is assigned as a print queue user. By default, the container in which a print queue resides is assigned as a user, so all objects within the container are also users of the queue.

A *print queue user* can do the following:

▸ Add jobs to a print queue

▸ See the status of all jobs in the queue

▸ Delete his or her job from the queue

A queue user cannot delete other users' print jobs from the queue.

A *print queue operator* is a special type of print queue user who has the ability to manage the print queue. A queue operator can delete other users' print jobs, put them on hold, and so on. The user Admin is the default queue operator.

You can add or remove users and operators from the list of print queue users by using the NetWare Administrator utility. You can also use the same utility to look at the current print jobs in the print queue.

To use the NetWare Administrator utility to change users and operators, double-click the Print Queue object (or choose Details from the Object menu), and then open the Users or Operator page. (See Figure 8.7 for an example of the Operator page for the queue named Q1.)

To see the current print jobs in the queue, open the print queue's Job List page. Here, users can delete their own print jobs or put them on hold. Queue operators can put on hold or delete any users' print jobs. Press the F1 key to read help on each of the available fields in the Job List screen. Figure 8.8 shows the Print Jobs page.

Unloading PSERVER.NLM

Unloading PSERVER.NLM is easy. From the NetWare Administrator utility, select the print server object. Then, from the Object menu, choose Details and click Unload.

To reload PSERVER, type the following command at the network server's console:

```
LOAD PSERVER printserver
```

where *printserver* is the name of the newly created print server.

FIGURE 8.7 *The Print Queue's Operator Page*

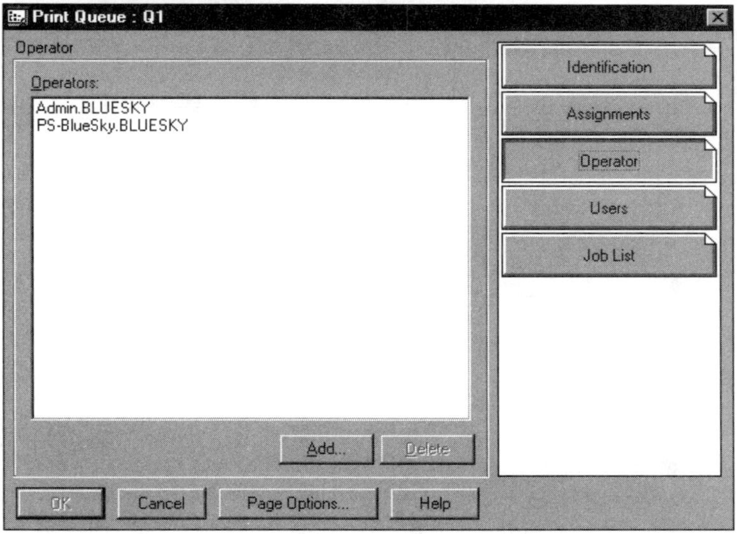

Beyond the Basics

This chapter explored the foundations of intraNetWare printing, and it also explained how to set up a quick and easy system of network printing.

Although the majority of network users can (and should) use the basic printing setup without making any customized changes, intraNetWare printing has numerous features built in that make it tremendously flexible. In fact, once you begin dabbling in customized printing setups, printing can become one of the more complex aspects of a network.

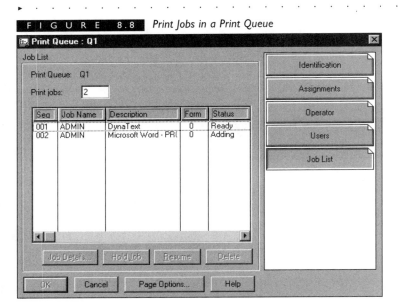

FIGURE 8.8 *Print Jobs in a Print Queue*

You can find more information about the following topics in Novell's online documentation (which came with your intraNetWare package) in *Novell's IntranetWare Administrator's Handbook* and *Novell's Guide to NetWare Printing* (both from Novell Press):

- ▶ Using the CAPTURE utility to redirect an LPT port to a network print queue. (You can also use CAPTURE to specify options such as whether or not to print a banner page, whether to use tabs, and so on.)

- ▶ Using print job configurations to predefine settings such as the designated printer, whether or not to print a banner page, and the type of paper form to print on (such as invoice forms, paychecks, legal-sized paper, and so on).

- ▶ Using the NPRINT utility to print a job from outside of an application (such as printing an ASCII file or a workstation screen).

- ► Using printer definition files if your applications don't have a printer driver for your type of printer.

- ► Customizing your printing environment, such as designating multiple queues that will be serviced by a single printer or multiple printers that will service a single queue

- ► Creating login scripts (for DOS and Windows 3.1 workstations) that let you specify certain files and programs that should load whenever the user logs in.

CHAPTER 9

Installing and Using the Novell Online Documentation

Instant Access

Installing

▸ To set up online documentation, first set up workstations to access the DynaText viewers, and then install the document collections on the server or the workstations.

▸ To install a DynaText viewer on a Windows 3.1 or Windows 95 workstation, run SETUPDOC.EXE (located on the *NetWare 4.11 Online Documentation* CD-ROM) on the workstation and choose the "DynaText Viewer" option.

▸ To install document collections on the server or a workstation, run SETUPDOC.EXE from a Windows 3.1 or Windows 95 workstation and choose the "Document Collections" option.

Using

▸ To use the DynaText viewer from a workstation, double-click the DynaText icon. Select the collection you want on the left panel of the viewer, and open any manual on the right side of the viewer.

Novell's Online Documentation

In an effort to save trees, bookshelf space, and the administrator's time, most of the documentation for intraNetWare is online — located on a CD-ROM. The only printed documentation that is included in the intraNetWare package is the documentation you'll need to get your server up and running. The rest of the documentation is located on the CD-ROM.

Having the documentation online allows you to access the documentation from anywhere on the network. Obviously, this is more handy than having to tote two dozen manuals with you to another user's office, and much cheaper than buying multiple sets of printed documentation for multiple users. In addition, the online documentation's search features can help you locate the information you need quickly.

To allow network users to access the online documentation, you can store the documentation files on the server in a network directory, or you can mount the online documentation CD-ROM as a NetWare volume and access the documentation directly from the CD-ROM. You can also install the documentation files directly onto a workstation. However, other network users won't be able to access the documentation if it's only on one workstation, so most administrators put the documentation into a network directory.

There are two main components of the online documentation package:

▶ The documentation itself (called "document collections"), which contains the text and graphics for all the Novell manuals

▶ A viewer (made by the software manufacturer DynaText), which is the application you use to read the documentation, search through it, print pages, and so on

For users to read the online documentation, they must have access to the DynaText viewer from each of their workstations. The DynaText viewers can be run from a local disk on a workstation, or from a directory (folder) on the network. If the viewer is installed on a workstation, only that workstation user can access it (therefore, a viewer must be installed on every user's workstation individually). If the viewer is installed in a network directory, all users will be able to use it.

Novell's intraNetWare includes DynaText viewers for both Windows (or OS/2) and Mac OS workstations. The following sections describe how to install the online documentation files onto the server and how to install and use the DynaText viewers from Windows 3.1 and Windows 95 workstations.

TIP

A full set of printed documentation, which you can purchase separately, is also available. To order the printed documentation, you can send in the order form that came in your intraNetWare box or call 800-336-3892 (in the United States) or 512-834-6905.

Setting Up the Online Documentation

Installing and accessing the online documentation is a two-step process. You will use a utility called SETUPDOC.EXE from your Windows 3.1 or Windows 95 workstation.

First, you will use this utility to set up the DynaText viewer on the workstation; then you will use it to copy the online documentation files themselves either onto the workstation or into a network directory. Figure 9.1 shows the most common way the Novell online documentation is set up on networks: The Novell document collections are stored on the server, and DynaText viewers are set up on each workstation.

TIP

Although the order in which you do these steps is not really important, it is usually easier if you set up the viewers on all the workstations first. That way, you won't have to configure the viewers to find the right document collections. When you install the document collections, they will automatically be assigned to the viewers that were already set up.

When you install the documentation files, you'll be asked to select the document collections you want. A *document collection* is simply a set of documentation. For example, all the manuals that were shipped with previous versions of NetWare were contained in a single collection. The manuals in intraNetWare are divided into six different collections: one for manuals about client software, one for reference manuals, and so on.

FIGURE 9.1
The Location of the Document Collections and DynaText Viewers

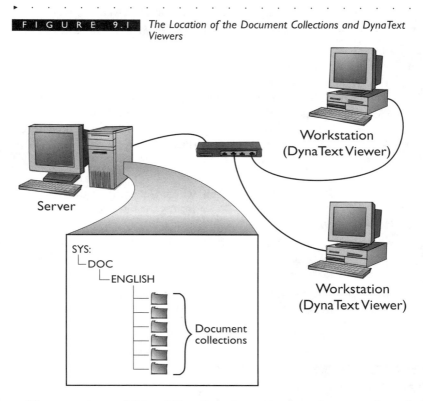

If you purchase additional Novell products, those products may have their own collections of documentation. You can add these collections to the same directory so you can access all of them from the same viewer session. You can also install document collections in more than one language, if you choose.

Setting Up the DynaText Viewer on a Workstation

The following steps explain how to set up a DynaText viewer for a Windows 3.1 or Windows 95 workstation.

TIP

You can also use this procedure to set up the DynaText viewer on an OS/2 workstation, if that computer is also running WIN-OS/2.

You can install the viewer in a network directory or on each individual workstation's hard disk. Once the viewer is set up, you can use this workstation to view the document collections — whether the collections are installed on a network directory, on a CD-ROM mounted as a NetWare volume, or on the workstation itself. (Windows-based workstations should support VGA or SVGA, be running Windows 3.1 or Windows 95, and have at least 8MB of memory.)

I. Start the SETUPDOC.EXE program, which is located on the *NetWare 4.11 Online Documentation* CD-ROM from your intraNetWare package (see Figure 9.2).

    a. If you're using Windows 3.1, choose File from the Windows Program Manager, select Run, and click Browse to choose SETUP-DOC.EXE from the documentation CD-ROM.

    b. If you're using Windows 95, click Start, choose Run, and then click Browse. Select SETUPDOC.EXE from the documentation CD-ROM.

FIGURE 9.2 *Start SETUPDOC.EXE.*

2. Following the messages that say the installation program is scanning for existing document collections and viewers, the initial installation screen appears, as shown in Figure 9.3. Under the DynaText Viewer heading, click the Install button.

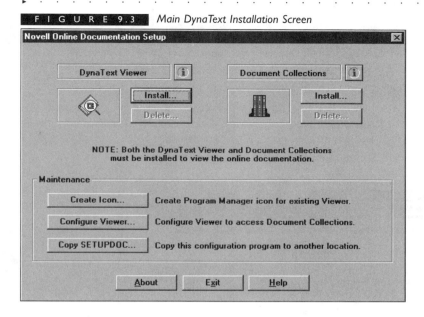

FIGURE 9.3 *Main DynaText Installation Screen*

3. Select the source directory for the DynaText viewer. The utility will display any possible source it finds or thinks you might have (such as the CD-ROM, a server's network directory, your workstation's hard disk, or diskettes). Select the CD-ROM directory, as shown in Figure 9.4.

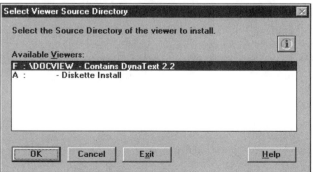

FIGURE 9.4 *Select the Source Drive for the DynaText Viewer.*

4. Select the destination directory (where you want to install the DynaText viewer). You can install it on either the local hard disk or in a network directory so all workstations can access it. By default, the proposed network directory will be a folder called DOCVIEW in the SYS volume.

5. Select the language for the viewer to use.

6. Next, you'll be shown a confirmation screen, as shown in Figure 9.5. This screen lets you confirm your source directory, destination directory, and language. Click OK to confirm your selections, and the viewer will be installed.

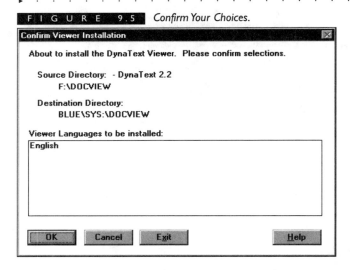

FIGURE 9.5 *Confirm Your Choices.*

7. When asked if you want to create a viewer icon, select Yes. This is the icon that will appear on your desktop. Whenever you double-click this icon, it will launch the viewer. This icon is located in a folder called DTAPPWIN, in the DOCVIEW folder, in volume SYS. (After the installation, if you use Windows 95, you may want to put a Shortcut to this icon on your desktop.)

8. After a few moments, a message appears telling you the DynaText viewer was installed successfully. Click OK.

9. When you arrive back at the main SETUPDOC menu, you can either click Exit to quit the installation program, or continue with the next section, "Installing the Online Document Collections."

10. If you've installed the viewer in a network directory, all you need to do for additional workstations to use this same viewer is to create viewer icons on their desktops. To create an icon on another workstation, run SETUPDOC on that workstation, choose Create Icon from the main menu, select the directory that contains the viewer, and choose OK. Repeat this process for additional workstations.

Installing the Online Document Collections

Now that you've installed the viewer, you can install the document collections, which contain all the online manuals.

You use the same SETUPDOC.EXE program to install the document collections. If you're still at the SETUPDOC.EXE main menu, you can skip to Step 2.

1. Start the SETUPDOC.EXE program, which is located on the *NetWare 4.11 Online Documentation* CD-ROM in your intraNetWare package.

   a. If you're using Windows 3.1, choose File from the Windows Program Manager, select Run, and click Browse to choose SETUP-DOC.EXE from the documentation CD-ROM.

   b. If you're using Windows 95, click Start, choose Run, and then click Browse. Select SETUPDOC.EXE from the documentation CD-ROM.

2. From the main installation screen, click the Install button under Document Collections.

3. Select the source directory for the document collections you want to install, as shown in Figure 9.6. The utility will display any possible source it finds or thinks you might have, such as the CD-ROM, a server's network directory if older document collections already exist, your workstation's hard disk, or diskettes. Select the CD-ROM directory.

F I G U R E   9 . 6   *Select the Source Directory for the Document Collections.*

Select Document Collection Source Directory   ☒

Select the Source Directory of the Document Collections to install.

Available **D**ocument Collection Directories:

```
F : \DOC - Contains Document Collections
A :         - Diskette Install
```

[OK]   [Cancel]   [E**x**it]   [**H**elp]

4. Select the destination for the document collections. If you want to install the files onto your workstation's hard disk, select your hard disk drive. If you want to install the files onto the network directory on the server, select that network directory. You can install the intraNetWare document collections into the same directory that contains older document collections, so you can access both sets.

5. Select the document collections you want to install. By default, all the intraNetWare 4.11 collections are selected in your language, as shown in Figure 9.7. Remember, intraNetWare and NetWare 4.11 are the same product.

6. Confirm your selections. The utility will begin copying the document collections to the destination you chose in Step 4.

7. When the document selections are successfully installed, you'll be returned to the main installation screen. You can either click Exit to quit the installation program, or you can click the Configure Viewer button to make sure the viewer is configured the way you want it. If you choose Configure Viewer, complete the following steps:

a. Select the path for the viewer you just installed (on the network directory or the workstation's local disk), and then click Configure. (Don't select the path to the CD-ROM.)

b. The top list shows the document collections that the viewer is currently configured to access. If you installed the viewer first, and then the document collections second, the document collections you installed should appear in the top list (see Figure 9.8).

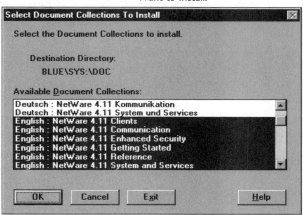

FIGURE 9.7 *Select the Document Collections You Want to Install.*

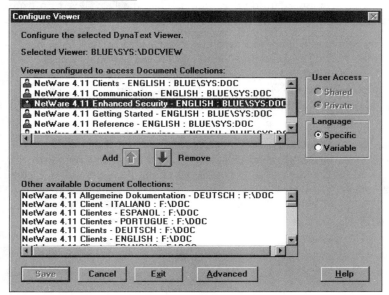

FIGURE 9.8 *Verify That the Document Collections Are Correct.*

The bottom list in this screen shows any additional document collections that may be installed — but aren't yet assigned to the viewer. To move a collection from the bottom ("Available") list into the top list, double-click the desired collection.

c. For the collections listed in the top list, make sure User Access is marked as Shared (instead of Private) if you want all network users to have access to the collections. Keep Language set to Specific (instead of Variable). (Highlight a collection to see if this button is marked.)

d. When you're finished making changes, select Save. If you didn't make any changes, click Exit to quit the installation program.

Now your viewer and your document collections are both installed. You can use the viewer to read the online documentation, as described in the next section.

Using the DynaText Viewer

After the viewers and the document collections are installed, you can access the online documentation. To do this, double-click the DynaText icon from your workstation to start up the viewer.

TIP By default, this icon is located in a folder called DTAPPWIN, in the DOCVIEW folder, in volume SYS. However, you may have selected a different location for the viewer during its installation. If so, look for the viewer in that location. (If you use Windows 95, you may want to put a Shortcut to this icon on your desktop.)

When the main DynaText window appears, it lists all the available document collections in the left-hand column. The right-hand column shows the individual books that are included in that collection. For example, in Figure 9.9, the collection called "NetWare 4.11 Clients" is highlighted in the left column. The right column lists all the manuals that are available in that collection.

The Main DynaText Screen Shows the Books Included in a
Document Collection.

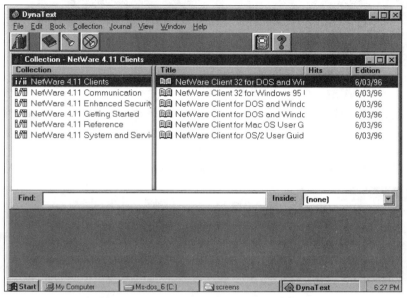

Highlight a different NetWare 4.11 collection in the left column to list all
of the manuals included in that collection.

To open a manual, simply double-click its title. The manual will appear on
the workstation screen. As illustrated in Figure 9.10, the manual's table of contents appears on the left side of the screen, and the chapter's text appears on
the right.

Once you've opened the book, you can navigate through it in the
following ways:

► Scroll through the text page by page, using the up-arrow and down-
  arrow keys or the scroll bar.

► Move quickly to different sections of the book by clicking a heading in
  the Table of Contents.

► Click a plus sign (+) next to a heading in the Table of Contents to display the subheadings beneath that topic.

► Search for specific words or phrases in a book by typing those words
  in the Find field, located toward the bottom of the DynaText screen.

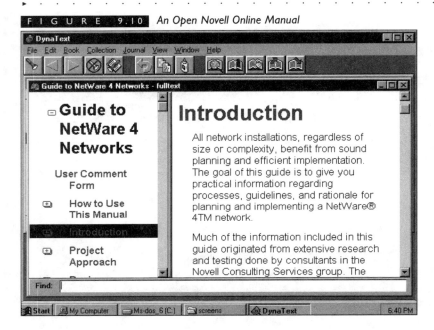

F I G U R E   9.10 *An Open Novell Online Manual*

▶ Click "links" (or cross-references) in a manual's text. These links will appear in a different color and will be underlined. If you click a link, it will take you to the location of the related information instantly. This information may be located in another section of the manual, or in a completely different manual. If the link takes you to another manual, DynaText will automatically open that book for you in a new, second window. To return to the previous book you were reading, close this second book's window.

▶ Choose Go Back from the Book menu if you want to return to a previous section you were reading in the same manual.

Beyond the Basics

You can find more information about the following topics in Novell's manual, *Installing and Using Novell Online Documentation*. This manual is available in printed form in your intraNetWare package; it is also available online after you've installed the Novell online documentation:

- ▶ Installing DynaText viewers on a Macintosh workstation
- ▶ Installing additional document collections, allowing access to multiple languages, or customizing other aspects of the online documentation

CHAPTER 10

Disaster Planning and Troubleshooting

Instant Access

Planning Disasters

▸ Write an emergency plan, including emergency contacts and procedures.

▸ Keep good records of your network, including hardware settings, inventory, and so on.

▸ When troubleshooting a problem, isolate the problem and try solutions one at a time.

Why Plan for Disasters?

Disasters come in many guises. A disaster that affects your network could be anything from a crashed hard disk on your server, to a security breach, to a fire that destroys your building. When it comes to computers, a malfunctioning water sprinkler system can cause as much damage as a hurricane.

If your company depends on your network to do business daily, every day — or even hour — that the network is out of commission means lost revenue. Therefore, getting the network back up and functioning is a priority for most businesses after a disaster.

The best way to recover from a disaster, regardless of the type of disaster, is to have planned for it ahead of time. Armed with a disaster plan, good backups, and accurate records of your network, the task of re-establishing your network will not seem nearly as daunting.

Planning Ahead

If you haven't already created a disaster plan — do it today. It doesn't need to be a difficult task, and it could save you a tremendous amount of wasted time, frustrated users, lost revenue, and sleepless nights. An earthquake or electrical fire isn't going to wait for a convenient time in your schedule to occur, so the sooner you plan for it, the better.

Be sure to document the plan. Write it down, get it approved by your organization's upper management, and then make copies and store them in several locations so you'll be able to find at least one copy if disaster strikes.

It's important to have a documented plan because having the plan in your head only works if you happen to be around, of course. In some cases, though, it's even more important to have the plan approved by management. If you've gotten the CEO to approve your plan to restore the production department's network before the administration department's, you won't have to deal with politics and egos while you're trying to restring cables.

What should be included in a disaster plan? Everyone's disaster plan will be different, but there are a few key points to consider when planning yours:

> ► Decide where you will store your emergency plan. It needs to be in a location where you or others can get to it easily. Ideally, there should be multiple copies of the plan, perhaps assigned to different individuals. Just storing the emergency plan in your office will not be adequate

if the building burns down, so you may consider storing a copy offsite, such as in a safety deposit box or even at your home.

- List people to call in case of an emergency and include their names, home phone numbers, pager numbers, and cellular phone numbers in your emergency plan. Remember to list key network personnel, such as any network administrators for various branches of the NDS tree, personnel who perform the weekly and daily backups, and so on. You may want to include names of security personnel who should be notified in case of a potential security breach.

- Plan the order in which you will restore service to your company. Who needs to be back online first? Is there a critical department that should be restored before any other? Are there key individuals who need to be reconnected first?

- Once you've identified the key people who need to be reconnected, determine if there is an order to the files or services they'll need. Which servers need to be restored first? What applications must those users have immediately? Which files will they need to access?

- Document the location of your network records. Where do you keep your hardware inventory, purchase requisitions, backup logs, and so forth?

- Document the location of your network backup tapes or disks. Don't forget to document instructions for restoring files — or indicate the location of the backup system's documentation — in case the backup operator is unavailable. Record your backup rotation schedule so other people can figure out how to restore the network files efficiently.

- Include a drawing of the network layout, showing the exact location of cables, servers, workstations, and other computers. Highlight the critical components, so anyone else reading your plan will know at a glance where to find the priority servers.

Keeping Good Records of Your Network

Another line in your defense against disaster is to maintain up-to-date records about your network. When something goes wrong with your network, it is much easier to spot the problem if you have accurate documentation.

Good network documentation isn't just helpful in an emergency. Doing paperwork is always a distasteful task, but you'll be thankful you did it the next time you have to add new hardware to the network, resolve an interrupt conflict, justify your hardware budget to management, get a workstation repaired under warranty, call for technical support, or train a new assistant.

How you track your network information is up to you. You may want to keep a three-ring binder with printed information about the network, or you may prefer to keep the information online in databases or spreadsheets.

However you document your network, be sure you keep the information in more than one location. If a disaster occurs, you don't want to lose your only copy of the information that can help you restore the network quickly. Try to keep copies of your network information in separate buildings, if possible, so you won't lose everything if you can't access one building.

What types of network information should you record? Again, networks vary, so your documentation needs will vary, too. However, the following types of information are recommended:

▶ An inventory of hardware and software purchases. Record the product's version number, serial number, vendor, purchase date, length of warranty, and so on. This can help you when management asks for current capital assets or budget-planning information. It can also help you with insurance reports and replacements if a loss occurs.

▶ A record of configuration settings for servers, workstations, printers, and other hardware. This information can save you hours that you would otherwise spend locating and resolving interrupt conflicts.

▶ A history of hardware repairs. You may want to file all paperwork associated with repairs along with the paperwork that documents your original purchase of the item.

▶ A drawing of the network layout. If you store this with your disaster plan, you (and others) will be able to locate critical components quickly. On the drawing, show how all the workstations, servers, printers, and other equipment are connected. The drawing doesn't have to be to scale, but it should show each machine in its approximate location. Label each workstation with its make and model, its location, and its user. Show the cables (and indicate the types of cable) that connect the hardware.

▶ Batch files and workstation boot files. Use a text editor or other program to print out these files and keep them with the worksheets that document the workstation. You may also want to store copies of the files on diskette. If you need to reinstall the workstation, you can re-create the user's environment quickly if you have archived these files.

▶ Backup information. It is important to record your backup rotation schedule, the location of backup tapes or disks, the names of any backup operators, the labeling system you use on your backup tapes or disks, and any other information someone may need if you're not around to restore the system.

Troubleshooting Tips

Unfortunately, despite the best possible planning, something may go wrong with your network. The majority of network problems are related to hardware issues — interrupt conflicts, faulty components, incompatible hardware, and so on. However, software creates its own set of problems, such as application incompatibility, Windows bugs and incompatibility, and installation errors.

There are endless combinations of servers, workstations, cabling, networking hardware, operating systems, and applications. This makes it impossible to predict and document every possible problem. The best anyone can do is to use a methodical system for isolating the problem, and then fixing it.

The following troubleshooting guidelines can help you isolate the problem and find solutions.

NARROW DOWN THE LIST OF SUSPECTS

First, of course, you need to try to narrow your search to suspicious areas by answering the following types of questions:

▶ Were there any error messages? If so, look up their explanations in the *NetWare 4.11 System Messages* online manual. This manual explains thousands of messages (some of them error messages, some of them simply informational) that may appear on the server or a workstation. Use the DynaText viewer from a workstation to read the Novell online documentation, as explained in Chapter 9.

▶ How many machines did the problem affect? If multiple machines were affected, the problem is affecting the network and could be related to the network cabling or network software. If the problem is isolated to one workstation, the problem is most likely contained within the workstation's own hardware or software configuration.

▶ Can you identify a particular cabling segment or branch of the Directory tree that has the problem? This will help you isolate likely problem candidates.

▶ Does the problem occur only when a user accesses a particular application, or does it occur only when the user executes applications in a particular order? This could indicate an application problem that has nothing to do with the network. It could be related to the workstation's memory, to a conflict between two applications or devices that both expect to use the same port or address, or the like.

▶ If the problem occurred when you installed new workstations or servers on the network, have you checked their network addresses and hardware settings for conflicts with other boards or with machines that already exist on the network? Also double-check the installation documentation to make sure you didn't misspell a command or accidentally skip a step.

▶ If a user is having trouble working with files or applications, have you checked the security features? Does the user have appropriate rights in the necessary directories? Are the files already opened by someone else? Have the files or directories been assigned attributes that restrict the user from some actions? See Chapter 6 for more information about network security.

▶ Is a user missing some of his or her DOS path commands? Look in the login scripts for search drive mappings that were mapped without using the INS keyword (which inserts the mapping into the DOS path instead of overwriting existing paths). See Chapter 5 for more information about login scripts and search drives.

▶ For printing problems, have you checked that the printer, print server, and print queue are all correctly assigned to each other? You can use the NetWare Administrator utility to check your printing setup. Select the print server from the Browser, choose Details from the object menu, and then open the Print Layout page to see whether the print server, printer, and queue are all assigned together correctly. See Chapter 8 for more information about network printing.

▶ Do you have a volume that won't mount? If so, you may need to run VREPAIR.NLM to fix it. (However, VREPAIR will usually run automatically if intraNetWare detects a problem with a volume.) See the Novell documentation for more information about running VREPAIR.

▶ Are all of the servers in the Directory tree running the same version of DS.NLM? If all servers are not running the same version, some conflicts could occur. See Chapter 4 for more information about NDS and DS.NLM.

▶ Have you verified that applications are using the correct print drivers for your printers? See Chapter 8 for more information about network printing.

CHECK THE HARDWARE

Hardware problems can be relatively common in networks. Network cables are notorious for developing problems, partly because of the abuse they get from being coiled up, walked on, bent around corners, and so on. A network analyzer, such as NetWare LANalyzer, can be a useful tool for diagnosing cable problems. As you diagnose hardware problems, keep the following tips in mind:

▶ Cables have an annoying tendency to work loose from their connectors — seemingly all by themselves — so check all connections between cables and boards first.

▶ Test suspicious cables by replacing them with cables you know are working, and then see if the problem persists.

▶ Ensure that cables are terminated correctly and don't exceed length limits. Also ensure that the cables are not connected into endless loops (unless you're using a topology that permits loops).

▶ If the problem is with a computer or printer, try disconnecting the problematic machinery from the network and running it in standalone mode. If the problem still shows up in standalone mode, it's probably not a problem with the network connection. You can then eliminate the network components and concentrate on the configuration of the machine itself.

▶ Isolate sections of the network segment until the problem disappears. Add each section back to the network one at a time until you have identified the problem cable, board, connector, terminator, or other component.

▶ If the problem occurred when you installed a new workstation or server, or added a board to an existing computer, check hardware settings for conflicts with other boards or with machines that already exist on the network.

REFER TO THE DOCUMENTATION

Forget the jokes about only reading the manual as a last resort. The intraNetWare online manuals contain explanations of the error messages that may occur. In addition, they include troubleshooting tips, configuration instructions, and so on.

Be sure to check the manufacturer's documentation for any network hardware or applications you're using. Some applications have special instructions for installing them on a network.

LOOK FOR PATCHES OR WORKAROUNDS

Despite rigorous testing, every software product on the market is subject to bugs or unexpected problems. Novell's intraNetWare is no exception. When Novell engineers find a problem with intraNetWare, they usually solve the problem with either a patch (a piece of software that loads as an NLM on your server and repairs it) or a recommended workaround.

Novell distributes these patches and workarounds on its Internet Web site, www.novell.com. It's a good idea to periodically check this Web site to see if there are any new downloadable files that can help solve your problems.

TRY EACH SOLUTION BY ITSELF

After you've isolated the problem, try implementing the solutions you've found one at a time. Start with the easiest, cheapest solution, and work up from there.

Most of us give in to the tendency to try several possible fixes simultaneously to save time. Trying solutions simultaneously may save time in the short run, but it could cost you extra money for unnecessary repairs or replacements. For example, if you change the cable, the network board, and reinstall the intraNetWare client software all at the same time, you will have no way of knowing which one was the real solution. You may have just wasted money on a new network board unnecessarily.

In addition, if you try several fixes at once, you won't know for sure what fixed the problem, so you'll have to start from scratch again if the problem reappears on another machine or at another time.

DOCUMENT THE SOLUTION

When you find a solution, write it down and store it with your network documentation. This may prevent you or someone else from going through the same troubleshooting process to fix a similar problem later.

Beyond the Basics

There is a wide variety of places you can go to get help, advice, tips, and fixes for your intraNetWare problems or questions. These resources range from Novell technical support, to Internet user groups, to classes, to publications that deal with intraNetWare support issues. If you're looking for help or information, try some of these ideas:

▶ You can often find the technical help you need online, through the Internet Usenet groups that focus on NetWare and intraNetWare or through the Novell Web site on the Internet, www.novell.com.

▶ Try calling your reseller or consultant for help.

▶ Novell's technical support is available by calling 1-800-NETWARE. However, Novell's technical support is not free. You'll be charged a fee for each incident, so have your credit card handy. (An incident may involve more than one phone call, if necessary.) Before you call technical support, be sure you've tried your other resources first — especially the documentation. It's embarrassing and expensive to have technical support tell you that the answer to your question is on page 25 of the installation manual.

▶ The main Novell information number, 1-800-NETWARE, is also your inroad to all types of information about Novell or its products. By calling this number, you can obtain information about Novell products, the locations of your nearest resellers, pricing information, and so on.

▶ To order the printed manuals for intraNetWare, you can use the order form that came in your intraNetWare box, or call 800-336-3892 (in the United States) or 512-834-6905.

▶ The *Novell Application Notes* is a useful resource for network management information. Called AppNotes for short, this is a monthly publication put out by the Novell Research Department, and each issue contains research reports and articles on a wide range of advanced topics. To order a subscription, call 1-800-377-4136 in the U.S.A., or 303-297-2725 worldwide.

▶ IntraNetWare classes are taught at over 1,000 Novell Authorized Education Centers (NAECs) throughout the world. These classes typically offer the best way to get some direct, hands-on training in just a few days. Some of the classes are also available in Computer-Based Training (CBT) form, in case you'd rather work through the material at your own pace, on your own workstation, than attend a class. For more information about Novell Education classes or to find the nearest NAEC near you, call 1-800-233-3382. To purchase a CBT version of a class, contact your nearest NAEC.

► There are also numerous organizations that provide classes and seminars on intraNetWare. Some of these unauthorized classes are quite good. Others are probably of lower quality, because Novell does not have any control over their course content or instructor qualifications. If you choose an unauthorized provider for your NetWare classes, try to talk to others who have taken a class from the provider before, so you'll have a better idea of how good the class is.

► NetWare Users International (NUI) is a nonprofit association for networking professionals. They sponsor more than 250 Novell user groups worldwide. NUI user groups provides a forum for networking professionals to meet face to face, to learn from each other, to trade recommendations, or just to share war stories. There's usually no fee — or a very low fee — for joining an NUI user group. Membership also gives you a free subscription to *NetWare Connection*, described in the next bulleted point. For more information or to join an NUI user group, call 800-228-4NUI or send a fax to 801-228-4577.

► *NetWare Connection* is a bimonthly magazine that provides feature articles on new technologies, network management tips, product reviews, NUI news, and other helpful information. Membership in NUI gives you a free subscription. However, you can also get a free subscription just by faxing your name, address, and request for a subscription to 801-228-4576. You can also mail NUI a request at:

NetWare Connection
P.O. Box 1928
Orem, UT 84059-1928
USA

intraNetWare Utilities and NLMs

Instant Access

Using Utilities

► IntraNetWare workstation utilities are applications or commands you run from a network workstation. There are different utilities for the different tasks you can perform on the network, and different utilities for each workstation platform (DOS, Windows 3.1, Windows 95, and so on).

► IntraNetWare console utilities are commands you execute from the server's console (or from a Remote Console session running on a workstation). These utilities are generally used to affect the server's operation.

► NLMs (NetWare Loadable Modules) are software modules that you load into the server's operating system to add or change functionality in the server.

Using intraNetWare Utilities

The three main types of intraNetWare utilities that you can use when working on the network are as follows:

- *Workstation utilities* — These utilities are applications or commands you run from a network workstation.

- *Console utilities* — These are commands you execute from the server's console (or from a Remote Console session running on a workstation).

- *NLMs (NetWare Loadable Modules)* — NLMs are software modules that you load into the server's operating system to add or change functionality in the server.

This appendix lists all of the available intraNetWare utilities in alphabetical order, regardless of type. Some are common utilities you will use often. Others are used less frequently or rarely, and may be associated with some of the more advanced or obscure features of intraNetWare that aren't discussed in this book, such as NetWare/IP, NetWare for Macintosh, or NetWare SFT III (System Fault Tolerant Level III). However, even these advanced utilities are listed here for your convenience.

Each type of utility (workstation, console, or NLM) is executed differently, as explained in the following sections.

NOTE In many cases, to execute the utility, you simply type the name of the utility at the DOS prompt (for workstation utilities) or at the server prompt (for console utilities and NLMs). Where there are parameters or options you must enter along with the utility name, the command format to use is indicated.

USING WORKSTATION UTILITIES

How you execute a workstation utility depends on the type of utility it is, and the workstation operating system you're using. Workstation utilities are generally used to work with network services, such as the NDS tree, printing services, and so on.

To execute an intraNetWare utility that runs in DOS (such as NCOPY), you type the utility's name, plus any additional parameters that may be necessary, at a DOS prompt on the workstation. (These are often called *command-line utilities*, because you execute them by typing a command.) Some intraNetWare utilities that run in DOS may display menus, from which you choose the tasks or options you want. (These are called *menu utilities*.)

TIP

If you're using Windows 3.1 or Windows 95, you may also be able to run a DOS-based intraNetWare utility from the MS-DOS Prompt feature inside Windows. (Accessing the MS-DOS Prompt from Windows is sometimes called *opening a DOS box*.) However, occasionally Windows 3.1 and Windows 95 exhibit some incompatibilities with DOS-based programs, so not all intraNetWare utilities may work from within a DOS box.

To execute an intraNetWare utility that runs in Windows or Windows 95 (such as NetWare Administrator), you have to add the utility to your workstation's desktop first. To do this, you use the normal Windows or Windows 95 method for adding a new application's icon. Most intraNetWare workstation utilities have online help.

► To read help for an intraNetWare command-line utility that runs in DOS, type the name of the utility, followed by /?. For example, to see help for the CAPTURE command, type **CAPTURE /?**.

► To read help for an intraNetWare menu utility that runs in DOS, press the F1 key while you're in the menu.

► To read help for intraNetWare utilities running in Windows 3.1 or Windows 95, click the Help button that appears on the utility's screen.

The following workstation utilities are described in this appendix:

ADDICON	MENUMAKE	NetWare User Tools
ATOTAL	MIGPRINT	NLIST
AUDITCON	MIGRATE	NLS Manager
CAPTURE	NCOPY	NMENU
COLORPAL	NCUPDATE	NPATH
CX	NDIR	NPRINT
DOSGEN	NDS Manager	NPRINTER.EXE
DS Migrate	NETADMIN	NPTWIN95.EXE
FILER	NETUSER	NVER
FLAG	NetWare Administrator	NWXTRACT
LOGIN	NetWare Application	PARTMGR
LOGOUT	Launcher	PCONCOLE
MAP	NetWare Application	PRINTCON
MENUCNVT	Manager	PRINTDEF
	NetWare File Migration	

PSC   SEND   UIMPORT
PURGE   SETPASS   WHOAMI
RCONSOLE   SETTTS   WSUPDATE
RENDIR   SETUPDOC
RIGHTS   SYSTIME

USING CONSOLE UTILITIES

Console utilities, such as MOUNT, are commands that you execute by typing a command at the server's console.

TIP

You can also execute console utilities from a Remote Console session running on a workstation. See Chapter 2 for instructions on setting up a Remote Console session on your workstation.

In general, you use console commands to change some aspect of the server or view information about it. Console utilities are built into the operating system, just as internal DOS commands are built into DOS.

To read online help for console utilities, use the HELP console utility. Use the following command format, substituting the name of the utility (such as SCAN FOR NEW DEVICES) for *utility*:

```
HELP utility
```

The following console utilities are described in this appendix:

ABORT REMIRROR   DISMOUNT   LOAD
ACTIVATE SERVER   DISPLAY NETWORKS   MAGAZINE
ADD NAME SPACE   DISPLAY SERVERS   MEDIA
ALIAS   DOWN   MEMORY
BIND   ENABLE LOGIN   MEMORY MAP
BINDERY   ENABLE TTS   MIRROR STATUS
BROADCAST   EXIT   MODULES
CD   HALT   MOUNT
CLEAR STATION   HCSS   NAME
CLS   HELP   OFF
CONFIG   INITIALIZE SYSTEM   PROTOCOL
DISABLE LOGIN   LANGUAGE   REGISTER MEMORY
DISABLE TTS   LIST DEVICES

REINITIALIZE SYSTEM	SEARCH	TIME
	SECURE CONSOLE	TRACK OFF
REMIRROR PARTITION	SEND	TRACK ON
	SERVER.EXE	UNBIND
REMOVE DOS	SET	UNLOAD
RESET ROUTER	SET TIME	UPS STATUS
RESTART	SET TIME ZONE	UPS TIME
RESTART SERVER	SPEED	VERSION
SCAN FOR NEW DEVICES	SPOOL	VOLUMES

USING NLMS

NetWare Loadable Modules (NLMs), such as INSTALL and MONITOR, are software modules that can add functionality to a server. They can allow the server to support Mac OS files, provide backup services, support different protocols, install new features, and so on.

Many NLMs are installed automatically with the intraNetWare operating system. Others are optional; you can load them if your particular situation requires them. One of the nice features of NLMs is that you can load and unload them while the server is running. You don't have to reboot the server to make the new NLMs take effect — they are immediately effective.

NOTE

Many NLMs that can be used on an intraNetWare server are also available from third-party companies. Third-party NLM products may include backup software, UPS management software, and the like. See the documentation that comes with these products for more information about their NLMs.

There are four types of NLMs that you can use to add different types of functionality to your server: NLMs, name space modules, LAN drivers, and disk drivers. These types of NLMs are described in Chapter 2.

Once loaded, many NLMs have their own status screen that displays continuously on the server. Because you can have multiple NLMs running simultaneously, you may have multiple active NLM screens, but you can only see one at a time. To move between active NLM screens on the server's console, press Alt-Esc to cycle through the available NLM screens. You can also press Ctrl-Esc to bring up a list of all available screens, from which you can select one.

load NLMs, type the following command, replacing *modules* with the name of the NLM (you do not need to type the .NLM extension in the LOAD command):

LOAD *module*

For example, to load MONITOR.NLM, type:

LOAD MONITOR

To unload an NLM, use the UNLOAD command in the same way. For example, to unload MONITOR.NLM, type:

UNLOAD MONITOR

This appendix describes the core NLMs. Many NLMs have related NLMs that automatically load when necessary. These "autoloaded" NLMs are not listed here, as you should never need to load them manually. The following NLMs are described in this appendix:

ADSP.NLM	FILTCFG.NLM	NFS.NAM
AFP.NLM	HCSS.NLM	NPAMS.NLM
AFPCON.NLM	HFSCD.NLM	NPRINTER.NLM
AIOCOMX.NLM	HFSCDCON.NLM	NWIP.NLM
APPLETLK.NLM	HFSLFS.NLM	NWIPCFG.NLM
ATCON.NLM	INETCFG.NLM	NWPA.NLM
ATCONFIG.NLM	INSTALL.NLM	PING.NLM
ATFLT.NLM	IPCONFIG.NLM	PSERVER.NLM
ATPS.NLM	IPFLT.NLM	PUPGRADE.NLM
ATPSCON.NLM	IPXCON.NLM	REMAPID.NLM
ATTOKLLC.NLM	IPXFLT.NLM	REMOTE.NLM
ATXRP.NLM	IPXPING.NLM	ROUTE.NLM
AURP.NLM	KEYB.NLM	RPL.NLM
CDROM.NLM	LONG.NAM	RS232.NLM
CONLOG.NLM	MAC.NAM	RSPX.NLM
DHCPCFG.NLM	MACFILE.NLM	SBACKUP.NLM
DS.NLM	MONITOR.NLM	SCHDELAY.NLM
DSMERGE.NLM	MPDRIVER.NLM	SERVMAN.NLM
DSREPAIR.NLM	NETSYNC3.NLM	SPXCONFG.NLM
EDIT.NLM	NETSYNC4.NLM	TCPCON.NLM

TCPIP.NLM	UNICON.NLM	V_MAC.NLM
TECHWALK.NLM	UPS.NLM	V_NFS.NLM
TIMESYNC.NLM	UPS_AIO.NLM	VIEW.NLM
TPING.NLM	V_LONG.NLM	VREPAIR.NLM

The Utilities and NLMs

The core intraNetWare utilities and NLMs are explained in the following sections.

ABORT REMIRROR (Console Utility)

Use this utility at the server to stop disk partitions from remirroring. Use the following command format, replacing *number* with the number of the logical disk partition you want to stop from remirroring:

```
ABORT REMIRROR number
```

NOTE

You can set up a server's hard disks so that they are "mirrored" to each other. (Actually, the disks' partitions are mirrored.) This means that all network data is copied to both hard disks, so that they are identical. That way, if one hard disk fails, the other disk takes over seamlessly, so that the network data is still available.

If the two disks have gotten out of sync so that they don't contain identical data, *remirroring* will bring them back into synchronization. See the Novell documentation for more information about disk mirroring.

ACTIVATE SERVER (Console Utility)

Use this utility on an SFT III server to load the MSENGINE on the servers, which synchronizes the servers' memory and mirrors their disks.

NOTE

SFT III is a flavor of intraNetWare that lets you install the network operating system on two identical servers that run simultaneously. The servers' hard disks and other hardware are "mirrored" to each other, so that they store identical information. That way, if one server goes down, the other server takes over seamlessly, so that network service is uninterrupted. See the Novell documentation for more information about SFT III.

ADD NAME SPACE (Console Utility)

Use this utility at the server console to add support for a name space (LONG.NAM for OS/2, Windows 95, and Windows NT files, MAC.NAM for Macintosh files, and NFS.NAM for UNIX files). See Chapter 2 for more information about name space modules.

Use the following command format, replacing *name* with the name of the name space module (such as MAC), and *volume* with the volume's name:

```
ADD NAME SPACE name TO volume
```

To display the name spaces currently loaded, just type:

```
ADD NAME SPACE
```

ADDICON (Workstation Utility)

Use this utility on a Windows 3.1 workstation to add icons to the Windows Program Manager. ADDICON can be executed at the DOS prompt or in a login script. It modifies an existing Program Manager group file (named with the extension .GRP) to add the icon to the group's window. Use the following command format, replacing *parameter* with one of the parameters shown in Table A.1:

```
ADDICON parameter
```

TABLE A.1 *ADDICON Parameters*

PARAMETER	DESCRIPTION
CMD=*parameters*	Indicates any command parameters necessary for the application.
DESC=*text*	Describes the application (the default is the executable file's name).
EXE=*filename*	Indicates the name of the executable file for the application.
GROUP=*group*	Indicates the name of the Program Manager group.
GROUPFILE=*filename*	Specifies the particular .GRP file to modify. Use this parameter instead of the GROUP and WINDOWS parameters.
/H	Displays online help.
ICON=*filename*	Specifies the file that contains the icon, if it isn't contained in the executable file for the application.

(continued)

TABLE A.1	ADDICON Parameters (continued)
PARAMETER	**DESCRIPTION**
MIN=yes/no	Set to Yes if you want to set the Minimize attribute. (Default is No.)
WINDOWS=path	Indicates the path to the Windows directory. If you omit this parameter, ADDICON searches the PATH environment for the WIN.COM file.
WORK=path	Indicates the working directory of the application.
@script	Indicates a script file that contains all of the necessary parameters. If you use this parameter, omit all other parameters from the ADDICON command.

ADSP (NLM)

Load this NLM on the server to load the AppleTalk Data Stream Protocol (if you are installing NetWare for Macintosh). This protocol allows applications to communicate over AppleTalk networks. If you are using the NetWare Client for Mac OS, you do not need to use this module.

NOTE NetWare for Macintosh is an older Novell product that lets you add Macintosh workstations to a Novell network via an AppleTalk router. NetWare for Macintosh is still supported by intraNetWare. However, intraNetWare contains new client software for Mac OS workstations that eliminates the need to install NetWare for Macintosh. This new client software lets you connect Mac OS workstations directly to the network using IPX. See the Novell documentation for more information about adding Macintoshes to your network.

AFP (NLM)

Load this NLM on the server to install support for the AppleTalk Filing Protocol 2.0 on the server, if you are using the NetWare for Macintosh product. If you are using the NetWare Client for Mac OS, you do not need to use this module.

NOTE NetWare for Macintosh is an older Novell product that lets you add Macintosh workstations to a Novell network via an AppleTalk router. NetWare for Macintosh is still supported by intraNetWare. However, intraNetWare contains new client software for Mac OS workstations that eliminates the need to install NetWare for Macintosh. This new client software lets you connect Mac OS workstations directly to the network using IPX. See the Novell documentation for more information about adding Macintoshes to your network.

AFPCON (NLM)

Load this NLM on the server to configure the AppleTalk Filing Protocol (AFP.NLM), if you are using the NetWare for Macintosh product. If you are using the NetWare Client for Mac OS, you do not need to use this NLM.

NOTE

NetWare for Macintosh is an older Novell product that lets you add Macintosh workstations to a Novell network via an AppleTalk router. NetWare for Macintosh is still supported by intraNetWare. However, intraNetWare contains new client software for Mac OS workstations that eliminates the need to install NetWare for Macintosh. This new client software lets you connect Mac OS workstations directly to the network using IPX. See the Novell documentation for more information about adding Macintoshes to your network.

AIOCOMX (NLM)

Load this NLM, which is a communications port driver, on the server to use with utilities such as Remote Console, if you are using asynchronous communications (for example, if you're using Remote Console to access a server across a modem). See Chapter 2 for more information about using Remote Console.

ALIAS (Console Utility)

Use this utility at the server to create an alias for a particular console utility or command, so you can type the alias — rather than the regular utility name — to execute the utility. Use the following command format, replacing *alias* with the new command you want to be able to type, and *command* with the original utility name or command you want to execute when you type the alias:

```
ALIAS alias command
```

APPLETLK (NLM)

Use this NLM to load the AppleTalk protocol stack on the server, if you are using the NetWare for Macintosh product. Use it to create an AppleTalk router on the server to support AppleTalk networks connected to the intraNetWare network. If you are using the NetWare Client for Mac OS, you do not need to use this NLM.

NOTE

NetWare for Macintosh is an older Novell product that lets you add Macintosh workstations to a Novell network via an AppleTalk router. NetWare for Macintosh is still supported by intraNetWare. However, intraNetWare contains new client software for Mac OS workstations that eliminates the need to install NetWare for Macintosh. This new client software lets you connect Mac OS workstations directly to the network using IPX. See the Novell documentation for more information about adding Macintoshes to your network.

ATCON (NLM)

Load this NLM on the server to monitor and configure the AppleTalk protocol stack and AppleTalk router on the server, if you are using the NetWare for Macintosh product.

ATCON lets you see the status of the AppleTalk Update-based Router protocol, which lets AppleTalk be tunneled through IP. ATCON also lets you see information about network interfaces, manage the error log files, do a Name Binding Protocol (NBP) look-up of network entities, see statistics about AppleTalk packets, display the configuration of the AppleTalk router, and so on.

When using ATCON, press the F1 key to read help for each option.

NOTE

NetWare for Macintosh is an older Novell product that lets you add Macintosh workstations to a Novell network via an AppleTalk router. NetWare for Macintosh is still supported by intraNetWare. However, intraNetWare contains new client software for Mac OS workstations that eliminates the need to install NetWare for Macintosh. This new client software lets you connect Mac OS workstations directly to the network using IPX. See the Novell documentation for more information about adding Macintoshes to your network.

ATCONFIG (NLM)

Load this NLM on the server to configure NetWare for Macintosh after installation. When you use INSTALL.NLM to install NetWare for Macintosh, this NLM is loaded automatically, allowing you to configure the newly installed product. You can also load ATCONFIG.NLM separately later to change the configuration. If you are using the NetWare Client for Mac OS, you do not need to use this NLM.

NOTE

NetWare for Macintosh is an older Novell product that lets you add Macintosh workstations to a Novell network via an AppleTalk router. NetWare for Macintosh is still supported by intraNetWare. However, intraNetWare contains new client software for Mac OS workstations that eliminates the need to install NetWare for Macintosh. This new client software lets you connect Mac OS workstations directly to the network using IPX. See the Novell documentation for more information about adding Macintoshes to your network.

ATFLT (NLM)

Load this AppleTalk filter NLM on the server to restrict how routers see and communicate with other AppleTalk routers, if you are using the NetWare for Macintosh product.

NOTE

NetWare for Macintosh is an older Novell product that lets you add Macintosh workstations to a Novell network via an AppleTalk router. NetWare for Macintosh is still supported by intraNetWare. However, intraNetWare contains new client software for Mac OS workstations that eliminates the need to install NetWare for Macintosh. This new client software lets you connect Mac OS workstations directly to the network using IPX. See the Novell documentation for more information about adding Macintoshes to your network.

ATOTAL (Workstation Utility)

Use this utility at a workstation's DOS prompt to create a report totaling the usage statistics tracked by the accounting feature on a server.

To display the totals on a workstation screen, type **ATOTAL**.

To redirect the output of ATOTAL's report to a text file, use the following command format, substituting a file name for *filename*:

```
ATOTAL > filename
```

NOTE

intraNetWare's accounting feature lets you keep track of how people are using your network and lets you charge them for that usage. With accounting you can charge for the time those users are logged in, the types of resources they use, and so on. See the Novell documentation for more information about setting up accounting on your network.

ATPS (NLM)

Load this NLM on the server to support AppleTalk Print Services, if you are using the NetWare for Macintosh product. If you are using the NetWare Client for Mac OS, you do not need to use this NLM.

NOTE

NetWare for Macintosh is an older Novell product that lets you add Macintosh workstations to a Novell network via an AppleTalk router. NetWare for Macintosh is still supported by intraNetWare. However, intraNetWare contains new client software for Mac OS workstations that eliminates the need to install NetWare for Macintosh. This new client software lets you connect Mac OS workstations directly to the network using IPX. See the Novell documentation for more information about adding Macintoshes to your network.

ATPSCON (NLM)

Load this NLM on the server to configure ATPS.NLM, if you are using the NetWare for Macintosh product. If you are using the NetWare Client for Mac OS, you do not need to use this NLM.

NOTE

NetWare for Macintosh is an older Novell product that lets you add Macintosh workstations to a Novell network via an AppleTalk router. NetWare for Macintosh is still supported by intraNetWare. However, intraNetWare contains new client software for Mac OS workstations that eliminates the need to install NetWare for Macintosh. This new client software lets you connect Mac OS workstations directly to the network using IPX. See the Novell documentation for more information about adding Macintoshes to your network.

ATTOKLLC (NLM)

Load this NLM on the server to support Mac OS workstations on a Token Ring network, if you are using the NetWare for Macintosh product. If you are using the NetWare Client for Mac OS, you do not need to use this NLM.

NOTE

NetWare for Macintosh is an older Novell product that lets you add Macintosh workstations to a Novell network via an AppleTalk router. NetWare for Macintosh is still supported by intraNetWare. However, intraNetWare contains new client software for Mac OS workstations that eliminates the need to install NetWare for Macintosh. This new client software lets you connect Mac OS workstations directly to the network using IPX. See the Novell documentation for more information about adding Macintoshes to your network.

ATXRP (NLM)

Load this NLM on the server to help set up printing if you are using the NetWare for Macintosh product. This NLM allows the intraNetWare print server to send a print job to an AppleTalk network printer from an intraNetWare print queue, taking advantage of PSERVER's benefits. ATXRP also allows AppleTalk printers to appear as objects in the NDS tree. If you are using the NetWare Client for Mac OS, you do not need to use this NLM.

NOTE

NetWare for Macintosh is an older Novell product that lets you add Macintosh workstations to a Novell network via an AppleTalk router. NetWare for Macintosh is still supported by intraNetWare. However, intraNetWare contains new client software for Mac OS workstations that eliminates the need to install NetWare for Macintosh. This new client software lets you connect Mac OS workstations directly to the network using IPX. See the Novell documentation for more information about adding Macintoshes to your network.

AUDITCON (Workstation Utility)

Use this menu utility from a workstation's DOS prompt to configure and view audit trails from a server's volume and container object. This utility lets an auditor see auditing information about NDS and file system or volume events. Auditors cannot, however, open or modify files without appropriate NDS or file system rights.

NOTE

intraNetWare's auditing feature tracks how your network is being used. An independent auditor can then access the information and evaluate it, much like a financial auditor might audit your financial books. With auditing, only the auditor has rights to read the auditing information — even the Admin user cannot access this information. See the Novell documentation for more information about setting up auditing on your network.

AURP (NLM)

Load this NLM on the server to allow AppleTalk to be tunneled through IP, which lets AppleTalk networks connect to each other through an IP internetwork. (AURP stands for AppleTalk Update-based Routing Protocol.) See the Novell documentation for more information about the AppleTalk and IP protocols.

BIND (Console Utility)

Use this utility to assign a protocol such as IPX or AppleTalk to a LAN driver or network board, so that the LAN driver or board knows which protocol to use. Any configuration parameters you specify when you load the LAN driver must also be added to the BIND command so that the protocol is bound to the correct board.

NOTE

When you install an intraNetWare server, the network board and LAN driver in the server are bound to the IPX/SPX protocol automatically. You only need to use this command if you want to make changes manually. See the Novell documentation for more information about loading and binding LAN drivers manually, and about protocol frame types.

Use the following command format, replacing *protocol* with the name of the protocol (such as IPS or APPLETLK), *driver* with the name of the LAN driver or network board, and *parameters* with any necessary driver or protocol parameters:

```
BIND protocol driver parameters
```

The most common protocol parameter for the IPX protocol is:

```
NET=number
```

Replace *number* with the unique network number for the network on which this board is running. (Each network board in a server will have a different network number.)

The most common driver parameters are described in Table A.2.

T A B L E A . 2	*Common Driver Parameters*
DRIVER PARAMETER	**DESCRIPTION**
DMA=*number*	Indicates the DMA channel the board should use.
FRAME=*type*	Indicates the frame type (Ethernet or Token Ring) this board should use. The available frames types are: Ethernet_802.2 (default) Ethernet_802.3 Ethernet_II Ethernet_SNAP Token-Ring (default) Token-Ring_SNAP
INT=*number*	Indicates the interrupt (in hex) that the board should use.
MEM=*number*	Indicates the memory address the board should use.
NODE=*number*	Indicates the board's node address.
PORT=*number*	Indicates the I/O port the board should use.
SLOT=*number*	Indicates the slot in which the board is installed.

BINDERY (Console Command)

Use this utility at the server to add or delete a bindery context in the list of bindery contexts this server uses. You can also use the SET BINDERY CONTEXT parameter to set a bindery context.

NOTE

A bindery context identifies a portion of NDS database and makes that portion look like a flat bindery database to specific applications that require network objects to be in a bindery format. This feature is provided so that older bindery-based applications can still function in an NDS environment. See the Novell documentation for more information about using bindery contexts.

BROADCAST (Console Utility)

Use this utility at the server to send a short message from the server console to users on the network. To send a message to a user, use the following command format, replacing *message* with the message you want displayed (no more than 55 characters long) and *user* with either the name of the user or that workstation's connection number (as seen in MONITOR.NLM):

```
BROADCAST "message" user
```

To send the message to multiple users, separate each user name or connection number with a comma or space. To send the message to all users, don't specify any user name at all. (You can also use the SEND console utility to accomplish the same thing.)

CAPTURE (Workstation Utility)

Use this utility at a workstation's DOS prompt to redirect the workstation's LPT port to a network print queue. Many network applications can redirect print jobs to a network print queue automatically, but others don't, so it's a good idea to put a CAPTURE command in the login script just in case. (See Chapter 8 for more information about printing.)

In general, you can use the following command format, replacing *port* with the number of the LPT port and *queue* with the name of the print queue (you may need to specify the complete Directory name of the queue, if it isn't in your own context). Replace *parameters* with one of the additional parameters listed in Table A.3.

```
CAPTURE L=port Q=queue parameters
```

TABLE A.3   *CAPTURE Parameters*

PARAMETER	DESCRIPTION
AU	End capture Automatically — Sends a print job to the printer when you exit the application.
B=*text*	Banner — Specifies that a banner page (displaying the *text* you specify) is printed before the print job. The default text is the print job file name.

PARAMETER	DESCRIPTION
C=number	Copies — Specifies how many copies are printed (1 to 999; the default is 1).
CR=*path*	Create — Redirects the print job to a file instead of to a printer. Replace *path* with the directory path and name of the file you want to create.
D	Details — Displays details of printing parameters for a capture, and shows whether a print job configuration was used.
EC	End Capture — Stops capturing data to the LPT1 port, and if the data was being captured to a file, closes the file. To end a capture to another port, use EC L=*n* and replace *n* with the LPT number. To end a capture and delete the data that was being captured, use ECCA. To end the capture of all LPT ports, use EC ALL.
F=*form*	Form — Specifies the number or name of the form (paper type) that this job should be printed on.
FF	Form Feed — Causes a form feed at the end of a print job so that the next job prints on the next page. This parameter is only necessary if the application doesn't cause a form feed automatically.
HOLD	Hold — Sends a print job to a queue, but doesn't print it. To release the Hold, use the NetWare Administrator utility.
J=*name*	Job configuration — Specifies the name of a print job configuration to use. This parameter is necessary only if you don't want to use the default print job configuration.
K	Keep — Instructs your workstation to keep all captured data in case your workstation loses power while capturing data. The network server will send the captured data to the printer if it detects that your workstation is down.
L=*number*	LPT port — Specifies which LPT port should be captured (1, 2, or 3).

(continued)

TABLE A.3   *CAPTURE Parameters (continued)*

PARAMETER	DESCRIPTION
NA	No Auto Endcap — Prevents the workstation from sending captured data to the printer when you exit an application.
NAM=*name*	Name — Specifies the name that should appear on the banner page (the default is your login name).
NB	No Banner — Eliminates the banner page.
NFF	No Form Feed — Eliminates the form feed.
NNOTI	No Notification — Prevents a message from appearing on your workstation telling you that the print job is finished. This parameter is necessary only if the print job configuration requests notification and you don't want it.
NOTI	Notify — Specifies that your workstation receives notification when a print job is finished. This parameter is disabled by default.
NT	No Tabs — This parameter is necessary only if your application has a print formatter, but has problems printing graphics or creates unexpected formats. It allows an application's print formatter to determine how many spaces are in a tab stop.
P=*printer*	Printer — Specifies a network printer.
Q=*name*	Queue — Specifies a network print queue.
S=*name*	Server — Specifies to which network server a print job should be sent.
SH	Show — Displays a list of your workstation's captured ports and the print queues to which they are redirected.
T=*number*	Tabs — Specifies how many spaces are in a tab stop. This is necessary only if your application has no print formatter.
TI=*number*	Timeout — Specifies the *timeout* — the number of seconds to wait before printing — instead of waiting for the user to exit the application. The default is 0, meaning that timeout is disabled.
/?	Help — Displays help for CAPTURE.

CD (Console Utility)

Use this utility at the server after you've loaded CDROM.NLM, to work with a CD-ROM on the server. (This command is only available if CDROM.NLM is already loaded.)

TIP

By using CDROM.NLM and CD together, you can mount a CD-ROM in the server's CD-ROM drive so that it looks like any other volume on the server. By doing this, users on the network can access the CD-ROM the same way they access the SYS volume or any other volume.

With this utility, you can mount a CD-ROM as a volume, dismount a CD-ROM, display a list of all CD-ROMs currently mounted, and so on. The variation of this command that you use depends on the task you want to accomplish. The different commands you can use are explained in Table A.4.

TABLE A.4 *CD Commands*

CD COMMAND	DESCRIPTION
CD CHANGE *name*	Allows you to remove one CD-ROM and replace it with another. Replace *name* with the name or number of the volume you're changing.
CD DEVICE LIST	Displays a list of the CD-ROM drives that are connected to the server, and shows the volume names and device numbers of the CD-ROMs in those drives.
CD DIR	Displays a list of the files and directories contained in the CD-ROM's root volume.
CD DISMOUNT *name*	Dismounts a CD-ROM volume. Replace *name* with either the CD-ROM's volume name or number. To eject the CD-ROM, add /EJECT to the end of the command. To remove the index file for the volume, add /PURGE to the end of the command.
CD GROUP *name*	Assigns a NetWare group as a trustee of the CD-ROM volume.
CD HELP	Displays a description of the CD commands you can use.

(continued)

T A B L E A . 4	CD Commands (continued)
CD COMMAND	**DESCRIPTION**
CD IMAGE	Lets you mount a CD-ROM image file as a CD, which lets you test the image before making a CD.
CD MOUNT name	Mounts a CD-ROM as a NetWare volume, so network users can access it. Replace name with either the CD-ROM's name or number (shown with CD DEVICE LIST).
CD PURGE	Purges the index and cache files created on the server when a CD-ROM is mounted as a volume. (Dismount all CD-ROM volumes first.)
CD RENAME /D= number newname	Renames a CD-ROM volume. To see names of mounted volumes, type **CD RENAME.** To change the volume name, dismount the volume and then use the **CD RENAME** command, replacing number with the volume's object number (shown with CD DEVICE LIST) and newname with the new volume name you want to use.
CD VOLUME LIST	Displays a list of the volumes on each CD-ROM device and shows whether those volumes are mounted.

CDROM (NLM)

Load this NLM on the server to mount a CD-ROM as a NetWare volume. This NLM supports the High Sierra and ISO 9660 formats, along with HFS (Apple) extensions. (This means you can access Macintosh files on the CD from a Mac OS workstation.) After you've loaded this NLM, you can use the CD console utility to mount a CD-ROM as a NetWare volume and perform other related tasks.

CLEAR STATION (Console Utility)

Use this command at the server to close a workstation's open files and remove the workstation's connection from the server. This is necessary only if the workstation has crashed and left files open and the user can't log out normally.

Use the following command format, replacing *number* with the workstation's connection number (as seen in MONITOR.NLM) or the word ALL to clear all connections:

```
CLEAR STATION number
```

CLS (Console Utility)

Use this utility at the server to clear the server's console screen (just as the CLS command works on DOS workstations).

COLORPAL (Workstation Utility)

Use this menu utility from a workstation's DOS prompt if the workstation uses a monochrome monitor from a composite color adapter, such as an AT&T 6300 computer, and the computer has trouble displaying the NetWare menu utilities in the default colors. COLORPAL lets you select the colors in which you want elements of the menus to be displayed. Each color scheme is called a palette.

See the Novell documentation for more information about using COLORPAL.

CONFIG (Console Utility)

Use this utility at the server to see configuration information about the server. This utility displays information such as:

- ▶ The server's name
- ▶ The server's internal network number
- ▶ The LAN drivers that are loaded on the server
- ▶ The server's hardware settings
- ▶ The protocols the server is currently supporting
- ▶ The node address of each network board installed in the server

CONLOG (NLM)

Load this NLM on the server to capture the console messages that occur during system initialization.

You can use this NLM if you want to see what error messages may be displayed when the server initializes. The messages are captured and sent to a file called CONSOLE.LOG in the SYS:ETC directory. You can use any text editor to open and read this file.

To stop capturing messages in this file, type UNLOAD CONLOG.

CX (Workstation Utility)

Use this utility at a workstation's DOS prompt to change your current context in the Directory tree. With CX, you can move up and down through containers in the Directory tree. This utility is similar to DOS's CD utility, which lets you move around in the file system's subdirectory structure. (See Chapter 4 for more information about name contexts.)

Use the following command format, replacing *context* with the NDS context you want to move to (such as .MKTG.RESEARCH.BIGTIME), or *parameter* with one of the parameters listed in Table A.5:

```
CX context /parameter
```

T A B L E   A.5   *CX Parameters*

PARAMETER	DESCRIPTION
/A	Includes all objects in the context (use with /T or /CONT).
/C	Causes the display to scroll continuously down the screen.
/CONT	Displays a list of containers in your current context, or in the context you specify in the command.
/R	Displays a list of the containers at the root level, or changes the context in relation to the root.
/T	Displays a list of the containers below your current context or the context you specify in the command.
/?	Displays help for CX.

DHCPCFG (NLM)

Load this NLM on the server to manage the NetWare DHCP service. DHCP (Dynamic Host Configuration Protocol) lets a TCP/IP workstation get configuration information, such as its IP address and network configuration, from the server automatically.

See the Novell documentation for more information about using DHCP and the IP protocol on your network.

DISABLE LOGIN (Console Utility)

Use this utility at the server to prevent users from logging in to the server (such as when you want to perform maintenance on the server). Users who are already logged in won't be affected, but additional users cannot log in. To allow users to log in again, use ENABLE LOGIN.

DISABLE TTS (Console Utility)

Use this utility at the server to disable TTS (NetWare's Transaction Tracking System). You should not need to disable TTS using this utility, unless you are an application developer and have a specific need to do so. If you disable TTS, you can turn it back on using ENABLE TTS.

NOTE TTS monitors the updates to database files, and keeps track of the updates so any unfinished updates can be safely backed out (undone) if the server fails during a database transaction. This prevents the database from being corrupted by unfinished updates. See the Novell documentation for more information about TTS.

DISMOUNT (Console Utility)

Use this utility at the server to dismount a volume (usually in preparation for repairing or deleting a volume). Use the following command format, replacing *volume* with the name of the volume you want to dismount:

```
DISMOUNT volume
```

DISPLAY NETWORKS (Console Utility)

Use this utility at the server to display a list of all the networks (shown by their network numbers) that this server recognizes. It also displays how many hops (cable segments between servers or routers) away these networks are, and the time (in ticks — approximately 1/18 of a second) it takes for a packet to reach these networks.

See the Novell documentation for more information about routers.

DISPLAY SERVERS (Console Utility)

Use this command to display a list of all the servers that this server recognizes and records in its router table. It also displays how many hops (cable segments between servers or routers) away those servers are.

The command DISPLAY SERVERS will list all servers on the network. To see information about a single server or set of servers that start with the same letters, use the following command format, replacing *server* with a server's name (or use the wildcard character * to display multiple servers that begin with the same letters, such as B*):

DISPLAY SERVERS *server*

See the Novell documentation for more information about routers.

DOSGEN (Workstation Utility)

Use this utility at a workstation's DOS prompt to create an image file of a boot disk and store it on the server. This way, diskless workstations can access the image and boot from the network instead of from a local disk.

See the Novell documentation for more information about installing diskless workstations.

DOWN (Console Utility)

Use this utility at the server to shut down the server cleanly. This command will close any open files, write any data left in the cache buffers to the disk, and so on, so that the server files will not be damaged when you shut it down.

After you've brought down the server with the DOWN command, you can use the EXIT console utility to return the computer to DOS. Then you can safely turn the computer off.

See Chapter 2 for more information about bringing down and rebooting the server.

DS (NLM)

This NLM (along with several related NLMs, such as DSBACKER.NLM, DSEVENT.NLM, and DSAPI.NLM) loads Novell Directory Services on the server. Networks will generally work more efficiently and have fewer conflicts if all servers in the tree are using the same version of DS.NLM. This NLM is loaded on the server automatically when the server starts up.

See Chapter 4 for more information about managing NDS.

DSMERGE (NLM)

Load this NLM on the server to merge two or more NDS trees into a single tree. (Do not use this utility to merge Directory partitions. This utility should only be used for merging two Directory trees.) You can also use this utility to rename a tree.

See the Novell documentation for more information about merging Directory trees.

DS MIGRATE (Workstation Utility)

Use this utility on a Windows 3.1 or Windows 95 workstation to migrate bindery information from a NetWare 2.*x* or 3.1*x* server to an existing NetWare Directory tree. This utility is actually an option under the Tools menu of the NetWare Administrator utility.

See the Novell documentation for more information about using DS Migrate.

DSREPAIR (NLM)

Load this NLM on the server to repair possible problems with the NDS database on individual servers. You have to run it on each server that has a problem. DSREPAIR can also perform replica synchronization operations and allow you to see the current status of this server's view of the network or Directory.

See the Novell documentation for more information about using DSRE-PAIR.NLM.

EDIT (NLM)

Load this NLM on the server to edit text files (such as AUTOEXEC.NCF or STARTUP.NCF) on the server. When you load EDIT, you will be prompted for the path and name of the file to edit. This NLM works like any other simple text editor.

ENABLE LOGIN (Console Utility)

Use this utility at the server to allow users to log in to the network. This is necessary only if you've used DISABLE LOGIN to prevent users from logging in.

ENABLE TTS (Console Utility)

Use this utility at the server to restart TTS (Transaction Tracking System) after the server has disabled TTS. The server will disable TTS if the SYS volume gets too full or if the server doesn't have enough memory to run TTS. (You can also disable TTS manually by using the DISABLE TTS console utility.)

NOTE

TTS monitors the updates to database files, and keeps track of the updates so any unfinished updates can be safely backed out (undone) if the server fails during a database transaction. This prevents the database from being corrupted by unfinished updates. See the Novell documentation for more information about TTS.

EXIT (Console Utility)

Use this utility at the server after using the DOWN console utility. EXIT will return the server to DOS. (If you removed DOS from the server using the REMOVE DOS command, EXIT will reboot the server instead of going to DOS.)

See Chapter 2 for more information about bringing down and rebooting the server.

FILER (Workstation Utility)

Use this menu utility from a workstation's DOS prompt to work with files, directories, and volumes on the network. With FILER, you can see and work with the following types of file and directory information:

- ▶ List of subdirectories and files within a directory
- ▶ Trustees
- ▶ File system rights
- ▶ File owners
- ▶ Creation dates and times
- ▶ Available disk space and directory entries for a volume
- ▶ File and directory attributes
- ▶ Salvageable files

FILTCFG (NLM)

Load this NLM on the server to set up and configure filters for IPX, TCP/IP, and AppleTalk protocols. Filters provide additional network security by limiting what type of information is broadcast across the network by routers.

See the Novell documentation for more information about protocols.

FLAG (Workstation Utility)

Use this utility at a workstation's DOS prompt to view and assign file and directory attributes. To use FLAG to set file and directory attributes, use the following command format:

FLAG *path attributes /options*

For *path*, indicate the path to the directory or file whose attributes you're changing. For *attributes*, insert the list of attributes you want to assign. (See Chapter 6 for a description of these file and directory attributes.)

You can also use FLAG to assign search modes for executable files. (Search modes are instructions that tell the workstation where to look for a particular file.) To specify a search mode, use the following command format:

`FLAG path /M=number`

For *path*, specify the path to the file or directory whose search mode you want to change. For *number*, insert the number of the search mode you want to be used for the executable files in this path. The search modes are explained in Table A.6.

T A B L E   A . 6   *FLAG Search Modes*

SEARCH MODE NUMBER	DESCRIPTION
0	Looks for search instructions in the NET.CFG file. (Default mode.)
1	Searches the path specified in the file. If no path is found, searches the default directory, and then all search drives.
2	Searches the path specified in the file. If no path is found, searches only the default directory.
3	Searches the path specified in the file. If no path is found, searches the default directory. Then, if the open request is read-only, searches the search drives.
4	Not used.
5	Searches the path specified, and then searches all search drives. If no path is found, searches the default directory, and then all search drives.
6	Not used.
7	Searches the path specified. If the open request is read-only, searches the search drives. If no path is found, searches the default directory, and then all search drives.

HALT (Console Utility)

Use this utility on an SFT III server to stop the IOEngine in one server and force the other server to take over.

NOTE

SFT III is a flavor of intraNetWare that lets you install the network operating system on two identical servers that run simultaneously. The servers' hard disks and other hardware are "mirrored" to each other, so that they store identical information. That way, if one server goes down, the other server takes over seamlessly, so that network service is uninterrupted. See the Novell documentation for more information about SFT III.

HCSS (NLM)

Load this NLM on the server to load support for HCSS (High-Capacity Storage System) on the server. This allows you to use an optical jukebox as file storage for the network.

See the Novell documentation for more information about HCSS.

HCSS (Console Utility)

Use this utility at the server to control HCSS support once you've loaded HCSS.NLM.

See the Novell documentation for more information about HCSS.

HELP (Console Utility)

Use this utility at the server to display help for console utilities. To see a list of available console utilities, type HELP at the server console. To display help for a specific console utility, use the following format, replacing *utility* with the name of the console utility whose help file you want to read:

HELP *utility*

HFSCD (NLM)

Load this NLM on the server to allow the server to mount an HPFS-formatted (High Performance File System) CD-ROM as a NetWare volume.

HFSCDCON (NLM)

Load this NLM on the server to configure HFSCD.NLM, which allows you to use HPFS-formatted CD-ROMs as NetWare volumes.

HFSLFS (NLM)

Load this NLM on the server, along with CDROM.NLM, to allow CDROM.NLM to support HPFS-formatted CD-ROMs.

INETCFG (NLM)

Load this NLM on the server to configure both data link and network protocols. INETCFG is a menu-driven NLM that makes it relatively easy to configure the protocols. You can also use the LOAD and BIND console commands (by either typing them at the console or adding them to AUTOEXEC.NCF), but you may find INETCFG easier to work with.

See the Novell documentation for more information about using INETCFG.

INITIALIZE SYSTEM (Console Utility)

Use this utility at the server to execute commands in NETINFO.CFG and to enable the multiprotocol router configuration.

See the Novell documentation for more information about using the multiprotocol router.

INSTALL (NLM)

Load this NLM on the server to install intraNetWare on a server. You can also use it to upgrade a NetWare 3.1*x* or 4.*x* server to intraNetWare, as well as to modify an existing intraNetWare server, create or modify volumes, install additional products (such as the NetWare Web Server), replace hard disks, or modify disk partitions.

See Chapter 2 for more information about using INSTALL to install or upgrade servers. See the Novell documentation for instructions on using INSTALL to modify volumes, replace hard disks, and so on.

IPCONFIG (NLM)

Load this NLM on the server to configure IP static routes.

NOTE

IntraNetWare supports the IPX protocol by default, but can support the IP protocol if you prefer. You can either add IP support to the server, so that it supports both protocols, or you can install NetWare/IP, which is a flavor of intraNetWare that runs only on IP. See the Novell documentation for more information about using IP on your network.

IPFLT (NLM)

Load this IP filter NLM on the server to restrict how routers see and communicate with other IP routers.

See the Novell documentation for more information about using the IP protocol and IP routers.

IPXCON (NLM)

Load this NLM on the server to monitor information about IPX. With this utility, you can configure SNMP parameters, display IPX statistics and error counts, display information about NLSP, RIP, and SAP on the server, and list information (such as known services and destination networks). When using IPXCON, press the F1 key to read help for each option.

See the Novell documentation for more information about the IPX protocol.

IPXFLT (NLM)

Load this IPX filter NLM on the server to restrict how routers see and communicate with other IPX routers.

See the Novell documentation for more information about IPX routers.

IPXPING (NLM)

Load this NLM on the server to send test messages (pings) to another node on the network to see if it is communicating with this server via IPX. You will need to specify the target node's IPX internal network number and its node number.

See the Novell documentation for more information about IPX.

KEYB (NLM)

Load this NLM on the server to indicate the type of keyboard that is attached to your server. The default type of keyboard supported by intraNetWare is the type used in the United States with the English language. Different countries and languages may require different types of keyboards. You only need to use this NLM if you're not using a United States/English keyboard on the server.

If you aren't using a United States keyboard with English, use the following command format to specify a different keyboard type, replacing *country* with the name of the country you want to choose:

```
LOAD KEYB country
```

To see a list of the countries from which you can choose, type LOAD KEYB without specifying any country.

LANGUAGE (Console Utility)

Use this utility at the server to change the language that displays when NLMs are loaded at the server console. This will not change the language of the operating system or of NLMs that are already loaded. It only affects those NLMs that are loaded after this utility is executed.

To display the current language being used by NLMs, type LANGUAGE.

To display a list of all available languages, type LANGUAGE LIST.

To change the language to be used by subsequently loaded NLMs, use the following command format, replacing *name* with either the name or number of the language:

```
LANGUAGE name
```

LIST DEVICES (Console Utility)

Use this utility at the server to display a list of all the storage devices you have installed on the server, such as CD-ROM drives, disk drives, and tape drives.

LOAD (Console Utility)

Use this utility at the server to load NLMs on the server. Use the following command format, replacing *module* with the name of the NLM you're loading (you don't need to include the .NLM extension in the module name):

```
LOAD module
```

To unload an NLM, use the UNLOAD console utility.

LOGIN (Workstation Utility)

Use this utility at a workstation to log in to the network. LOGIN authenticates you to the network and it can also execute login scripts to set up your work environment. There are two versions of this utility. The DOS-based version is a command you execute at the DOS prompt of your workstation. For DOS, use the following command format, replacing *tree* with either a Directory tree name or a server name (this is not necessary if you want to log in to the default tree or server), and *username* with your login name:

```
LOGIN tree/username
```

If you are using Windows 3.1 or Windows 95 on your workstation, you can log in to the network using graphical version of LOGIN. The graphical Login program for Windows 3.1 and Windows 95 is installed as part of the intraNetWare client software. To log in using the graphical Login program, use one of the following methods (depending on your workstation's OS):

▸ To log in to the network from Windows 3.1, double-click the Login Program icon, and specify a login name and a password.

▸ From Windows 95, open the Network Neighborhood, right-click the desired server or tree, click either Authenticate or Login to NDS Tree, and then enter a login name and password.

For more information about logging in to the network and about login scripts, see Chapter 5.

LOGOUT (Workstation Utility)

Use this utility at a workstation to log out of the network. How you log out depends on the operating system you're using on your workstation:

▸ If you're using a DOS workstation, simply type the following command at the DOS prompt:

    LOGOUT

▸ If you're using a Windows 3.1 workstation, you can either go to DOS and type LOGOUT at the DOS prompt, or you can use the NetWare User Tools utility to log out. Double-click NetWare User Tools, select NetWare Connections, choose the server or tree from which you want to log out, and choose Logout.

▸ If you're using a Windows 95 workstation, double-click the Network Neighborhood icon, right-click the NDS tree or server from which you want to log out, and choose Logout.

See Chapter 5 for more information about logging out.

LONG.NAM (NLM)

Load this NLM on the server to make the server support OS/2, Windows NT, and Windows 95 long file names. After you've loaded this NLM, use the ADD NAME SPACE console command to assign the name space to a particular volume.

See Chapter 2 for more information about loading name spaces.

MAC.NAM (NLM)

Load this NLM on the server to make the server support Mac OS long file names and file formats on the server. After you've loaded this NLM, use the ADD NAME SPACE console command to assign the name space to a particular volume.

See Chapter 2 for more information about loading name spaces.

MACFILE (NLM)

Load this NLM on the server to control the desktop for Mac OS files on the server.

See the Novell documentation for more information about using this NLM.

MAGAZINE (Console Utility)

If the server prompts you to insert a new media magazine during some task, use this utility to indicate to the server that you've inserted or removed a media magazine. Use the following command format, replacing *parameter* with one of the parameters listed in Table A.7:

`MAGAZINE parameter`

TABLE A.7   *MAGAZINE Parameters*

PARAMETER	DESCRIPTION
Inserted	Tells the server you've inserted the media magazine.
Not Inserted	Tells the server that you have not inserted the media magazine.
Removed	Tells the server that you have removed the media magazine.
Not Removed	Tells the server that you have not removed the media magazine.

MAP (Workstation Utility)

Use this utility at a workstation to map drive letters on the workstation to network directories. You can execute MAP commands at the workstation's DOS prompt, or you can put MAP commands in a login script, so that the same drives are mapped every time the user logs in.

The MAP utility and drive mappings are explained in Chapter 5.

MEDIA (Console Utility)

If the server prompts you to insert a specified storage medium during some task, use this utility to indicate to the server that you've inserted or removed the medium. Use the following command format, replacing *parameter* with one of the parameters listed in Table A.8:

```
MEDIA parameter
```

TABLE A.8	*MEDIA Parameters*
PARAMETER	**DESCRIPTION**
Inserted	Tells the server you've inserted the medium.
Not Inserted	Tells the server that you have not inserted the medium.
Removed	Tells the server that you have removed the medium.
Not Removed	Tells the server that you have not removed the medium.

MEMORY (Console Utility)

Use this utility at the server to see the total amount of memory currently installed in the server.

MEMORY MAP (Console Utility)

Use this utility at the server to see how much of the server's memory is allocated to DOS and to the server.

MENUCNVT (Workstation Utility)

If you have menu programs that you created in NetWare 3.11 using the older MENU utility (whose files have the extension .MNU), use this utility at a workstation's DOS prompt to convert the old menus into the newer-style menu programs supported by intraNetWare's NMENU utility.

NOTE A menu program is a program you can create in order to let DOS users select tasks from a menu instead of typing commands at the DOS prompt. Menus are not used for Windows 3.1 or Windows 95 workstations. See the Novell documentation for more information about creating menu programs.

MENUMAKE (Workstation Utility)

Use this utility at a workstation's DOS prompt to create a menu program for users to use when they work on the network. Create a text utility with the necessary commands first, and then run this utility to compile the text file into a menu program. Use the following command format, replacing *file* with the name of the text file (leave off the file's extension when you type its name):

```
MENUMAKE file
```

NOTE A menu program is a program you can create in order to let DOS users select tasks from a menu instead of typing commands at the DOS prompt. Menus are not used for Windows 3.1 or Windows 95 workstations. See the Novell documentation for more information about creating menu programs.

MIGPRINT (Workstation Utility)

Use this utility at a workstation's DOS prompt to migrate NetWare 2.*x* or NetWare 3.*x* printers, print queues, print job configurations, and print servers to an intraNetWare Directory tree. During a server upgrade, the printing objects are not upgraded from previous versions of NetWare to the Directory tree by default. You must use this utility to migrate those objects.

In the MIGPRINT command format, replace the variables with the correct information, as indicated:

▶ Replace *source* with the name of the server from which you're migrating printing information.

▶ Replace *destination* with the name of the intraNetWare server.

▶ Replace *volume* with the name of the volume that will hold the print queues (only if you don't want to use the default SYS volume).

▶ Replace *file* with the name of an output file to store messages about the migration (only if you don't want to use the default file, called MP*nnn*.RPT).

Use the following command format to execute MIGPRINT:

```
MIGPRINT /S=source /D=destination /VOL=volume /O=file
```

MIGRATE (Workstation Utility)

Use this utility at a workstation to migrate NetWare 2.*x* bindery information to an intraNetWare Directory tree. See the Novell documentation for more information about using MIGRATE.

MIRROR STATUS (Console Utility)

Use this utility at a server to list all the disk partitions on the server and display their mirror status. The following five states are possible:

▶ Being Remirrored — This means the disk partition is being synchronized with another and will soon be mirrored.

▶ Fully Synchronized — This means the disk partitions are mirrored and working correctly, so that both partitions contain identical data.

▶ Not Mirrored — This means the disk partition isn't mirrored with any other partition.

▶ Orphaned State — This means the disk partition used to be mirrored with another, but isn't now. The integrity of this partition's data may not be ensured anymore.

▶ Out of Synchronization — This means the two disk partitions that are mirrored do not have identical data and, therefore, need to be remirrored.

NOTE

You can set up a server's hard disks so that they are "mirrored" to each other. (Actually, the disks' partitions are mirrored.) This means that all network data is copied to both hard disks, so that they are identical. That way, if one hard disk fails, the other disk takes over seamlessly, so that the network data is still available. See the Novell documentation for more information about disk mirroring.

MODULES (Console Utility)

Use this utility at a server to display a list of all the NLMs currently loaded on the server. If you want to see information about a single NLM or set of NLMs that start with the same letters, use the following command format, replacing *module* with an NLM's name:

```
MODULES module
```

You can use the wildcard character * to display multiple NLMs that begin with the same letter or letters. For example, to see all the loaded NLMs that start with the letters DS, type **MODULES DS***.

MONITOR (NLM)

Load this NLM on the server to monitor the server's performance. This is one of the most frequently used management utilities for NetWare servers. In addition to letting you track and modify your server's performance characteristics, it lets you run a screen saver on the console and lock the console so that a password is required to use it.

To load MONITOR.NLM, use the following command format, replacing *parameter*, if necessary, with one of the optional parameters listed in Table A.9:

```
LOAD MONITOR parameter
```

TABLE A.9 *MONITOR Parameters*

PARAMETER	DESCRIPTION
L	Locks the server console when MONITOR is loaded. Use the Admin user's password to unlock the console.
M	Activates the screen saver only if MONITOR's screen is currently displayed on the console. Without this option, the screen saver will activate regardless of what screen is currently displayed.
N	Disables the screen saver.
T*nnn*	Sets the number of seconds of keyboard inactivity MONITOR waits before activating the screen saver. Replace *nnn* with the number of seconds. The default is 600 seconds if the console is unlocked, 60 seconds if the console is locked.

MOUNT (Console Utility)

Use this utility at a server to mount a volume on a server so network users can access it. Use the following command format, replacing *volume* with the volume's name (or with ALL to mount all volumes):

```
MOUNT volume
```

MPDRIVER (NLM)

Load this NLM on the server to enable processors in a multiprocessor server. You can use this NLM only if you have installed the NetWare SMP (Symmetric Multiprocessing) version of intraNetWare on your server. Use the following command format, replacing *number* with the number of the processor you want to enable, or with the word ALL to enable all licensed processors:

```
LOAD MPDRIVER number
```

NOTE
NetWare SMP is a flavor of intraNetWare that runs on computers that contain more than one processor chip. These computers are high-end computers, allowing NetWare SMP to take advantage of the multiple processors so some network tasks can span the processors and run more quickly. See the Novell documentation for more information about using NetWare SMP.

MSERVER (.EXE)

This executable file starts up an SFT III server. (It works just like SERVER.EXE running on a regular intraNetWare server.)

When the server computer first boots up, it is running DOS. From DOS, you type MSERVER to execute MSERVER.EXE, which will load the SFT III network operating system and turn the computer into a server.

You can add the command MSERVER to the server's AUTOEXEC.BAT file so the server loads automatically when the computer is booted.

NOTE
SFT III is a flavor of intraNetWare that lets you install the network operating system on two identical servers that run simultaneously. The servers' hard disks and other hardware are "mirrored" to each other, so that they store identical information. That way, if one server goes down, the other server takes over seamlessly, so that network service is uninterrupted. See the Novell documentation for more information about SFT III.

NAME (Console Utility)

Use this utility at the server to display the server's name.

NCOPY (Workstation Utility)

Use this utility at a workstation's DOS prompt to copy files and directories from one drive or disk to another. To use NCOPY, use the following command format:

```
NCOPY source/filename destination/filename /parameters
```

The parameters that can be used with the NCOPY utility are listed in Table A.10.

TABLE A.10 *NCOPY Options*

PARAMETER	DESCRIPTION
/A	Archive Bit Only — Copies only those files that have the Archive Needed attribute (also called the modify bit). NCOPY does not, however, remove the attribute from the source file, so the file will still have the Archive Needed attribute.
/C	Copy — Copies files, but does not preserve extended attributes or name space information.
/F	Force Sparse Files — Forces the operating system to copy sparse files, which aren't normally copied.
/I	Inform — Notifies the user when extended attributes or name space information can't be copied because the destination volume doesn't support those features.
/M	Archive Bit Set — Copies files that have the Archive Needed attribute, and removes the attribute from the source file. This allows NCOPY to be used as a backup tool.
/R	Retain Compression — Keeps compressed files compressed, rather than decompressing them during the copy process.
/R/U	Retain Unsupported Compression — Keeps compressed files compressed even if they are copied to a destination volume that doesn't support compression.
/S	Subdirectories — Copies all of the subdirectories (except empty subdirectories) as well as the files in the specified path.
/S/E	Subdirectories, Empty — Copies all the subdirectories, including empty subdirectories, as well as files in the specified path.
/V	Verify — Verifies that the original and the new files are identical. This option is useful for copies made on local DOS drives only.

For example, to copy all the files from drive G to drive L, use the following command:

```
NCOPY G:*.* L:
```

To copy all of the files, plus the subdirectories (including empty ones) from drive G to drive L, use the following command:

```
NCOPY G:*.* L: /S/E
```

NCUPDATE (Workstation Utility)

Use this utility at a workstation's DOS prompt to update a workstation's NET.CFG file with a new name context automatically, if you have moved or renamed the user's container. You can execute this utility from a login script if desired.

For more information about name contexts, see Chapter 4. For more information about login scripts, see Chapter 5.

NDIR (Workstation Utility)

Use this utility at a workstation's DOS prompt to list a directory's files, subdirectories, and related information. With it, you can see the following types of information about files and directories:

- ► List of subdirectories and files within a directory
- ► Inherited Rights Filters
- ► Effective file system rights
- ► File owners
- ► Creation dates and times
- ► File sizes
- ► File and directory attributes
- ► Archive information
- ► File version (for Novell files)
- ► Volume information

With NDIR, you can sort the display of files so they appear in different orders, such as from largest to smallest, newest to oldest, all those owned by a particular owner, and so on.

To use NDIR, use the following command format:

```
NDIR path /option
```

For example, to list all the files in the directory that is mapped to drive G, use the following command:

```
NDIR G:
```

To display the NDIR help screens, use the following command:

```
NDIR /?
```

The following are some of the most common options:

▶ To list any files in the directory's subdirectories, add the option /SUB.

▶ To list only the files in the directory, add the option /FO.

▶ To list only the subdirectories in the directory, add the option /DO.

▶ To list files in the order of their sizes, from smallest to largest, add the option /SORT SI.

▶ To list files in the order of their sizes, from largest to smallest, add the option /REV SORT SI.

▶ To list only the files owned by user Mick, add the option /OW EQ Mick.Sales.BigTime (EQ stands for "equals").

▶ To list only Macintosh files, add the option /MAC.

NDS Manager (Workstation Utility)

Use this utility on a Windows 3.1 or Windows 95 workstation to analyze and repair (if necessary) Directory partitions and replicas. This utility can be executed by itself, or as a feature of the NetWare Administrator utility under the Tools option.

NDS Manager automatically executes DSREPAIR.NLM for repair options, so you may prefer to use NDS Manager from a workstation instead of using DSREPAIR from the console.

By default, NDS Manager is not part of NetWare Administrator, but you can add it easily. If you don't want to add it to NetWare Administrator, you must add NDS Manager to your workstation desktop as its own icon before you can use it.

For more information about NDS Manager, see Chapter 4.

NETADMIN (Workstation Utility)

Use this utility at a workstation's DOS prompt. This is the DOS-based version of the NetWare Administrator utility. It is much more limited than the Windows-based NetWare Administrator, but you can still use it from a DOS workstation to work with NDS objects, login scripts, and so on.

NETSYNC3 (NLM)

Load this NLM on a NetWare 3.1x server to synchronize its bindery objects with an intraNetWare server, so that you can manage the NetWare 3.1x users from NetWare Administrator.

NOTE
NetSync is an intraNetWare feature that allows you to manage the objects in the binderies of up to 12 NetWare 3.1x servers just as if they were in the NDS database. See the Novell documentation for more information about NetSync.

NETSYNC4 (NLM)

Load this NLM on an intraNetWare server to turn the server into a host for a NetSync network of NetWare 3.1x servers.

NOTE
NetSync is an intraNetWare feature that allows you to manage the objects in the binderies of up to 12 NetWare 3.1x servers just as if they were in the NDS database. See the Novell documentation for more information about NetSync.

NETUSER (Workstation Utility)

Use this utility from a DOS-based workstation to perform common network tasks, such as selecting print queues, sending messages to other users, changing passwords, mapping drive letters to directories, and logging in and out of the network. This is the DOS-based version of the NetWare User Tools utility, which runs in Windows 3.1. (Most Windows 95 users will use the Windows Explorer and Network Neighborhood instead of NETUSER or the NetWare User Tools to complete network tasks.)

For more information about the NetWare User Tools utility, see Chapter 5.

NetWare Administrator (Workstation Utility)

Use this utility on a Windows 3.1 or Windows 95 workstation to manage your network. NetWare Administrator enables you to do tasks, such as:

- ► Create, delete, or modify NDS objects
- ► Set up print services
- ► Assign NDS rights
- ► Modify login scripts

Before you can use NetWare Administrator, you need to install it on your workstation. The Windows 3.1 version of NetWare Administrator (which can also run on OS/2) is called NWADMN3X.EXE, and it's located in SYS:PUBLIC. The Windows 95 version is called NWADMN95.EXE, and it can be found in SYS:PUBLIC\WIN95.

For information on setting up and using NetWare Administrator on your workstation, see Chapter 4.

NetWare Application Launcher (Workstation Utility)

Use this utility on a Windows 3.1 or Windows 95 workstation to allow users to find and launch network applications easily.

Once you have the NetWare Application Launcher set up on each user's workstation, you can use NetWare Administrator to make an application become an object in the NDS tree. Then, the icon for the Application object will appear automatically on the desktop of each user you assign to that application.

The users don't need to know where the application is located; they don't need to map drives or enter launch parameters; and you don't need to update login scripts. When you update the application, the icons in all of the desktops will continue to point to the new application.

For more information, and for instructions on setting up the NetWare Application Launcher, see Chapter 5.

NetWare Application Manager (Workstation Utility)

Use this utility on a Windows 3.1 or Windows 95 workstation to set up Application objects so that users can execute them from the NetWare Application Launcher installed on their workstations. This utility is actually executed as a feature of the NetWare Administrator utility when you create an Application object. You don't execute this utility separately.

For more information about creating Application objects and setting up the NetWare Application Launcher, see Chapter 5.

NetWare File Migration (Workstation Utility)

Use this utility at a workstation to migrate network data files from a NetWare 3.1x server to a new intraNetWare server. You will use this utility after you have migrated all of the NetWare 3.1x server's bindery information to the intraNetWare server.

See the Novell documentation for more information about NetWare file migration.

NetWare User Tools (Workstation Utility)

Use this utility from a Windows 3.1-based workstation to perform common network tasks, such as selecting print queues, sending messages to other users, changing passwords, mapping drive letters to directories, and logging in and out of the network. There is also a DOS-based version of this utility, called NETUSER. (Most Windows 95 users will use the Windows Explorer and Network Neighborhood instead of NETUSER or the NetWare User Tools to complete network tasks.)

For more information about the NetWare User Tools utility, see Chapter 5.

NFS.NAM (NLM)

Use this NLM to load support for UNIX long file names on the server. After you've loaded this NLM, use the ADD NAME SPACE console command to assign the name space to a particular volume.

See Chapter 2 for more information about using name spaces.

NLIST (Workstation Utility)

Use this utility at a workstation's DOS prompt to display a variety of information about network objects, such as users, groups, servers, and volumes. Use the following command format, replacing *class* with the type of object you want to display (such as SERVER, USER, or GROUP):

NLIST *class*

You can also specify a specific object name (or use wildcards to list those that begin with the same letters) by using the following command format:

NLIST *class=name*

You can use additional parameters and variations of this command to display many kinds of information. To read help screens and see examples of NLIST commands, type:

NLIST /? ALL

For more information about NDS object classes, see Chapter 4.

NLS Manager (Workstation Utility)

Use this utility at a Windows 3.1 or Windows 95 workstation to manage NetWare Licensing Services (NLS).

You can use NLS Manager to install license certificates, create metering certificates, display licensing information, and so on. This lets you track and limit the number of users that are allowed to use a particular product. Few third-party applications have taken advantage of this feature yet, however. See the Novell documentation for more information about NLS.

NMENU (Workstation Utility)

Use this utility at a workstation's DOS prompt to execute a menu program that you've created. Use the following format, replacing *filename* with the path and name of the menu file:

```
NMENU filename
```

To have workstations automatically execute the menu program when users log in, add the following line to the end of the login script:

```
EXIT "NMENU filename"
```

A menu program is a program you can create in order to let DOS users select tasks from a menu instead of typing commands at the DOS prompt. Menus are not used for Windows 3.1 or Windows 95 workstations. See the Novell documentation for more information about creating menu programs.

NPAMS (NLM)

Load this NLM on the MSEngine of an SFT III server to allow a CD-ROM to be mounted as a NetWare volume.

SFT III is a flavor of intraNetWare that lets you install the network operating system (NOS) on two identical servers that run simultaneously. The servers' hard disks and other hardware are "mirrored" to each other, so that they store identical information. That way, if one server goes down, the other server takes over seamlessly, so that network service is uninterrupted. See the Novell documentation for more information about SFT III.

NPATH (Workstation Utility)

Use this utility at a workstation's DOS prompt to see the search path that a particular utility is using. This lets you determine why your workstation can't find a particular file, why it's finding the wrong version of the file, or why it's executing in a foreign language.

Use the following command format, replacing *utility* with the name of the utility whose search sequence you want to see, *filename* with the name of the file your workstation says it can't find, and *parameter* with any of the parameters listed in Table A.11:

```
NPATH utility filename /parameters
```

TABLE A.11 NPATH Parameters

PARAMETER	DESCRIPTION
A	All — Lists the path to all occurrences of the file.
D	Details — Displays the language, version number, date, and time of the file.
Uni	Unicode — Displays all paths to Unicode files.
/Uni /D	Unicode Details — Displays the country code and code page for your workstation, the utility's needed Unicode files, and the path to the first occurrence of each file.

NPRINT (Workstation Utility)

Use this utility at a workstation's DOS prompt to print a job from outside of an application (such as printing an ASCII file or a workstation screen). Use the following command format, replacing *parameters* with parameters from Table A.12:

```
NPRINT parameters
```

TABLE A.12 NPRINT Parameters

PARAMETER	DESCRIPTION
B=text	Banner — Specifies that a banner page (displaying the *text* you specify) is printed before the print job. The default text is the print job file name.
C=number	Copies — Specifies how many copies are printed (1 to 65,000; the default is 1).
D	Details — Displays the printing parameters for the print job, and shows whether a print job configuration was used.

PARAMETER	DESCRIPTION
DEL	Delete — Specifies that the file is deleted after it's printed.
F=*form*	Form — Specifies the number or name of the form (paper type) that this job should be printed on.
FF	Form Feed — Causes a form feed at the end of a print job, so that the next job prints on the next page. This parameter is necessary only if the application doesn't already cause a form feed.
HOLD	Hold — Sends a print job to a queue, but doesn't print it. To release the Hold, use the NetWare Administrator utility.
J=*name*	Job configuration — Specifies the name of a print job configuration to use. This parameter is necessary only if you don't want to use the default print job configuration.
NAM=*name*	Name — Specifies the name that should appear on the banner page (the default is your login name).
NB	No Banner — Eliminates the banner page.
NFF	No Form Feed — Eliminates the form feed.
NNOTI	No Notification — Prevents a message from appearing on your workstation telling you that the print job is finished. (This is only necessary if the print job configuration requests notification and you don't want it)
NOTI	Notify — Specifies that your workstation receives notification when a print job is finished. Disabled by default.
NT	No Tabs — Allows an application's print formatter to determine how many spaces are in a tab stop. This parameter is necessary only if your application has a print formatter, but has problems printing graphics or creates unexpected formats.
P=*name*	Printer — Specifies a printer.
Q=*name*	Queue — Specifies a network print queue.
S=*name*	Server — Specifies which network server to send a print job to.
T=*number*	Tabs — Specifies how many spaces are in a tab stop. This parameter is necessary only if your application doesn't have a print formatter.
/?	Help — Displays help for NPRINT.

NPRINTER.EXE (Workstation Utility)

Use this utility on a DOS or Windows 3.1 workstation to load a port driver on the workstation. The port driver is software that routes jobs out of the print queue, through the proper port on the workstation, to the printer.

See Chapter 8 for more information about printing.

NPRINTER (NLM)

Load this NLM on the server to load a port driver on the server. The port driver is software that routes jobs out of the print queue, through the proper port on the server, to the printer.

See Chapter 8 for more information about printing.

NPTWIN95.EXE (Workstation Utility)

Use this utility on a Windows 95 workstation to load a port driver on the workstation. The port driver is software that routes jobs out of the print queue, through the proper port on the workstation, to the printer.

See Chapter 8 for more information about printing.

NVER (Workstation Utility)

Use this utility at a workstation's DOS prompt to display the version number of the following types of programs running on the workstation or server:

- ► NetBIOS
- ► IPX and SPX
- ► LAN drivers
- ► IntraNetWare client software
- ► The workstation's operating system
- ► The version of intraNetWare running on the server

NWIP (NLM)

Load this NLM on the server to support NetWare/IP on the server.

NOTE

IntraNetWare supports the IPX protocol by default, but can support the IP protocol if you prefer. You can either add IP support to the server, so that it supports both protocols, or you can install NetWare/IP, which is a flavor of intraNetWare that runs only on IP. See the Novell documentation for more information about using IP on your network.

NWIPCFG (NLM)

Load this NLM on the server to configure the NetWare/IP server software, start the NetWare/IP service, or configure the server as a NetWare Domain Name System (DNS) client.

NOTE IntraNetWare supports the IPX protocol by default, but can support the IP protocol if you prefer. You can either add IP support to the server, so that it supports both protocols, or you can install NetWare/IP, which is a flavor of intraNetWare that runs only on IP. See the Novell documentation for more information about using IP on your network.

NWPA (NLM)

Load this NLM on the server to allow the server to support the NetWare Peripheral Architecture, which allows disk drivers and CD-ROM drivers to work with intraNetWare.

See the Novell documentation for more information about NWPA.NLM.

NWXTRACT (Workstation Utility)

Use this utility at a workstation's DOS prompt to extract an individual file from the intraNetWare CD-ROM and copy it to a network directory or your hard disk. The files on the CD-ROM are compressed, so you cannot simply copy the file directly from the CD-ROM. This utility will locate the file on the CD-ROM, decompress it, and then copy it to the location you specify.

The NWXTRACT utility is located on the CD-ROM, in the following directory: PRODUCTS\NW411\INSTALL\IBM*ostype*\XXX\ENGLISH. (Replace *ostype* with either DOS or OS2, depending on which operating system your workstation is currently using. You can also replace ENGLISH with the language directory you prefer.)

To use NWXTRACT, first go to this directory on the CD-ROM. Then, use the following command format, replacing *source* with the path to the CD-ROM, *filename* with the name of the file you want, and *destination* with the path you want the file copied to (or omit the destination if you want it copied to the default location on the server):

```
NWXTRACT source filename destination /parameters
```

Replace *parameters* with one of the following, if necessary:

▶ S=*server* — Replace *server* with the name of the server to which you want the file copied.

▶ T=*type* — Copies files of the specified *type*: DOS, MAC, OS2, SER (server), UNX, or WIN.

To read the online help, type:

NWXTRACT /?

OFF (Console Utility)

Use this utility at the server to clear the server's console screen. You can also use the CLS utility to accomplish the same thing.

PARTMGR (Workstation Utility)

Use this utility at a workstation's DOS prompt to manage Directory partitions and replicas. You may prefer to use the NDS Manager utility (which runs on Windows 3.1 and Windows 95 workstations) to work with Directory partitions and replicas because NDS Manager is more graphical and easy to use. It also automatically launches DSREPAIR.NLM when necessary.

See Chapter 4 for more information about using NDS Manager.

PCONCOLE (Workstation Utility)

Run this menu utility from a workstation's DOS prompt to set up and modify printing services. You may prefer to use the NetWare Administrator utility from a Windows 3.1 or Windows 95 workstation to work with printing services, however, because its graphical interface is often easier to use.

See Chapter 8 for more information about using NetWare Administrator's printing features.

PING (NLM)

Load this NLM on the server to test if the server can communicate with an IP node on the network. PING sends an ICMP (Internet Control Message Protocol) echo request packet to an IP node.

NOTE

IntraNetWare supports the IPX protocol by default, but can support the IP protocol if you prefer. You can either add IP support to the server, so that it supports both protocols, or you can install NetWare/IP, which is a flavor of intraNetWare that runs only on IP. See the Novell documentation for more information about using IP on your network.

PRINTCON (Workstation Utility)

Use this utility at a workstation's DOS prompt to create and use print job configurations. You may prefer to use the NetWare Administrator utility to set up print job configurations, however, because its graphical interface is often easier to use.

See Chapter 8 for more information about using NetWare Administrator's printing features.

PRINTDEF (Workstation Utility)

Use this utility at a workstation's DOS prompt to define the printer you're using, if necessary, and to define paper forms (types of paper, such as paychecks, invoices, legal-size paper, and so on). You may prefer to use the NetWare Administrator utility to work with printer definitions and paper forms, however, because its graphical interface is often easier to use.

See Chapter 8 for more information about using NetWare Administrator's printing features.

PROTOCOL (Console Utility)

Use this utility at the server register a new protocol or frame type with the server so that the server will support it. You don't need to use this utility to register IPX, IP, or AppleTalk because they are registered automatically during installation or configuration, but you may need to use this if you use a different protocol. See the protocol's manufacturer for more details.

To list all the protocols that are currently registered on the server, simply type PROTOCOL.

To use this utility to register a new protocol, use the following command format, replacing *protocol* with the name of the protocol, *frame* with the frame type, and *id* with the Protocol ID (PID, also called Ethernet Type, E-Type, or SAP) number assigned to the protocol:

```
PROTOCOL REGISTER protocol frame id
```

See the Novell documentation for more information about protocols.

PSC (Workstation Utility)

Use this utility at a workstation's DOS prompt to control print servers and network printers. This utility allows you to execute many of the same functions as PCONSOLE and the NetWare Administrator utility, but in a command-line format so that the commands can be used in a batch file. Use one of the following command formats:

PSC PS=*printserver parameters*

or

PSC P=*number parameters*

Replace *printserver* with the name of the print server you want to control, or replace *number* with the number of the printer you want to control. Replace *parameters* with any of the parameters from Table A.13.

TABLE A.13	PSC Parameters
PARAMETER	**DESCRIPTION**
AB	Abort — Aborts the current print job and deletes it from the print queue.
CD	Cancel Down — If you chose the option in PCONSOLE or NetWare Administrator to have the printer go down after current print jobs are finished, this command will prevent the printer from going down.
FF	Form Feed — Causes a form feed to occur if the printer is stopped or paused.
L	Layout — Displays a tree layout of how printing is currently set up.
M *character*	Mark — Prints a line of the character you specify so you can see on which line the printer will begin printing. The default character is *.
MO F=*form*	Mount Form — Indicates to the printer that you have mounted a new form on the printer. Replace *form* with the number of the form you mounted.
PAU	Pause — Pauses the printer.
PRI	Private — Changes the printer to a local printer, removing it from the print server's list of network printers, so only the workstation to which the printer is attached can use it.
SHA	Shared — Removes the PRI (Private) attribute so the printer can once again be used by other network users.
STAR	Start — Restarts a paused or stopped printer.

PARAMETER	DESCRIPTION
STAT	Status — Displays the status of the print server's printers.
S=server	Server — Specifies which intraNetWare server contains the print server you want to manage.
STO	Stop — Stops a printer and deletes the current print job from the print queue.

PSERVER (NLM)

Use this NLM to load a print server on the server, so that the print server can regulate network print queues and printers. Use the following command format, replacing *name* with the name of the print server you created by using the NetWare Administrator utility:

```
LOAD PSERVER name
```

See Chapter 8 for more information about using PSERVER.

PUPGRADE (NLM)

Load this NLM on the server to upgrade NetWare 3.1x print servers and printers to intraNetWare NDS objects and to upgrade NetWare 3.1x PRINT-CON and PRINTDEF databases to the format used by intraNetWare. You must run PUPGRADE after you've upgraded the rest of your NetWare 3.1x server and bindery information to intraNetWare, if you want to upgrade your printing objects.

See Chapter 8 for more information about upgrading printing objects.

PURGE (Workstation Utility)

Use this utility at a workstation's DOS prompt to permanently erase files from the server. Usually, when files are deleted, they are retained in a salvageable state until the server needs the disk space and automatically purges them. To completely remove these files without waiting for the server to run out of disk space, you can use either the PURGE utility or the NetWare Administrator utility.

To use PURGE, use the following command format, replacing *path* with the path to the files you want to purge, and *filename* with a file name for the specific file or files (wildcards are acceptable):

```
PURGE path\filename /option
```

If desired, you can replace *option* with one of the following:

- ▸ /A — Purges all files in the current directory and all of its subdirectories.
- ▸ /? — Displays help screens for PURGE.

For more information about purging and salvaging files, see Chapter 7.

RCONSOLE (Workstation Utility)

Use this utility at a workstation's DOS prompt to start a Remote Console session from a workstation.

For more information about Remote Console and using RCONSOLE, see Chapter 2.

REGISTER MEMORY (Console Utility)

Use this utility on ISA (AT bus) servers to register memory above 16MB so that intraNetWare can address it. This command is unnecessary for EISA or MCA computers because intraNetWare automatically registers memory above 16MB on EISA machines. On a PCI computer, intraNetWare recognizes up to 64MB. (Refer to your manufacturer's documentation to verify whether your computer uses ISA, EISA, MCA, or PCI technology.)

Use the following command format, replacing *start* with the hexadecimal address of where the memory above the limit begins (16MB starts at 1000000, 64MB starts at 4000000), and *length* with the hexadecimal length of the memory above 16MB or 64MB. (See Table A.14 for some *length* numbers for different amounts of memory.)

```
REGISTER MEMORY start length
```

NOTE

Hexadecimal numbers can use the numerals 0 through 9 and the letters A through F.

TABLE A.14	*Length Values for Memory*
MEMORY ABOVE THE MINIMUM (16MB OR 64MB)	**LENGTH**
4	400000
8	800000
12	C00000
16	1000000

MEMORY ABOVE THE MINIMUM (16MB OR 64MB)	LENGTH
20	1400000
24	1800000
48	3000000
96	6000000
112	7000000
240	F000000
384	18000000
984	3D800000
2936	B7800000
2984	BA800000

REINITIALIZE SYSTEM (Console Utility)

Use this utility at the server to re-enable the multiprotocol router configuration after you've used INETCFG.NLM to make changes to NETINFO.CFG.

See the Novell documentation for more information about using the multiprotocol router.

REMAPID (NLM)

Load this NLM on NetWare 3.1x servers that are being managed by NetSync. This NLM is used to control how passwords are synchronized, so you shouldn't unload it or you will have to change every user's password on the server.

Make sure the AUTOEXEC.NCF file loads REMAPID.NLM to ensure that it doesn't get removed if you remove NetSync. The command to load REMAPID should have been added to the file during NetSync installation.

NOTE

NetSync is an intraNetWare feature that allows you to manage the objects in the binderies of up to 12 NetWare 3.1x servers just as if they were in the NDS database. See the Novell documentation for more information about NetSync.

REMIRROR PARTITION (Console Utility)

Use this utility at the server to restart the remirroring process if something halted the server's remirroring of its disk partitions. Use the following command format, replacing *number* with the number of the disk partition you want to remirror:

```
REMIRROR PARTITION number
```

NOTE

You can set up a server's hard disks so that they are "mirrored" to each other. (Actually, the disks' partitions are mirrored.) This means that all network data is copied to both hard disks, so that they are identical. That way, if one hard disk fails, the other disk takes over seamlessly, so that the network data is still available. See the Novell documentation for more information about disk mirroring.

REMOTE (NLM)

Load this NLM on the server to allow an intraNetWare server to support Remote Console sessions from a workstation. This NLM will ask you to specify a password that a Remote Console user will have to provide in order to start a Remote Console session from his or her workstation.

See Chapter 2 for more information about using Remote Console.

REMOVE DOS (Console Utility)

Use this utility at the server to remove DOS from the server's memory. This prevents anyone from using commands or files on the server's DOS partition. It also frees up the memory that DOS was using.

RENDIR (Workstation Utility)

Use this utility at a workstation's DOS prompt to rename a directory. Use the following command format, replacing *oldname* with the original directory name (or a period if you want to rename your current directory), and *newname* with the name to which you want the directory renamed:

```
RENDIR oldname newname
```

RESET ROUTER (Console Utility)

Use this utility at the server to clear the router table and force a new table to be built on the server, updating any changes to servers or routers that have gone down or come back up. The table is rebuilt every two minutes automatically, so you only need to use this utility if you don't want to wait for the next automatic rebuild.

See the Novell documentation for more information about using routers.

RESTART (Console Utility)

Use this utility on an SFT III server to reload a stopped IOEngine while the IOEngine in the other server continues to run. You can also use this utility to force an SFT III server to switch from being primary to secondary.

NOTE

SFT III is a flavor of intraNetWare that lets you install the network operating system (NOS) on two identical servers that run simultaneously. The servers' hard disks and other hardware are "mirrored" to each other, so that they store identical information. That way, if one server goes down, the other server takes over seamlessly, so that network service is uninterrupted. See the Novell documentation for more information about SFT III.

RESTART SERVER (Console Utility)

Use this utility at the server to restart the server after you have brought it down.

See Chapter 2 for more information about bringing down and rebooting the server.

RIGHTS (Workstation Utility)

Use this utility at a workstation's DOS prompt to see your effective rights in a directory. Use the following command format, replacing *path* with the path to the directory or path you want (you can omit the *path* if you want to see your rights in your current directory), and *parameters* with any of the parameters shown in Table A.15:

```
RIGHTS path /parameters
```

TABLE A.15 *RIGHTS Parameters*

PARAMETER	DESCRIPTION
C	Causes the display to scroll continuously down the screen.
F	Displays the Inherited Rights Filter (IRF).
I	Shows from where the inherited rights came.
NAME=*username*	Replace *username* with the name of a user or group whose rights you want to see or change.
S	Lets you see or change subdirectories below the current directory.
T	Displays trustee assignments for a directory.

See Chapter 6 for more information about rights, and for instructions on using NetWare Administrator to work with rights.

ROUTE (NLM)

Load this NLM on the server to allow intraNetWare to support an IBM bridge on a Token Ring network using Source Routing. Load this NLM once for every Token Ring network board you have installed in your server. Use the following command format, replacing *parameters* with one or more of the parameters shown in Table A.16:

```
LOAD ROUTE parameters
```

TABLE A.16 *ROUTE.NLM Parameters*

ROUTE.NLM PARAMETER	DESCRIPTION
BOARD=*number*	Indicates the network board's number, if the Token Ring LAN driver wasn't the first LAN driver loaded.
CLEAR	Clears all information from the Source Routing table so that it can be rebuilt with updated information.
DEF	Causes frames (packets) with unknown destination addresses to be forwarded as All Routes Broadcast packets, which means they won't be sent across Single Route IBM bridges.

ROUTE.NLM PARAMETER	DESCRIPTION
GBR	Causes General Broadcast frames to be sent as All Routes Broadcast frames, instead of being sent as Single Route Broadcast frames.
MBR	Causes Multicast Broadcast frames to be sent as All Routes Broadcast frames, instead of being sent as Single Route Broadcast frames.
NAME=*board*	Specifies the name of the network board.
REMOVE=*number*	If a bridge has gone down, use this parameter to remove a node address from the server's Source Routing table, forcing the server to find a new route.
RSP=*response*	Indicates how the server must respond to a broadcast request. Replace *response* with:
	NR (Not Required). Default: Respond to all requests directly.
	AR (All Routes). Respond with an All Routes Broadcast frame.
	SR (Single Route). Respond with a Single Route Broadcast frame.
TIME=*seconds*	Determines how often to update the server's Source Routing table. Default: 03. Range: 03 to 255.
UNLOAD	Removes Source Routing support from a network board. (Specify the board you want first by using the BOARD= parameter, and then use this UNLOAD parameter.)
XTX=*number*	Sets how many times to transmit on a timed-out route using the old route. Default: 02. Range: 00 to 255.

RPL (NLM)

Load this NLM on the server to allow diskless workstations to boot from the server instead of from a local boot disk.

See the Novell documentation for more information about setting up disk-less workstations.

RS232 (NLM)

Load this NLM on the server to allow the server to support Remote Console sessions over an asynchronous connection (via a modem). Use the following command format, replacing *port* and *baud* with the appropriate communications port number (1 or 2) and baud rate being used by your modem:

```
LOAD RS232 port baud
```

See Chapter 2 for more information about running Remote Console.

RSPX (NLM)

Load this NLM on the server to allow the server to support Remote Console sessions over a direct network connection (in other words, if the workstation is connected directly to the network and doesn't require a modem to access the server).

See Chapter 2 for more information about running Remote Console.

SBACKUP (NLM)

Load this NLM on the server to back up and restore data from the network. To use SBACKUP, you must also have a TSA (Target Service Agent) loaded on the server you intend to back up or restore.

See Chapter 7 for more information about using SBACKUP.

SCAN FOR NEW DEVICES (Console Utility)

Use this utility at the server to cause the server to look for and recognize any new storage devices (disk drives, CD-ROM drives, and so on) that may have been added since the server was booted.

SCHDELAY (NLM)

Load this NLM on a server to list all server processes and to see which ones have consistently high Load values. If you want to change some of the values on the scheduling information screen, you may find it easier to use the Scheduling Information option of MONITOR.NLM.

See Chapter 2 for more information about using MONITOR.

SEARCH (Console Utility)

Use this utility at the server to set the paths that the server should search through when looking for an .NCF (configuration) file or an NLM. The default search path is SYS:SYSTEM. If volume SYS isn't mounted, the default search path becomes the DOS boot directory on the server.

To display the server's current search paths, simply type SEARCH.

To add a search path, use the following command format, replacing *path* with the directory path you want the server to search:

```
SEARCH ADD path
```

To delete a search path, use the following command format, replacing **number** with the number of the search drive you want to remove (drive numbers are displayed when you type SEARCH):

```
SEARCH DEL number
```

SECURE CONSOLE (Console Utility)

Use this utility at the server to prevent anyone from loading NLMs from anywhere but SYS:SYSTEM. (This prevents unauthorized users from loading NLMs from an area where they may have more rights than in SYS:SYSTEM, such as from a diskette in the server's diskette drive.) This utility also prevents anyone from accessing the operating system's debugger from the server's keyboard, and allows only the administrator to change the server's date and time. To disable this feature, reboot the server.

SEND (Workstation Utility)

Use this utility at a workstation's DOS prompt to send a short message from your workstation to other users on the network. To send a message to a user or group, use the following command format, replacing *message* with the message you want displayed (no more than 44 characters long) and *user* with the name of the user or group:

```
SEND "message" user
```

To send the message to multiple users or groups, separate each name with a comma.

SEND (Console Utility)

Use this utility at the server to send a short message from the server console to users on the network. To send a message to a user, use the following command format, replacing *message* with the message you want displayed (no more than 55 characters long) and *user* with either the name of the user or that workstation's connection number (as seen in MONITOR.NLM):

```
SEND "message" user
```

To send the message to multiple users, separate each user name or connection number with a comma or space. To send the message to all users, don't specify any user name at all. (You can also use the BROADCAST console utility to accomplish the same thing.)

SERVER (.EXE)

This is the command that loads the intraNetWare server from DOS. When the server computer first boots up, it is running DOS. From DOS, you type SERVER to execute SERVER.EXE, which will load the network operating system and turn the computer into a server.

You can add the command SERVER to the server's AUTOEXEC.BAT file so that the server loads automatically when the computer is booted.

SERVMAN (NLM)

Load this NLM on the server to set server parameters, also called SET parameters, to optimize your server's performance. SET parameters control things, such as how buffers are allocated and used, how memory is used, and so on. You can change these parameters by loading SERVMAN.NLM and selecting the SET parameters you want from menus. SERVMAN will automatically save the command in the correct server startup file.

See the Novell documentation for more information about SET parameters.

SET (Console Utility)

Use this utility at the server to change performance parameters on the server. You may prefer to use the SERVMAN.NLM to change SET parameters, because SERVMAN allows you to select the parameters from menus rather than having to type long commands. SET commands can also be added to the AUTOEXEC.NCF and STARTUP.NCF files so that they are executed every time the server is rebooted.

See the Novell documentation for more information about SET parameters.

SET TIME (Console Utility)

Use this utility at the server to change the server's date and time. Use the following command format:

`SET TIME mm/dd/yy hour:minute:second`

SET TIME ZONE (Console Utility)

Use this utility at the server to change the server's time zone information. When using this utility's command format, replace the variables with the correct information:

▶ Replace *zone* with the three-letter abbreviation for your time zone (such as EST, CST, MST, or PST).

▶ Replace *hours* with the number of hours you are east or west of Greenwich Mean Time (use a - [minus] sign before the number if you're east).

▶ Replace *daylight* with the three-letter abbreviation for your area's daylight saving time (only if you are currently on daylight saving time).

Use the following command format:

`SET TIMEZONE zone hours daylight`

For example, to set the time zone to Eastern Daylight Saving Time, type:

`SET TIMEZONE EST5EDT`

SETPASS (Workstation Utility)

Use this utility at a workstation's DOS prompt to change your network password. When you execute this utility, follow the prompts to type in your old and new passwords.

See Chapter 6 for more information about using and changing passwords.

SETTTS (Workstation Utility)

Use this utility at a workstation's DOS prompt to set the number of logical and physical record locks that TTS (NetWare's Transaction Tracking Service) ignores before beginning to track a transaction. This utility lets TTS work with an application that requires you to set new transaction beginning points. (Most applications do not require this utility.)

Use the following command format, replacing *logical* with the number of logical record locks you want TTS to ignore, and *physical* with the number of physical record locks you want TTS to ignore:

```
SETTTS logical physical
```

NOTE

TTS monitors the updates to database files, and keeps track of the updates so any unfinished updates can be safely backed out (undone) if the server fails during a database transaction. This prevents the database from being corrupted by unfinished updates. See the Novell documentation for more information about TTS.

SETUPDOC (Workstation Utility)

Use this utility on a Windows 3.1 or Windows 95 workstation to install the intraNetWare online documentation and the documentation viewers. See Chapter 9 for more information on using SETUPDOC.

SPEED (Console Utility)

Use this utility at the server to display the server's processor speed.

SPOOL (Console Utility)

Use this utility at the server to display or create spooler mappings so applications that print to printer numbers will direct their print jobs to print queues instead. Most current network applications do not require this utility to be executed. If used, this utility also specifies the default print queue for NPRINT and CAPTURE.

Use the following command format, replacing *number* with the printer number (which will also be the spooler number), and *queue* with the name of the print queue:

```
SPOOL number TO QUEUE queue
```

See Chapter 8 for more information about printing.

SPXCONFG (NLM)

Load this NLM on the server to configure SPX parameters. You can also configure the same parameters using INETCFG.NLM. To display help screens for using SPXCONFG, use the following command:

```
LOAD SPXCONFG H
```

See the Novell documentation for more information about protocols and SPX.

SYSTIME (Workstation Utility)

Use this utility at a workstation's DOS prompt to synchronize a workstation's time with the server's time. Use the following command format, replacing *server* with the name of the server to which you want your workstation synchronized:

```
SYSTIME server
```

TCPCON (NLM)

Load this NLM on the server to monitor information about the TCP/IP protocol suite that is loaded on the server. You can view information about the protocols in the TCP/IP suite, SNMP configuration information, user statistics, and so on.

NOTE

IntraNetWare supports the IPX protocol by default, but can support the IP protocol if you prefer. You can add IP support to the server so it supports both protocols, or you can install NetWare/IP, which is a flavor of intraNetWare that runs only on IP. See the Novell documentation for more information about using IP on your network.

TCPIP (NLM)

Load this NLM on the server to load TCP/IP support on the network server.

NOTE

IntraNetWare supports the IPX protocol by default, but can support the IP protocol if you prefer. You can add IP support to the server so it supports both protocols, or you can install NetWare/IP, which is a flavor of intraNetWare that runs only on IP. See the Novell documentation for more information about using IP on your network.

TECHWALK (NLM)

Load this NLM on the server to record INETCFG settings in a file called TECHWALK.OUT in the SYS:ETC directory. It may take this utility anywhere from 5 to 60 minutes to record all your information. If you want to record configuration information for a specific NLM, use the following command format, replacing *module* with the name of the NLM:

```
LOAD TECHWALK module
```

See the Novell documentation for more information about using INETCFG.

TIME (Console Utility)

Use this utility to display the server's date, time, daylight saving time status, and time synchronization information. (To change the date or time, use the SET TIME console utility. To change the server's time zone information, use the SET TIMEZONE console utility.)

TIMESYNC (NLM)

This NLM is automatically loaded when the server boots, and is used to control the server's time services. You should not need to load or unload this NLM.

TPING (NLM)

Load this NLM on the server to send ICMP packets to an IP node to see if the server can communicate with that node. Use the following command format, replacing *host* with the symbolic host name or IP address of a TCP/IP system, *size* with the size (in bytes) of the ICMP packets, and *retries* with the number of times the packet should be sent to the host if it doesn't reply to the first (default is 5):

```
LOAD TPING host size retries
```

NOTE

IntraNetWare supports the IPX protocol by default, but can support the IP protocol if you prefer. You can add IP support to the server so it supports both protocols, or you can install NetWare/IP, which is a flavor of intraNetWare that runs only on IP. See the Novell documentation for more information about using IP on your network.

TRACK OFF (Console Utility)

Use this utility at the server to turn off the display of routing information (which is displayed if you used the TRACK ON console utility).

See the Novell documentation for more information about routers.

TRACK ON (Console Utility)

Use this utility at the server to display the routing information that your server is broadcasting and receiving.

See the Novell documentation for more information about routers.

UIMPORT (Workstation Utility)

Use this utility at a workstation's DOS prompt to create User objects in the Directory database by importing user information from another database. This can be a quick way to create multiple users if you've already defined all of their information in some other database.

Use the following command format, replacing *controlfile* with the name of the file that contains information on how to load user data into the directory, and *datafile* with the name of the text file that contains the actual user data (property values):

```
UIMPORT controlfile datafile
```

See the Novell documentation for more information about using UIMPORT.

UNBIND (Console Utility)

Use this utility at the server to unbind a protocol, such as IPX or AppleTalk, from a network board. Use the following command format, replacing *protocol* with the name of the protocol, *driver* with the name of the LAN driver or network board from which you want the protocol unbound, and *parameters* with the same parameters you originally specified when you loaded the driver (so the UNBIND command knows exactly which LAN driver or network board you intend):

```
UNBIND protocol FROM driver parameters
```

See the explanation of the BIND console utility for more information about driver parameters.

UNICON (NLM)

Load this NLM on the server to manage the NetWare Domain Name System and the NetWare/IP Domain SAP/RIP Service, if you have installed NetWare/IP on your server.

NOTE

IntraNetWare supports the IPX protocol by default, but can support the IP protocol if you prefer. You can add IP support to the server so it supports both protocols, or you can install NetWare/IP, which is a flavor of intraNetWare that runs only on IP. See the Novell documentation for more information about using IP on your network.

UNLOAD (Console Utility)

Use this utility at the server to unload an NLM that's been previously loaded. Use the following command format, replacing *module* with the name of the NLM you want to unload (you can omit the .NLM extension of the NLM's file name):

```
UNLOAD module
```

UPS (NLM)

Load this NLM on the server to allow the server to be supported by a UPS (Uninterruptible Power Supply). Some UPS manufacturers supply their own software to be used instead of UPS.NLM. If so, you do not need to use UPS.NLM.

See Chapter 2 for more information about using a UPS with your server.

UPS_AIO (NLM)

Load this NLM on the server instead of UPS.NLM if your UPS is attached to your server's serial port.

See Chapter 2 for more information about using a UPS with your server.

UPS STATUS (Console Utility)

Use this utility at the server to display the status of a UPS (Uninterruptible Power Supply) that is attached to your server. When you use this utility, you can see the following types of information:

► The type of power the server is currently using (regular power or the UPS's battery)

► The discharge time remaining (how much time the server can safely run on the UPS's battery power)

► The battery's status (recharged, low, or being recharged)

> ▸ The recharge time remaining

> ▸ The current network power status

See Chapter 2 for more information about using a UPS with your server.

UPS TIME (Console Utility)

Use this utility at the server to change the amount of time required to discharge and recharge a UPS battery. The discharge time is the amount of time that the server can run on the battery's power if commercial power stops. The recharge time is the amount of time required to fully recharge a battery after it's been used. See the UPS manufacturer's documentation for the recommended times for your UPS.

When you execute this utility, you will be asked to specify the amount of recharge and discharge time necessary.

See Chapter 2 for more information about using a UPS with your server.

V_LONG (NLM)

This NLM is used on the server by VREPAIR.NLM to repair volumes that use the LONG.NAM name space module. LONG.NAM allows the server to support Windows NT, Windows 95, and OS/2 long file names and formats, and it is loaded by default when you install intraNetWare. You may want to copy this support NLM, along with VREPAIR, to the server's DOS boot partition so you can use them even if volume SYS is down. (VREPAIR and its support NLMs are located in SYS:SYSTEM by default.)

See the Novell documentation for more information about repairing volumes.

V_MAC (NLM)

This NLM is used on the server by VREPAIR.NLM to repair volumes that use the MAC.NAM name space module. MAC.NAM allows the server to support Mac OS long file names and formats. If you store Mac OS files on your server, you may want to copy this support NLM, along with VREPAIR, to the server's DOS boot partition so you can use them even if volume SYS is down. (VREPAIR and its support NLMs are located in SYS:SYSTEM by default.)

See the Novell documentation for more information about repairing volumes.

V_NFS (NLM)

This NLM is used on the server by VREPAIR.NLM to repair volumes that use the NFS.NAM name space module. NFS.NAM allows the server to support

UNIX long file names and formats. If you store NFS files on your server, you may want to copy this support NLM, along with VREPAIR, to the server's DOS boot partition so you can use them even if volume SYS is down. (VREPAIR and its support NLMs are located in SYS:SYSTEM by default.)

See the Novell documentation for more information about repairing volumes.

VERSION (Console Utility)

Use this utility at the server to see the version of intraNetWare that is running on the server.

VIEW (NLM)

Load this NLM on the server to display a file on the server console. You cannot edit or create a file with VIEW.NLM, however. You must use EDIT.NLM to edit or create a file. Use the following command format, replacing *filename* with the name of the file you want to see:

```
LOAD VIEW filename
```

VOLUMES (Console Utility)

Use this utility at the server to display a list of all the volumes currently mounted on the server. The display also indicates which name spaces each volume supports.

See Chapter 2 for more information about name spaces, and see Chapter 7 for more information about volumes.

VREPAIR (NLM)

Load this NLM on the server to repair minor problems with a volume or to remove a name space from a volume. If the server detects a volume problem when it boots, it will run VREPAIR automatically. You can also run VREPAIR manually if you need to, but you can only run it on dismounted volumes. VREPAIR also requires the name space support modules (V_MAC.NLM, V_LONG.NLM, or V_NFS.NLM) if the volume supports any of those name spaces.

You may want to copy VREPAIR.NLM and these support NLMs to the server's DOS boot partition so you can use them even if volume SYS is down. (VREPAIR and its support NLMs are located in SYS:SYSTEM by default.)

Use the following command format, replacing *name* with the name of the volume you want to repair:

`LOAD VREPAIR name`

See the Novell documentation for more information about repairing volumes.

WHOAMI (Workstation Utility)

Use this utility at a workstation's DOS prompt to display information, such as the servers you're logged in to, your login name on each of those servers, and the times you logged in. To see a list of all the servers you're logged in to, simply type **WHOAMI**. To see more detailed information, use the following command format:

`WHOAMI /ALL`

WSUPDATE (Workstation Utility)

Use this utility on a workstation's DOS prompt to update files on users' workstations. WSUPDATE compares the dates of the files on the workstation with the source files on the server, and copies the newer version to the workstation if necessary.

Use the following command format, replacing *source* with the path and name of the source file you want to use to update the workstation with, *destination* with the workstation drive on which you want the utility to look for the older file, and *parameters* with any of the parameters listed in Table A.17:

`WSUPDATE source destination /parameters`

T A B L E   A . 1 7   *WSUPDATE Parameters*

PARAMETER	DESCRIPTION
C	Copies the newer file over the old, and doesn't keep a backup copy of the old file.
F=*path\filename*	Sends WSUPDATE to a file that contains commands for updating the workstation's files.
/I	Makes WSUPDATE interactive, so that it asks the user whether to update an old file. (Default)
L=*path\filename*	Creates a log file containing the messages generated during updates.
N	Creates a new path and file if an older version doesn't already exist.

(continued)

T A B L E A . 1 7	WSUPDATE Parameters (continued)
PARAMETER	**DESCRIPTION**
R	Renames the old file with the extension .OLD, and then copies the new file to the workstation.
S	Searches for the old files in all subdirectories of the workstation's drive.
V=drive	Updates the workstation's CONFIG.SYS file.

See the Novell documentation for more information about using WSUPDATE.

GLOSSARY

Abend (Abnormal End): An unexpected, serious error that causes the server to quit running.

Account restrictions: Properties of a User object that control when the user logs in, how often the user must change passwords, and so on.

Accounting: An intraNetWare feature lets you keep track of how people are using your network and lets you charge them for that usage. With accounting turned on, you can charge for the time those users are logged in, the types of resources they use, and so on.

AppleTalk: A networking protocol suite built into every Macintosh. AppleTalk networks can run on several different flavors of network architectures: LocalTalk, EtherTalk, and TokenTalk. AppleTalk provides peer-to-peer networking (serverless networking) between all Macintoshes and Apple hardware.

Architecture: See *Network architecture*.

Attribute, file and directory: A property of a file or directory that controls what can happen to that file or directory. Attributes, which are also called flags, can be used to restrict users from deleting files, renaming files, changing files, or the like. Attributes can also be used to identify files and directories that have been changed since their last backup, that should be purged immediately if deleted, and so on.

Attribute, NDS object: See *Property*.

Auditing: An intraNetWare feature that tracks how your network is being used. An independent auditor can access this information and evaluate it, much like a financial auditor might audit your financial books. With auditing, only the auditor has rights to read the auditing information — even the Admin user cannot access this information.

AUTOEXEC.BAT file: A DOS batch file on a computer, which runs when the computer is booted and executes necessary commands to make the computer boot up correctly, load necessary programs, and so on.

AUTOEXEC.NCF file: A startup file on the server that executes every time the server is rebooted. This file loads the server's LAN drivers, specifies the server name and internal network number, mounts volumes, loads any NLMs you want automatically loaded, and executes additional server parameters. This file is created during the server installation, and contains commands that reflect the choices you made during the installation.

Backup: A copy of a file or set of files that you archive and keep as a precaution, in case the original files are lost or corrupted. A full backup backs up all network files, and removes the Archive Needed file attribute from all files and directories. A differential backup backs up only files that were modified since the last full backup, and does not remove the Archive Needed attribute from these files. An incremental backup backs up only files that were modified since the last full or incremental backup, and removes the Archive Needed attribute. A custom backup lets you specify particular directories to back up or restore, and lets you specify whether or not to remove the Archive Needed attribute.

Bindery: The database of network information that was used in previous versions of NetWare (version 3.12 and earlier). The bindery is a flat database, which means it cannot recognize container objects that help organize other network entities. In addition, the bindery is specific to a server. Each server has its own unique bindery, and cannot recognize objects in another server's bindery. The bindery was replaced by the NDS database in NetWare 4 and intraNetWare.

Bindery context: A portion of the NDS database assigned to look like a flat bindery database to specific applications that require network objects to be in a bindery format. This feature is provided so that older bindery-based applications can still function in an NDS environment.

Board: See *Network board*.

Bridge: The connection between two networks where data can flow from one network to the other. A bridge can join two networks that are using different network architectures. See also *Router*.

Browser, Internet: An application that runs on a workstation, allowing the user to search, access, and view information stored on the Internet or an intranet. Netscape Navigator and Microsoft Internet Explorer are two popular brands of Internet browsers.

Browser, NetWare Administrator: The view of the NDS tree and its objects, as displayed by the NetWare Administrator utility. You can see information about NDS objects by opening objects from within the Browser.

Cable: Used to connect all of the hardware components (workstations, servers, printers, and so on) of a network together. Network cabling comes in a wide variety of forms, such as coaxial cable (like your TV cable), twisted pair and shielded twisted pair cable, and fiber optic cable.

Capture: To redirect a workstation's parallel port so that print jobs sent to that port are directed to a print queue instead of an actual printer.

Client: Often used to refer to a workstation, client indicates a computer or application that requests services from a network resource (such as a server). For example, the intraNetWare client software is a set of programs installed on a workstation so that the workstation can communicate with and request services from the rest of the network.

Command-line utility: A utility that is executed by typing a command at the DOS prompt.

Concentrator: A piece of network equipment into which workstation cables must feed before being connected to the main network cable. Concentrators boost the signals before sending them on their way. Concentrators are sometimes called active hubs.

Connectors: Hardware that joins cables together or connect them to other pieces of hardware.

Console utility: A command you type at the server's console (keyboard and monitor) to change some aspect of the server or view information about it. Console utilities are built into the operating system, just as internal DOS commands are built into DOS.

Container Login script: See *Login script*.

Container object: An NDS object that contains other NDS objects. Organization objects and Organizational Unit objects are both container objects. See also *Leaf object*.

Context: See *Name context*.

Controller board: A circuit board on a storage device, such as a hard disk, that plugs into the computer. Each hard disk or other type of storage device installed in your server has its own controller board. The computer and the disk communicate through this controller board.

Device driver: See *Driver*.

Differential backup: See *Backup*.

Directory attribute: See *Attribute, file and directory*.

Directory context: See *Name context*.

Directory Services: See *NDS*.

Directory Tree: See *NDS tree*.

Disk controller board: See *Controller board*.

Disk driver: Software that allows a disk drive (such as a hard disk drive or a CD-ROM drive) to communicate with the computer (via the disk's controller board). Each brand of disk controller board has a unique disk driver associated with it.

Disk mirroring: Setting up a server's hard disks so that they are "mirrored" to each other. (Actually, the disks' partitions are mirrored.) This means that all network data is copied to both hard disks, so that they are identical. That way, if one hard disk fails, the other disk takes over seamlessly, so that the network data is still available.

Disk partition: See *Partition, disk*.

Dismount: To bring down a volume so users cannot see or access it on the network.

DNS: See *Domain name service (DNS)*.

Document collection: The files that contain the full text and graphics for a set of Novell online manuals.

Domain name service (DNS): An Internet protocol that allows administrators to associate Internet addresses with names that people can remember. A DNS server stores the names and their corresponding IP addresses, and responds to clients that need name services.

DOS partition: See *Partition, disk*.

Drive mapping: The assignment of a drive letter (such as G or H) to a specific network directory. Mapping a drive letter to a network directory works the same way as making drive C point to your hard disk, or drive E point to a CD-ROM. See also *Search drive*.

Driver: A software program that lets a piece of hardware communicate with other parts of a computer or with the network. For example, a mouse driver is the software that controls how a mouse works with the computer, a LAN driver controls how the network board communicates with the computer, and a disk driver controls how the disk drive communicates with the computer. Sometimes called a device driver.

DynaText viewer: A workstation application that allows a user to read, search through, and print the Novell online documentation.

Effective rights: The combination of trustee rights that the user can ultimately execute. A user can have effective rights to NDS objects, as well as effective rights to files and directories. A user's effective rights to an object, directory, or file are determined in one of two ways: the user's inherited rights minus any rights blocked by the IRF, or the sum of all the user's direct trustee assignments and security equivalences to other objects. See also *Trustee rights; Inherited Rights Filter (IRF)*.

Ethernet: Currently the most common network architecture. It provides good performance at a reasonable cost, and is relatively easy to install.

Fake root: A special type of drive mapping to an application's directory. A fake root makes the application's directory appear to be a root directory, even though the directory may be located under other directories. See also *Drive mapping*.

File attribute: See *Attribute, file and directory*.

Full distinguished name: An object's full name, which also indicates its position in the tree. An object's full distinguished name (or full name) consists of the object's name, followed by the names of each of the container objects above it in the tree. Each name is separated by a period, such as Eric.Sales.BlueSky.

Gateway: Connects one network to a completely different type of network or computer system, through a single point. The gateway takes a request from a network client and transfers it to the other system, reversing the process when the other system replies back to the network client. For example, the IPX/IP Gateway in intraNetWare lets all workstations on the intraNetWare network connect to the Internet through the gateway, eliminating the need for each workstation to have its own IP address.

Group object: An NDS object that contains a list of users who belong to the Group object. Groups allow you to manage security, printer assignments, and other issues that may affect many or all of the users in the same way.

Hexadecimal number: A number that uses the numerals 0 through 9 and the letters A through F. Hexadecimal numbers are often used to specify addresses or locations in computer programs.

Home directory: A directory (folder) on the network created especially for a specific user. All users can have their own home directories, in which they can store their applications, work files, or personal files. Users generally have full trustee rights to their own home directories.

Host server: When using SBACKUP to back up network files, a host server is the server that is running SBACKUP, and which is attached to the backup device (such as a tape drive or optical disk drive).

HTML (HyperText Markup Language): The type of formatting used in preparing documents to be published on the Web or on intranets. HTML documents can be read by browsers running on workstations.

HTTP (HyperText Transfer Protocol): A protocol that allows a Web server to communicate with browsers.

Hub: A piece of network equipment into which workstation cables must feed before being connected to the main network cable. Passive hubs simply gather the signals and relay them. Active hubs actually boost the signals before send-ing them on their way. Active hubs are also sometimes called concentrators.

Incremental backup: See *Backup*.

Inheritance: The gaining of trustee rights at a lower level of the NDS tree or file system, because you were granted those rights at a higher level. NDS trustee rights can be inherited, as well as file system trustee rights. If you are granted a new trustee assignment at a lower level, you no longer inherit rights from a higher level.

Inherited Rights Filter (IRF): A way to restrict the rights that a user can inherit from a higher level in the NDS tree or file system. If you remove a right from an object's or directory's IRF, users can no longer inherit and use that right at this level.

Internet: A global network, originally started as a way to link various research, defense, and education systems together. Since then, it has expanded greatly as thousands of other networks have connected into it. Universities, corpora-tions, individual users, small businesses, nonprofit organizations, and others can all access the Internet to research libraries of information stored all over the world, or to communicate with other users via e-mail.

Intranet: A private network that provides information to its users in the same formats available on the Internet. Users can use normal Internet browsers to view the information posted on an Intranet — the only difference is that out-side users are not permitted to access the Intranet.

Intruder detection: A feature of intraNetWare that lets you limit the number of times a user can attempt to log in without succeeding. This prevents users from guessing passwords or from using a password generator to try to break into the network.

IP: The suite of network protocols used by the Internet. IntraNetWare sup-ports the IPX protocol by default, but can support the IP protocol if you pre-fer. You can either add IP support to the server, so it supports both protocols, or you can install NetWare/IP, which is a variation of intraNetWare that runs only on IP.

IP address: A unique number that identifies a computer on the Internet.

IPX/IP Gateway: A software gateway that lets administrators allow IPX-based workstations to access TCP/IP-based resources, such as the World Wide Web, without installing or configuring TCP/IP on those workstations. The gateway

IPX/SPX: The default network protocol supported by intraNetWare.

IRF: See *Inherited Rights Filter (IRF)*.

LAN driver: Software that allows a network board to communicate with its computer. Each brand of network board has a unique LAN driver associated with it. Sometimes called a network driver.

Leaf object: An NDS object that can't have any other objects beneath it in the NDS tree. Users, groups, printers, and print queues are all examples of leaf objects. See also *Container object*.

Login script: A set of commands that execute when the user logs in. Login scripts automatically set up the users' workstation environments with necessary drive mappings and other types of useful environmental settings. Container login scripts execute for all objects within a container. User login scripts execute for specific users. Profile login scripts can be created to execute for a group of users.

Major TSA resource: A volume. (This term is used in the SBACKUP program, which is used to back up network files.)

Mapping: See *Drive mapping*.

Menu program: A program you can create in order to let DOS users select tasks from a menu instead of typing commands at the DOS prompt. Menus are not used for Windows 3.1 or Windows 95 workstations.

Menu utility: A utility that runs in DOS, which lets a user select a task to perform by choosing an option from a menu.

Migration: Transferring data from one machine or storage device to another. Specifically in intraNetWare, *server migration* means transferring all network information off of an old server machine, across the network, onto a new machine. This process lets you upgrade to intraNetWare from an older version of NetWare, while at the same time utilizing a brand new server machine. *Data migration* is an advanced feature of intraNetWare that can move older, unused files from a primary storage device onto a secondary storage device (such as an optical disk storage system) automatically. This saves disk space on the primary storage device.

Mirroring. See *Disk mirroring*.

Mount: To bring up a volume so users can see and access it on the network.

MultiProtocol Router 3.1: An intraNetWare feature that provides WAN (Wide Area Network) connectivity, routing multiple protocols over leased lines, frame relay, or ISDN lines. This capability allows you to connect network users to an Internet Service Provider (ISP).

NAL: See *NetWare Application Launcher (NAL)*.

Name context: An NDS object's location in the NDS tree. For example, if user Eric is located in an Organizational Unit object called Sales, under the Organization object called BlueSky, Eric's name context is Sales.BlueSky. The names of the container objects in a name context are separated by periods.

Name space module: A software program (loaded on the server) that allows a server's volumes to store files created in nonDOS operating systems. These nonDOS files may have different file formats (such as Macintosh files) or may support longer file names than DOS (such as Windows 95).

NDS: A database that contains information about every object in the intraNetWare network. Using this database, intraNetWare can identify each object, know where it's supposed to be in the network, know who's allowed to use it, know what it's supposed to be connected to, and so on.

NDS object: An entity defined in the NDS database that represents a physical network resource (such as a server, workstation, or printer), a software network resource (such as a printer server, print queue, or volume), or a human or organizational resource (such as a user, group, or department). An NDS object contains properties that define the object, specifying such characteristics as the object's name, security rights, and so on.

NDS object class: A particular type of object that has been defined, such as Server object, User object, Print Queue object, or Volume object.

NDS schema: The overall plan that defines and describes the allowable NDS object classes, their properties, and the rules that govern their creation and existence. The schema determines how objects can inherit properties and trustee rights of other container objects above it. In addition, the schema defines how the Directory tree is structured and how objects in it are named.

NDS tree: The figurative representation of the NDS database's hierarchical structure, showing the Root object at the top, and container objects forming branches beneath the root.

NetSync: An intraNetWare feature that allows you to manage the objects in the binderies of up to 12 NetWare 3.1x servers just as if they were in the NDS database. The objects in the binderies are maintained in the NDS database by a host server, and you can use the NetWare Administrator utility to manage those bindery objects just as you do NDS objects.

NetWare Administrator: An intraNetWare utility that allows you to work with NDS objects on the network. This is one of the primary utilities used in intraNetWare for management tasks, and can be run on workstations using Windows 3.1, Windows 95, OS/2, or Windows NT.

NetWare Application Launcher (NAL): An application in intraNetWare that lets you set up an icon on users' desktops that points directly to network applications. Then the users can simply launch the application from their desktops without having to know where the application is, which drives to map, and so on.

NetWare for Macintosh: An older Novell product that lets you add Macintosh workstations to a Novell network via an AppleTalk router. NetWare for Macintosh is still supported by intraNetWare. However, intraNetWare contains new client software for Mac OS workstations that eliminates the need to install NetWare for Macintosh. This new client software lets you connect Mac OS workstations directly to the network using IPX.

NetWare Loadable Module (NLM): A software module that you load into the server's operating system to add or change functionality. Many NLMs are automatically installed with the intraNetWare operating system. Others are optional, which you can load if your particular situation requires them. Other manufacturers also produce NLMs for products such as backup software.

NetWare partition: See *Partition, disk.*

NetWare Peripheral Architecture (NWPA): A standard supported by intraNetWare that allows disk drivers and CD-ROM drivers to work with intraNetWare.

NetWare SFT III: A variation of intraNetWare that lets you install the network operating system on two identical servers that run simultaneously. The servers' hard disks and other hardware are "mirrored" to each other, so they store identical information. That way, if one server goes down, the other server takes over seamlessly, so that network service is uninterrupted.

NetWare SMP: A variation of intraNetWare that runs on computers containing more than one processor chip. In these high-end computers, NetWare SMP takes advantage of the multiple processors so that some network tasks can span the processors and run more quickly.

NetWare User Tools: An intraNetWare utility that runs only on Windows 3.1. It is used primarily by network users, to help them manage their network drive mappings, print capture assignments, and so on.

NetWare/IP: A variation of intraNetWare that runs only on the IP protocol suite.

Network architecture: The cabling scheme that specifies the types of cabling, connectors, and network boards used in a network. Ethernet, Token Ring, and AppleTalk are all examples of network architectures.

Network board: A special type of circuit board installed in a computer. A network board is connected to the network cable, and allows the computer to send data onto the network and receive data from the network. Also called network interface boards, network cards, and network adapters.

Network Neighborhood: The Windows 95 program that allows users to see the intraNetWare network, log in to it, locate network directories, and so on.

Network operating system: The intraNetWare software that runs on the server. The network operating system replaces the regular operating system (such as DOS or Windows 95) on the computer, and manages the communication that takes place over the entire network. IntraNetWare controls data transfer, file storage, security (to make sure only authorized users access the right files), communication between multiple networks, and other network activities.

NFS: The protocol used to support UNIX files on a network.

NLM: See *NetWare Loadable Module (NLM)*.

Novell Directory Services: See *NDS*.

Novell Internet Access Server (NIAS): A set of intraNetWare features that turn intraNetWare into a comprehensive platform for a full-service intranet. These features include the IPX/IP Gateway, MultiProtocol Router 3.1, and the Netscape Navigator browser.

NWAdmin: See *NetWare Administrator*.

NWPA: See *NetWare Peripheral Architecture (NWPA)*.

Object: See *NDS object*.

Organization object: An NDS container object, located immediately beneath the Root object in the NDS tree, which generally represents the company or organization to which the network belongs. The Organization object contains all other container objects, as well as all the leaf objects (such as servers, users, and printers) that reside within that organization.

Organizational Unit object: An NDS container object that is located beneath an Organization object or another Organizational Unit object. The Organizational Unit object often represents a department, division, or project team within a larger organization. The Organizational Unit object can contain leaf objects (such as users or printers), as well as other Organizational Unit objects.

Packet: The unit in which data is packaged to be sent across the network. Each packet includes a small amount of data, plus addressing information to make sure the data gets to the right destination. In addition, packets may include information that will help the receiving station know that the data arrived safely without corruption, and other types of helpful tidbits. A protocol dictates exactly how these packets should be formed, so that all devices on the network can understand the packets they receive.

Partial name: See *Relative distinguished name*.

Partition, Directory: Portions of the NDS database that can be replicated on different servers. A Directory partition is a branch of the Directory tree, beginning with any container object you choose. Partitions can also hold subpartitions beneath them (called child partitions). If you have a smaller NDS database, the whole database can reside in a single partition. Using partitions can improve network performance, especially if the network spans across a WAN (wide area network). Partitions also can make it easier to manage portions of the tree separately.

Partition, disk: A portion of the hard disk (in most cases, the entire disk belongs to the partition) that is formatted in such a way that it can store and handle files. The intraNetWare server's hard disk contains a DOS partition (which contains the DOS operating system and DOS-formatted files) and at least one NetWare partition (which contains the intraNetWare network operating system, intraNetWare files, and all network files and applications).

Peripherals: Equipment (such as printers, plotters, scanners, or modems) that can be attached to a network or to a computer.

Port driver: Software that routes print jobs out of the print queue, through the correct port on the server, to the printer.

Print driver: Software that converts the print job into a format that the printer can understand.

Print job configuration: Instructions that tell the printer a unique way to print different jobs. Print job configurations can specify printing characteristics, such as the print queue to use and the type of paper to use.

Print queue: A special network directory (folder) that stores print jobs temporarily before they are printed. Multiple network users can have their jobs stored in the same print queue. The print queue receives all incoming print jobs from various users, and stores them in a first-come, first-served order.

Print queue operator: A user that has been granted additional rights to manage a print queue. A print queue operator can delete other users' print jobs, put them on hold, and so on.

Print queue user: A user that has been granted rights to use a print queue.

Print server: A software program (called PSERVER.NLM) running on the intraNetWare server that manages how print jobs are handled by the network and its printers. The print server takes print jobs from print queues and sends them to network printers when those printers are ready. It controls print traffic, manages the order and priority of print jobs, verifies that users are allowed to use the printers they select, and so on.

Profile login script: See *Login script.*

Property: A piece of information associated with an NDS object, that helps to define that object. For example, a User object's properties could include the user's last name, trustee assignments, login script, and e-mail address. Properties are sometimes called attributes.

Protocol: A set of defined rules that control how processes or machines communicate. Different protocols control different levels of communication on the network. For example, some protocols regulate how two computers establish a connection so they can communicate and how they terminate the connection when they're finished. Other protocols control how data is transferred across network cabling, and still others control how applications communicate.

Purge: Permanently removing a deleted file from the network. Deleted files are normally stored in a salvageable, but hidden, state until the files are either purged or salvaged (restored).

Relative distinguished name: A shortened version of an NDS object's full name, showing the name context only partway up the NDS tree. Also called partial name.

Remote Console: A feature of intraNetWare that lets you temporarily transform your workstation into a console (monitor and keyboard) for the server, so that you can control the server from your workstation.

Replica: A copy of the NDS database stored on a server. You can have several replicas of the NDS database so that if one server goes down, all the other servers can still access the NDS database from another replica on another server.

Restore: To retrieve a backup file from its archived location, and place it back onto the network so it can be accessed.

Rights: See *Trustee rights; Effective rights.*

Root object: The highest-level object in the NDS tree.

Router: A software program (sometimes housed in its own hardware device, sometimes running inside a network server) that allows network communication to travel across mixed networks. Routers take packets of data from one network, reformat the packets if necessary to conform to the next network's protocol requirements, and then send those packets along to their destination. Routers also manage routes between servers or networks, tracking the shortest routes between two servers so network communication isn't slowed. The router software controls the actual routing of packets from one network to the other. The router hardware forms the necessary physical connection by linking the cabling systems together.

Salvage: To retrieve and restore a deleted network file. Deleted files are normally stored in a salvageable, but hidden, state until the files are either purged (permanently erased) or salvaged.

Schema: See *NDS schema.*

Search drive: A special type of drive mapping, which acts like a DOS path command. Search drives are used to indicate directories that contain applications or utilities. They let users execute an application without having to know where the application is; the network searches through the designated search drives for the application's executable file when the user types the program's execution command. See also *Drive mapping.*

Security, file system: A set of intraNetWare security features that control how users work with files and directories. File system security includes trustee rights (which grant users rights to work with files) and file and directory attributes (which restrict any users from performing specified activities on files). See also *Trustee rights.*

Security, login: A set of intraNetWare security features that control whether or not users can log in to the network (and, optionally, when they can log in, what kind of passwords they use, and so on).

Security, NDS: IntraNetWare access rights that regulate how NDS objects can use other objects (for example, whether or not one user can change another user's allowable login times, or whether one user can delete or change a print server). See also *Trustee rights.*

Security equivalence: An assignment that grants you the same trustee rights as another user. Your trustee rights become "equivalent" to the other user's rights.

Server: A software product, installed in a computer, that provides services to clients. The network server is the most commonly recognized to type of server. Other types of servers include Web servers, fax servers, and e-mail servers; often these specialty types of servers run inside the intraNetWare network server.

Server, network: A computer with the intraNetWare network operating system installed on it. The server controls the network, managing data transfer over the network, network file storage, network security, communication between networks, and so on.

SET parameter: A server option you can change to optimize your server's performance. SET parameters control things such as how buffers are allocated and used, how memory is used, and so on. You can change these parameters by loading SERVMAN.NLM and selecting the SET parameters you want from menus. SET parameters are also called server parameters.

SFT III: See *NetWare SFT III*.

SMP: See *NetWare SMP*.

Standalone: Not attached to a network.

STARTUP.NCF: A startup file on the server that executes whenever the server is booted. STARTUP.NCF automates the initialization of the intraNetWare operating system. It loads disk drivers, loads name space modules to support different file formats, and executes some additional parameters that modify default initialization values. This file is created during the server installation, and contains commands that reflect the choices you made during the installation.

Storage device: The hardware into which storage media is inserted in order to be formatted and used. For example, CD-ROM drives, tape drives, and disk drives are considered storage devices.

Storage media: Tapes, disks, CD-ROMs, or other types of products that can be used to store data.

Surge suppressor: A device that helps protect computer equipment from damage caused by surges in electrical power.

System login script: A type of login script used in previous versions of NetWare. This was replaced in intraNetWare by container login scripts. See also *Login script*.

Target server: When using SBACKUP to back up network files, a target server is the server whose files you intend to back up.

Target Service Agent (TSA): An NLM that runs on a server (called the target server) whose files you want to back up. The TSA allows the target server to communicate with the host server.

TCP/IP: A type of protocol that can run on intraNetWare workstations and servers, allowing them to communicate with the Internet's IP protocol suite.

Terminator: A special type of cable connector that should be attached to the open end of certain types of network cable. It keeps electrical signals from reflecting back across the network, corrupting information or communications.

Token Ring: A network architecture with the reliability to work well in situations involving heavy data traffic. It is fairly easy to install, but it is more expensive than Ethernet networks.

Transaction Tracking System (TTS): An intraNetWare feature that monitors updates to database files, and keeps track of the updates. This way, if the server fails during a database transaction, any unfinished updates can be safely backed out (undone). This prevents the database from being corrupted by unfinished updates.

Tree: See *NDS tree*.

Trustee: A user (or other object) who has been given trustee rights to an object, file, or directory.

Trustee rights: Permissions that allow users or objects to perform specified tasks. NDS trustee rights control whether users can work with other NDS objects and their properties, such as viewing other objects, changing their properties, deleting them, and so on. File system trustee rights control how users can work with files and directories, specifying whether a user can delete a file, change it, open it, and so on. See also *Effective rights*.

TTS: See *Transaction Tracking System (TTS)*.

Uninterruptible power supply (UPS): A device that provides the server with a backup battery that takes over in case of a power outage. This backup battery allows enough time for the UPS to shut down the server cleanly, leaving no open files exposed to corruption. A good UPS also protects against spikes, surges, brownouts, and line noise (interference on the wire).

User account: The information about a user that allows the user to log in to the network. When a User object is created in the NDS tree, the user's account is automatically created.

User login script: See *Login script*.

Utility: An application or command used to configure or manage some aspect of intraNetWare or other operating system.

Viewer: See *DynaText viewer*.

Volume: A root directory on the intraNetWare server's hard disk — the highest level of directory in the file system. The SYS volume is created automatically by the Simple Installation. If the server has more than one hard disk attached, each additional disk will have its own separate volume, named VOL1, VOL2, and so on. (If you use the Custom Installation of intraNetWare, you can specify different sizes or names of volumes.)

WAN: See *Wide Area Network (WAN)*.

Web authoring: The act of creating Web pages, including writing the text, formatting the pages, creating links to other pages, and so on.

Web server: A software product, installed in an intraNetWare network server, used to post and control information in such a way that it's available on the World Wide Web or on an intranet. The NetWare Web Server is included with intraNetWare.

Wide Area Network (WAN): A network that covers a territory so large that it requires some of the network connections to be made over telephone lines.

Workstation: A computer (attached to a network) that users must use to complete their normal work. A workstation contains a network board, which is connected to the network cabling, and runs intraNetWare client software on it, which communicates with the server. An intraNetWare workstation still uses its own operating system, and can be running DOS, Windows 3.1, Windows 95, Windows NT, OS/2, Mac OS, or UNIX.

Index

E

O

T

V

X

Z

my2cents.idgbooks.com

Register This Book — And Win!

Visit **http://my2cents.idgbooks.com** to register this book and we'll automatically enter you in our fantastic monthly prize giveaway. It's also your opportunity to give us feedback: let us know what you thought of this book and how you would like to see other topics covered.

Discover IDG Books Online!

The IDG Books Online Web site is your online resource for tackling technology — at home and at the office. Frequently updated, the IDG Books Online Web site features exclusive software, insider information, online books, and live events!

10 Productive & Career-Enhancing Things You Can Do at www.idgbooks.com

- Nab source code for your own programming projects.
- Download software.
- Read Web exclusives: special articles and book excerpts by IDG Books Worldwide authors.
- Take advantage of resources to help you advance your career as a Novell or Microsoft professional.
- Buy IDG Books Worldwide titles or find a convenient bookstore that carries them.
- Register your book and win a prize.
- Chat live online with authors.
- Sign up for regular e-mail updates about our latest books.
- Suggest a book you'd like to read or write.
- Give us your 2¢ about our books and about our Web site.

You say you're not on the Web yet? It's easy to get started with IDG Books' *Discover the Internet,* available at local retailers everywhere.